Interface between English Language Education Policies and Practice

Eric Enongene Ekembe
Lauren Harvey • Eric Dwyer
Editors

Interface between English Language Education Policies and Practice

Examples from Various Contexts

Editors
Eric Enongene Ekembe
Higher Teacher Training College (ENS)
Université de Yaoundé I
Yaounde, Cameroon

Lauren Harvey
University of Arizona
Tucson, AZ, USA

Eric Dwyer
College of Arts, Sciences & Education
Florida International University
Miami, FL, USA

ISBN 978-3-031-14309-0   ISBN 978-3-031-14310-6   (eBook)
https://doi.org/10.1007/978-3-031-14310-6

© The Editor(s) (if applicable) and The Author(s), under exclusive licence to Springer Nature Switzerland AG 2022

This work is subject to copyright. All rights are solely and exclusively licensed by the Publisher, whether the whole or part of the material is concerned, specifically the rights of translation, reprinting, reuse of illustrations, recitation, broadcasting, reproduction on microfilms or in any other physical way, and transmission or information storage and retrieval, electronic adaptation, computer software, or by similar or dissimilar methodology now known or hereafter developed.

The use of general descriptive names, registered names, trademarks, service marks, etc. in this publication does not imply, even in the absence of a specific statement, that such names are exempt from the relevant protective laws and regulations and therefore free for general use.

The publisher, the authors, and the editors are safe to assume that the advice and information in this book are believed to be true and accurate at the date of publication. Neither the publisher nor the authors or the editors give a warranty, expressed or implied, with respect to the material contained herein or for any errors or omissions that may have been made. The publisher remains neutral with regard to jurisdictional claims in published maps and institutional affiliations.

Cover illustration: imageBROKER / Alamy Stock Photo

This Palgrave Macmillan imprint is published by the registered company Springer Nature Switzerland AG.
The registered company address is: Gewerbestrasse 11, 6330 Cham, Switzerland

Contents

1. English Language Policies and Practice in the World: From Problems Toward Solutions ... 1
   Eric Enongene Ekembe, Justina Njika, and Alan Mackenzie

Part I Change Process in ELT Policy ... 19

2. Teaching at—Not to—the Middle in Japan: Examining How ELT Policies Aimed at Extremes Influence Mid-Tier Institutions ... 21
   Giancarla Unser-Schutz, Beni Kudo, and Samuel Rose

3. The Implementation of the 4+4+4 Educational Policy in Turkey: Reflections from English Classrooms ... 39
   Tuğba Birdal and Seniye Vural

4. Teachers' Appreciation of ELT Policies and Practices in Egypt ... 59
   Islam M. Farag and Mohamed Yacoub

5 ELT Policies in Multilingual Contexts: An Analysis of
   Rural-Urban Experience in Ghana 85
   Raymond Karikari Owusu and Andrea Sterzuk

Part II Practice Steering the Wheel 105

6 Integrating Communicative Language Teaching Activities
   in Overcrowded Classrooms: Policy and Practice Issues in
   South Sudan Secondary Schools 107
   Alex D. D. Morjakole

7 ELT Policies and Practices in Superdiverse Central Ohio:
   From "Flexible" to "English-Centric" 127
   Brian Seilstad

8 English Language Teaching in Colombia: From Policy to
   Reality 151
   Daniel Ramírez Lamus

9 Broken Promises? The Florida Consent Decree,
   Multilingual Learners in Mainstream Classes, and
   Assimilationist Practice 169
   Eric Dwyer and Carolyn O'Gorman-Fazzolari

Part III Teachers' Position in Policy Innovation 201

10 Policy on Global Issues in Sub-Saharan Africa: A Possible
   Role for ELT from Examples in Guinea Bissau, Senegal
   and DRC 203
   Linda Ruas and Ali Djau

11 English Language Proficiency for All University Graduates Stipulated by Law: A Realistic or Idealistic Goal? An Appraisal of a Tertiary ELT Policy from Montenegro   221
Vesna Bratić and Milica Vuković-Stamatović

12 Assessing Teachers' Perceptions of Relevant ELT Policies in Cameroon   243
Eric Enongene Ekembe

Part IV Interface   267

13 So … What's the Interface? The Specter of Smush and Poof   269
Eric Dwyer

Index   295

Notes on Contributors

Tuğba Birdal is a graduate of the Linguistics department at Hacettepe University, Turkey. She works as an English instructor at the School of Foreign Languages of Abdullah Gül University. She holds an MA in English Literature from Erciyes University and has a TESOL certificate.

Vesna Bratić is an Assistant Professor of English Language and Literature at the Faculty of Philology of the University of Montenegro. She obtained her MA and PhD from the Faculty of Philology, University of Belgrade (Serbia). Her MA thesis focused on the narratives of death and suffering in William Faulkner and Serbian author Aleksandar Tišma, while her PhD research was centered around the image of America in the plays of Sam Shepard and David Mamet. She teaches undergraduate courses in eighteenth- and nineteenth-century English literature and graduate courses in American Literature at the English Department of the Faculty of Philology, as well as ESP at the Faculty of Electrical Engineering and Faculty of Metallurgy and Technology of the University of Montenegro. Her professional interests lie within contemporary American and eighteenth-century English literature, gender studies in literature, and metaphor and discourse analysis.

Ali Djau has 12 years' experience as a secondary school teacher of English in Guinea Bissau. He has different degrees, both in ELT and in

Environmental Management. His interests lie in combining blending environmental issues with ELT. He is currently director of a secondary school in Bissau.

Eric Dwyer is a program leader and Associate Professor in Foreign Language Education at Florida International University in Miami, where he in an instructor of foreign language teaching methods and a researcher in multilingual education.

Eric Enongene Ekembe holds a PhD in Applied Linguistics from the University of Yaounde 1, Cameroon and is a senior lecturer at the Higher Teacher Training College, Yaounde, Cameroon. He runs the Cameroon English and Literature Teachers Association (CAMELTA) Research Group and is the outreach coordinator of the International Association of Teachers of English as a Foreign Language (IATEFL) ReSIG. He is an ELT consultant with TransformELT and a steering committee member for the International Festival of Teacher Research. His research interest is postcolonial ELT, EMI, and CPD. He is co-editor of *Interdisciplinarity in the 21st Century Global Dispensation: Research in Language, Literature, & Education in Africa*.

Islam M. Farag is an Arabic instructor at the University of Pittsburgh and a PhD candidate in Composition and Applied Linguistics at Indiana University of Pennsylvania. He has 12 years of experience teaching English and Arabic as additional languages in Egypt and the United States. His research interests include writing expertise, bilingual education, and critical pedagogy.

Beni Kudo is an associate professor in the Department of Business Administration in Rissho University with research interest in English education, English culture, and English Literature. She has published research papers in international journals and is a member of JALT, The English Literary Society of Japan, The Brontë Society of Japan, as well as the Thomas Hardy Society of Japan.

Alan Mackenzie is the director of TransformELT and Senior Consultant for NILE and Module Leader for Developing Autonomy on the MA in Professional Development for Language Education. I have been advisor to the boards of Thailand TESOL, the Philippines Association for Language Teaching (PALT), the Society of Pakistan English Language Teachers (SPELT), and English Language Teacher's Association of India (ELTI). He has also worked with multiple state ministries of education across East and South Asia, and is a member of Eaquals, IATEFL, and BALEAP.

Alex D. D. Morjakole holds an MA in Educational Policy Studies from the University of Wisconsin-Madison, an MA in Teaching English to Speakers of Other Languages (TESOL) from the University of Warwick (UK), and a Bachelor's degree in Education from Makerere University, Kampala (Uganda). He has taught teacher trainees in Arapi National Teacher Training Institute (NTTI) and teacher education and development projects with the Windle Trust International and the Jesuit Refugee service (JRS). His research interests include teacher education and development, teacher management, educational policies, and their implications on the working conditions of the teacher.

Justina Njika is Professor of Applied Linguistics in the Department of English at the Higher Teacher Training College Yaounde, Cameroon. She is equally the Inspector General in Charge of Teaching in the Ministry of Basic Education, Cameroon. She has had her work published in international journals. Her research interest is classroom interaction and language-in-education policies.

Carolyn O'Gorman-Fazzolari serves as Professor of Teacher Education and ESL on the US-Mexico border in California. Her active research agenda and creative interests include exploring and identifying the socio-elements (cultural, political, and linguistic) that diverse learners bring to bilingual, biliteracy, and bicultural learning environments. Research and action merge while the spirit of authorship is awakened, and students celebrate their voices as published authors in the *Borderlands: Local Literacies* book series.

Raymond Karikari Owusu is a PhD candidate at the University of Regina. He has a Teachers' certificate, a BEd degree, and Master's in Educational Administration and Management. He has many years of high school and junior high school teaching experience in Ghana and

Canada. His research interests focus on language policy and language of instruction in postcolonial countries and how these impact teaching and learning.

Daniel Alfonso Ramírez Lamus is an English teacher at Universidad de Los Andes in Bogotá, Colombia, and holds an EdD in Teaching English to Speakers of Other Languages (TESOL) from Florida International University (FIU). His doctoral dissertation, Foreign Language Education in Colombia: A Case Study, was published in 2015. He is also a member of the musical project called Filigranas, which blends rock, folk, and Brazilian popular music, and is available on all music streaming platforms.

Samuel Rose is an associate professor in the Department of Sociology at the Rissho University. His research interest is in post-colonial literature and instructed second language learning. He is critical about the relationship between the human mind and the environment.

Linda Ruas is a highly experienced teacher trainer (having run and assessed many CELTA and DELTA courses), who holds an MA. She continues to work on her teaching by still teaching ESOL classes, and has taught ELT in several countries, including Brazil and Japan. She has written several books and has had teaching materials published related to global issues, and manages the Easier English New Internationalist website: eewiki.newint.org. Linda has presented at several international conferences, including the Pakistan SPELT travelling conference and AfricaELTA, and has recently been working with many groups of teachers in West Africa.

Brian Seilstad received his PhD from the Ohio State University's Department of Education/Teaching and Learning, with a focus on Multicultural and Equity Studies. He is the Director of Internationalization and Partnerships at Al Akhawayn University in Ifrane, Morocco. Prior to this position, he received his MA in Classical Languages from Bryn Mawr College, Pennsylvania, taught high school Greek and Latin, served in the Peace Corps in Morocco, was the Deputy Director of Youth Service California, and held teaching and leadership positions at Al Akhawayn University and American Academy/College Casablanca. He focuses on linguistic diversity and equity, specifically with respect to refugees/migrants.

Andrea Sterzuk is a professor in the Faculty of Education at the University of Regina, Canada. Her research projects and teaching focus on issues of power, identity, and language in education, particularly as they relate to settler colonialism.

Giancarla Unser-Schutz is an associate professor in the Department of Interpersonal and Social Psychology, Faculty of Psychology, Rissho University, a four-year, private Buddhist college in Tokyo, Japan. She has had her work published extensively in international journals in the fields of research cultural studies as well as sociolingustics.

Milica Vuković-Stamatović is Associate Professor of English Language and Linguistics 1 at the Faculty of Philology, University of Montenegro. She teaches Discourse Analysis and English for Specific Purposes (ESP). Her main research interests lie in the field of critical discourse analysis, conceptual metaphor, pragmatics, and ESP.

Seniye Vural is an assistant professor at the Department of English Language and Literature of Erciyes University, Turkey. She holds an MA in English Literature from Erciyes University, Turkey, an MA in Teaching English as a Foreign Language (TEFL) from Bilkent University, Turkey, and a PhD in TEFL from Middle East Technical University, Turkey.

Mohamed Yacoub is an assistant teaching professor in the Writing and Rhetoric Program in the English Department at Florida International University. Dr. Yacoub has English teaching experience in Egypt, China, Saudi Arabia, and the United States. Dr. Yacoub has had his work published on different topics in the English language in different scholarly journals.

Abbreviations

CEFR	Common European Framework of Reference
COFE	Colombian Framework for English
DRC	Democratic Republic of Congo
EBSs	Emergent Bilingual Students
ECOWAS	Economic Community of West African States
ELLs	English Language Learners
ELT	English Language Teacher or English Language Teaching
ESOL	English to Speakers of Other Languages
FEN	Foundation *Escuela Nueva*
FGM	Female Genital Mutilation
GISIG	Global Issues Special Interest Group: http://gisig.iatefl.org/about-us
IATEFL	International Association of Teachers of English as a Foreign Language
MEN	*Ministerio de Educación Nacional*
MEXT	Japanese Ministry of Education
MoE	Ministry of Education
MoNE	Ministry of National Education
OC	Octavio Calderón (OC), is a school in Medellín implementing the *Escuela Nueva* model
PFDCLE	*Programa de Fortalecimiento al Desarrollo de Competencias en Lenguas Extranjeras* or Program to Strengthen the Development of Competencies in Foreign Languages

PNB	National Program of Bilingualism, known as the *Programa Nacional de Bilingüismo*, instituted by the Colombian Ministry of Education
SINAPROF	*Sindicato Nacional dos Professores*—National Teachers Union of Guinea Bissau
SINDEPROF	*Sindicato Democrático dos Professores*—Democratic Union of Teachers
TENOR	Teaching English for No Obvious Reason
TESOL	Teachers of English to Speakers of Other Languages International Association
TEYL	Teaching English to Young Learners

List of Figures

Fig. 7.1	Ms. Popov's home language test	139
Fig. 7.2	Ms. Popov's vocabulary building sheet	140
Fig. 8.1	Language-policy research and the spread of English	156
Fig. 9.1	Exploratory sequential design. (Based on Creswell & Creswell, 2017: 217)	172
Fig. 9.2	Screenshot of prototypical 5th-grade mainstream lesson plan	189
Fig. 9.3	Screenshot of mainstream lesson plan with highlighted ESOL codes	190
Fig. 11.1	Entry level of Montenegrin students (in %) (Božović & Piletić, 2020)	232
Fig. 11.2	Exit level of students from four departments of the University of Montenegro (in %)	234
Fig. 13.1	The goal: mastering content in both one's home language and English	276
Fig. 13.2	EMI syllabus planning: attention to both language and content objectives	276
Fig. 13.3	EMI: convergence of both language and content objectives	277
Fig. 13.4	Collaborative EMI: equitable smushing and negotiation of language and content objectives	278
Fig. 13.5	Content area specialist dominant EMI: content objectives maintained with language objectives tangentially addressed	279

List of Tables

Table 2.1	Descriptions of Participating Faculty	27
Table 2.2	Understanding of MEXT's Policies	28
Table 2.3	English Language Teachers and Faculty Relations	31
Table 3.1	Crosswalk displaying the design of the study	45
Table 3.2	Teachers' perceived needs	47
Table 3.3	Classroom practices	48
Table 3.4	Source of class success in 2nd, 3rd, and 4th grades	49
Table 4.1	Timeline of key MoE mandates regarding ELT	63
Table 4.2	Timeline of key MoE mandates regarding technology	64
Table 4.3	School tuition	64
Table 4.4	Interview questions	69
Table 4.5	Demographic information of the participants	70
Table 6.1	Semi-structured interview question guides	112
Table 6.2	Participants' description of their classes and their preferred class size	113
Table 7.1	Program actors	135
Table 7.2	Transcript of Ms. Popov and six students discussing a vocabulary building sheet	140
Table 9.1	In-class strategies, identified by theme and by student base	177
Table 9.3	Proportion of classes per strategy	181
Table 9.2	Times each ESOL approach was observed among 40 classes	185
Table 10.1	Relevant policy excerpts	211
Table 12.1	Frequency of suggestions according to themes	260

1

English Language Policies and Practice in the World: From Problems Toward Solutions

Eric Enongene Ekembe, Justina Njika, and Alan Mackenzie

Introduction

English is increasingly gaining space as the world's superhighway language (Crystal, 2003; Richards, 2015; Melitz, 2016). This has prompted many countries in the world to shift their language policies and practice from English as a foreign language (EFL) toward English as a medium of instruction (EMI), especially in higher education (Rose, 2019). This is usually based on exclusive perception of the range of the socio-economic

---

E. E. Ekembe (✉)
Higher Teacher Training College (ENS), Université de Yaoundé I, Yaounde, Cameroon

J. Njika
Higher Teacher Training College, Yaounde/Inspectorate General in charge of Teaching, Ministry of Basic Education, Yaounde, Cameroon

A. Mackenzie
TransformELT, Norwich, UK
e-mail: amackenzie@transformelt.com

benefits policy makers associate with higher English language proficiencies (Hu, 2005; Nomlomo & Vuzo, 2014; Erling et al., 2017) commonly described in EMI discourse as the instrumentalist view (see Milligan & Tikly, 2016). The appreciation of advantages by policy makers in many respects ignores existing local realities and tends to disregard long-term negative effects, some of which generate multiple waves of complications, with potentially adverse effects on individuals, institutions, and the society at large (Milligan & Tikly, 2016; Walkinshaw et al., 2017). Diachronically, there exists no universally institutionalized framework for the adoption of English language policies and EMI in different contexts although issues arising from the interface between language policy innovations tend to be common, regardless of context (Dearden, 2016). Apart from this, a more complicated issue is the inconsistent evolution in policy innovation in different contexts. For example, Cunningham and Hatoss (2005) regret the non-existence of a language policy in Australia by 2005 when it had the best in the late 1980s. This, to them, is in contrast to South Africa, which counts 11 official languages policies, far distant from the multilingual United States with an unofficial monolingual English policy. To address such issues, research in English language teaching (ELT) and English Language education policies has persistently suggested grassroots stakeholder inclusion in the policy innovation process although this is yet to be seen as a consistent practice.

In fact, given limited data on the language and/or linguistic realities of the classroom (Simpson, 2019) and the consistent disregard for community needs in policy designs (Baldauf & Kaplan, 2005), language policy implementation around the world is most likely to remain experimental for some decades. More evidence on the link between policy and practice from different contexts is required to be able to understand the policy-practice interface.

This volume seeks to examine the above concerns with data-driven research from multiple contexts across the globe. The aim is from diverse perspectives to understand contextual implications in policy innovations and how innovation processes complicate the narrow ELT and broader English Language education policy-practice interface.

English Language Policies and the EMI Question

Most countries in the world are struggling to keep pace with increasing technological development and globalization (Sah & Li, 2018). The growing interest in maintaining home languages seriously contradicts and problematizes the need for global inter-connectivity. The imposition of the learning of a non-local language on people, is probably against their wishes and may prevent learning. This is fast growing at a time when research has demonstrated that learning achievement is more productive in mother tongue education (Refs?). All of these factors raise challenges associated with which language to prioritize in education in multilingual contexts; the scope of use of the other available languages; proficiencies of those charged with language policy implementation (Erling et al., 2017); and appreciation from local communities (Tembe & Norton, 2008; Davis et al., 2013). These complications are echoed by Simpson (2019):

> Introducing EMI into public education systems characterised by severe resource constraints, untrained and unqualified teachers, large classes, limited time on task, etc. risks exacerbating the adverse impact of these other important factors on the quality of teaching and learning – a serious risk that arguably is best avoided by not agreeing to support EMI at primary school level, whether through its introduction or expansion. (p. 7)

Language policy narrative is far from being straightforward. For example, research evidence suggests high learning achievement and increased societal advantages with mother tongue education (Laitin et al., 2019) when local communities show limited support to mother tongue education and rather prefer EMI (Tembe & Norton, 2008). In fact, though the spread of English is concomitantly related to increasing institutional English language and EMI consciousness across the globe, narratives on this are contentious and controversial (Bullock, 2020). Walkinshaw et al. (2017) cites Madhavan Brochier (2016) as suggesting that EMI is clearly not just a linguistic change but a geopolitical, economic, and ideological phenomenon. Simpson (2019) is more critical as to whether EMI discourse is not largely description and/or perception-based, given limited data on its real time practice in the classroom. Knagg (2020) attempt to clarify this by differentiating contexts of EMI. The discussion on the different EMI contexts is consistent with Walkinshaw et al.'s (2017) understanding that EMI practice has often been experimental. This is largely possible for five major reasons:

1. Many countries—even those with fragile economies and educational systems—are gaining consciousness on the comfortable position English has established as the world's lingua franca and the fashion for rapid EMI growth.
2. There exists no specific framework for language policy innovation, as narratives on policy innovation processes demonstrate.
3. EMI discourse is contentious and controversial.
4. Policy innovations are fashionably more driven by universally perceived economic advantages than learning achievement standards.
5. Issues arising from EMI practice and links between policy and practice are not widely acknowledged by education stakeholders (Probyn, 2001).

Although researchers continue to recommend baseline research for policy makers before innovation, there are still large numbers of cases of innovations that lack proper consideration of local realities across multiple contexts. In so many contexts, recurrent innovations are reported to be based on transplantation and policy makers' individual convictions about what is believed to be good. While this change process has remained the practice for some time, efforts invested in policy innovation and practice as well as teachers' involvement in policy innovation still lack practical impact assessments and reliable feedback processes. This volume is organized around common concerns connected with reconstructing the relationship between existing themes in ELT. The three main parts contain research studies from different contexts examining the multiple aspects of the interface between policy and practice:

> *Change process in ELT policy* looks at the way in which innovations come about; the way in which they are structured and the degree to which they take into account local realities

Practice steering the wheel focuses on the inconsistent link between existing policies and practice either because practice tries to be more realistic than policies, or because, in the absence of a guiding framework to innovative policies, teachers follow their traditional cycles of teaching.

Teacher involvement in policy innovation examines teachers' voices in existing policies including how they are consulted and what impact (if any) they have on policy.

The concluding chapter draws all of these themes together and looks at commonalities of experience.

Change Processes in ELT Policy

Some scholars have tried to differentiate 'innovation' from 'change' (Wedell, 2009; Waters, 2009; Bolitho, 2012; Carless, 2013) although the tendency has been to use the terminologies interchangeably as is operationalized here. The process of policy innovation, whether from learning English as a foreign language to EMI or from early English to mother tongue education, is fundamentally top-down in practice (Hagerman, 2009). One main argument to support the desire to the switch toward EMI is the need to attract international students (Dearden, 2016; Milligan & Tikly, 2016; Walkinshaw et al., 2017) especially in higher education, perhaps with little or no consideration to community needs, and the effects of such transitions on indigenous peoples. This explains why policy innovation processes have long been criticized as lacking credible backing. What obtains in most contexts is simple transfer of what has been rated successful elsewhere (Baldauf & Kaplan, 2005; Bolitho, 2012; Schweisfurth, 2013). However widely this has been discussed, evidence demonstrating how policy innovation affects the recipient cultures and how it is translated into concrete reality is yet to be comprehensive. Four chapters in this volume crucially illustrate this.

In Chap. 2, Unser-Schutz, Kudo, and Rose assess the Japanese Ministry of Education's (MEXT) policies moving from a grammar-oriented to a more communication-oriented curriculum; the development of English language programs intended to prepare Japanese students to work in international contexts; as well as the lowering of linguistic hurdles involved in studying at Japanese international universities. Deriving from multiple data sources, the authors claim the over-ambitious nature of the policy, as student achievement in 2017 did not seem to have met policy expectations. Some institutions required to implement the policy are reported to been unaware of the policy demands. The categorical stance in describing the proficiencies of students in the institutions required to implement the policy as noted in the chapter is seen from dual fronts: MEXT's association of students' English language achievement on a profile of high-to-low was done on an institutional level as well as labeling institutions by English language competence of their students. This dichotomizes English language competences and achievement on non-language use basis, which poses further concerns for teachers at the level of implementation.

Birdal and Vural (Chap. 3) offer insights on how teachers struggle with the requirements of a new English language policy, which lowers the learning level of English from the 4th to 2nd grade in Turkey, with no prior teacher preparation on how to teach young learners. Other major issues raised in the chapter are insufficient contact teaching time, and the terse nature of the grammar content of the curriculum compared with learners' cognitive dispositions. The question of non-realistic curriculum and evidence demonstrating non-readiness of teachers to implement the curriculum almost always result in 'tissue rejection' (Schweisfurth, 2013), and some tension between policy makers and policy implementers. This is described in Chap. 4 to be the case in Egypt. In this chapter, Farag and Yacoub draw from a history of reputed educational policies that gave Egypt the status of main exporter of education to the Middle East to chart how change of policies led to a downward slope of education in the country. The decentralization of education, in addition to the inconsistency in policies, is argued to have further weakened the educational system rather than strengthen it. Among all of the policy innovations, the greatest turbulence in reforms is reported to have taken place between 2012 and 2018 with excessive change of political decisions that established a culture of chaos both at the level of the change processes and implementation. The chapter notes crucial complications that emerged as various changes initiated by different ministers of education have affected teachers' self-belief about their participation in policy innovation.

Using a qualitative research design, Uwusu and Sterzuk in Chap. 5 examine the introduction of an EMI policy in a rural-urban multilingual Ghanaian context alongside nine local languages taught as school subjects within a context of multiple waves of policy innovations. The chapter describes a trend in Africa, where EMI was considered fashionable. Very few of such fashion-derived policy innovations survived the transition to full nationhood, other than Malawi. EMI policies follow an African elite's agenda to create spaces for their children in the global economy given their high English language proficiencies. The chapter compares the effects of current EMI programs on learners with monolingual indigenous backgrounds and those from multilingual backgrounds while examining the effects of the rural-urban divide. The authors noticed evidence of resistance to EMI-only-policy from the learners, which forced teachers to negotiate translanguaging strategies to increase uptake. The authors warn that EMI policy in a low-resourced context such as Ghana fosters exclusivity in the benefits accruing from policy innovations.

The chapters in this part all demonstrate the effects of the oversimplification of policy innovation processes. Randall (2013) warns that policy reform must not be considered as a written document that is easily translated into complete action. No matter the depth and transparent nature of the policies, the easily envisaged link between policy intention and classroom practice is often problematic (Schweisfurth, 2013). This is because evidence related to what actually promotes innovations is limited and it is difficult to identify any single catalyst and/or prompt to change initiatives and processes (Randall, 2013).

Where Policy Becomes Irrelevant and Practice Steers the Wheel

The broken link between policy and practice seems to paint a dismal picture of dysfunctionality in education systems affected by policy innovations. Policy rejection or non-implementation suggests the existence of alternative options. When policy fails, implementers are most likely to be involved in something that links with their judgment of immediate necessity or relevance. A huge barrier to policy implementation is teacher ability or quality and/or qualification. It is yet to be settled whether teacher quality and qualifications are directly linked with training or experience. Teacher quality and/ability are crucially linked with output and learner achievement (Laitin et al. 2019). Learners' achievement is reported to have dropped in South Africa due to poor quality teachers (Holmarsdottir, 2005). Teacher inability to implement policy may not be directly linked to quality or qualification. When prevailing circumstances tend to be challenging or when teachers cannot interpret policy, the likelihood is rejection or misapplication, and a resort to what is realistic. The chapters in this part describe how practice tries to be more realistic than policies or because, in the absence of a guiding framework to implement policies, teachers continue to teach what and how they know.

Morjakole in Chap. 6 noticed inconsistent opinions between teachers' perceptions of large classes and their pedagogic practices. The findings in the chapter reveal that student achievement, teacher quality, and internal conflicts have significant incidence on teachers' perception of class sizes, and these perceptions changed with school enrollment. The variety of strategies his subjects used to manage the commonly stated challenges in low-resourced classrooms included doing out-of-class activities, rearranging the seating space, sampling a few learners to assess the degree of uptake in class, calling out introverted learners to be engaged in lesson activities, and increasing the use of communicative activities such as debates. They also reported photocopying texts as a measure to deal with lack of textbooks. A crucial issue raised in the chapter is the awareness of teachers on the constraints of the work contexts and how their decision to adopt strategies is generated from their understanding of their context and not by 'sound pedagogic procedures'. This is suggestive of 'reasonable' practice. Being 'reasonable' in practice is practically based on a teachers' appreciation of the range of resources at their disposal and working within the limits of those resources.

Seisltad (Chap. 7) examines how attempts to satisfy the education needs of a growing adolescent immigrant population from plural cultures in the multilingual Ohio population in the U.S. are reported to have failed because of the unavailability of both technical and material resources. The author demonstrates, using both institutional ethnography and discourse analysis on a longitudinal design from 2016 to 2017, that English remains the procedural and instructional language in classroom settings, contrary to the policy intention of meeting the diverse linguistic needs of the learners. He notes that billboards on the campus give the impression of a micro context that is sensitive to the linguistic needs of its users while the projects represented by the billboards are essentially English-centric. Analysis of videos provides evidence of prohibition of home language even though the teacher appeared to show no negative attitudes toward the home languages. The author, however, describes some form of support for use of home languages, which does not follow any policy recommendation or institutional guidelines, but rather demonstrates the teachers' sensitivity to classroom realities.

In Chap. 8, Ramírez-Lamus pits the successes of an ambitious Colombian national English language policy locally known as PNB, against the relative value of a locally generated educational model known as the *Escuela Nueva* within the context of policy innovation. Based on qualitative investigation, the major beneficiaries of the policy innovation see English as a universal language, but are uncertain as to why it is imposed, especially with the disconnect in policy guidelines between elementary and high school levels. The misinterpretation of policy is demonstrated by teachers who see foreign language teaching from a monolingual English perspective. Their perception of the policy as top-down raises an issue: Why would ELT policies in the twentieth century be top-down in a country that has a well-appreciated bottom-up initiative—the *Escuela-Nueva*? This demonstrates disregard for local initiatives at the expense of internationalization of education that is present in many other contexts. A major pitfall of the policy innovation is the policy requirements of increased proficiency, which pushed teachers to expect more proficiency from learners than existing and previous classroom practices could offer. The university requires B2 for graduation. The effect is students developing a general sense of deficiency, frustration, and demotivation to learn English due to excessive policy requirements. Far more than the perceived advantages of English, the language causes frustration. Contrary to the curriculum targets, achievement tests demonstrate that only 8% attain the targeted B1 level of English. Given the learners' experiences, the chapter posits the exclusive and discriminatory effects of the policy both at the schooling and employment levels. The Chapter posits the benefits of the *Escuela Nueva* as a solution with clearly stated arguments. This is a clinical illustration of how grassroots-generated pedagogies can be more realistic than top-bottom policy initiatives.

The final chapter in this part explains how the Florida Consent Decree was passed to ensure that emergent bilinguals in schools in Florida received adequate English language support in the classroom as a reaction to the legal measures against the Florida Department of Education in 1990 for the non-implementation of an English language policy to support emergent bilinguals in Florida. Up to 2020, the decree was noted to have yielded inadequate results, as only moderate emergent bilinguals graduated successfully. Dwyer and O'Gorman-Fazzolari (Chap. 9) thus designed an ethnographic quantitative study to investigate how well the policy was implemented in the English language classrooms. Specifically, they noted that native-English-speaker-focused techniques characterized classroom practice more than double the techniques recommended for emergent bilinguals.

The chapters in this part raise major concerns when policy cannot be implemented: first, it is observed that practitioners do not quickly reject policies; they find alternatives that may be more responsive to local contexts when the policies are found to be non-responsive. A major issue raised is whether the policies themselves are totally non-responsive, or the problem generally arises from inability to translate the policies into practice. Whether or not these are justifications, this raises more arguments for teacher involvement at the conceptual phase of any policy design (Schweisfurth, 2013; Bolitho, 2012).

Teacher Involvement in Policy Innovation

Failed English language policies cut across many contexts (e.g., Yoshioda, 2003; Ayafor, 2005; Vavrus, 2009; Robayo Acuña, & Cárdenas, 2017; etc.) and grassroots stakeholders' involvement in policy innovation is believed to be a major step toward successful policy implementation (Bolitho, 2012; Schweisfurth, 2013). The argument for engaging teachers in policy crafting is that it gives them a sense of ownership that can easily be translated into concrete action (Schweisfurth, 2013). Equally, the realization of language policies in the classroom is not as homogeneous as the policy itself may assume. In a stricter sense, the levels, both pertaining to creating policies and those affected by policies are not always easily defined (Kennedy, 2011). Policy interpretation and implementation all depend on multiple teacher perceptions and understandings of the policy and appreciation of local resource provision, as well as teacher quality. However, very few studies have demonstrated the relationship between teachers' involvement in policy innovation and better classroom practices (see Tohidian & Nodooshan, 2021 for a notable example). The chapters in this part examine teacher involvement in policy designs, ranging from their opinions to actual agency in policy innovation.

To investigate the feasibility of extending the English language curriculum to cover global issues, Chap. 10 explains the researchers' position about teachers in three sub-Saharan African countries—Guinea Bissua, Senegal, and the DRC—who were yet to become sensitive to the possibilities of integrating global issues. They also verified the type of support required for teachers in driving the initiative through. The chapter sampled teacher and learner opinions about the relevance of including global issues topics in ELT in classrooms through a qualitative study involving nine teachers, three from each of the participating countries. WhatsApp discussions were also organized around global issues in a bid to see how the participants felt about integrating them into their language lessons. Based on the grassroots stakeholders' evidence, the chapter argues for the need to introduce global issues in ELT as an extension of the narrow long traditional approach to ELT which was at confluence with learner expectations.

There have been reports of failed policies with teachers demonstrating a feeling of pressure from policies (Kikuchi & Browne, 2009). In this chapter, however, Ruas and Djau strongly argue that this can be realized through supporting teachers to connect with change initiatives around the world.

In Chap. 11, Bratić and Stamatović observe that, in order to link Montenegro to the larger world and increase access to knowledge, policy makers decided to make English language a mandatory subject with increased teaching hours at all levels of study, targeting C2 as the required student exit proficiency level. Before 2017, there was no university English language policy and teachers taught whatever they thought necessary. To assess the degree of adoption of the new policy, Bratić and Stamatović's study consisted of semi-structured interviews involving 30 university staff teaching content courses. They found overwhelming teachers' resistance against the introduction of EFL lessons and an assessment of students' entry point to be far below the curriculum target. The intended collaboration between mainstream English language courses and those teaching main course equally met resistance. Based on their experiences both as ELT stakeholders and researchers, Bratić and Stamatović recommend a drop in exit requirement for graduating and an increase in the exit point of high school students. This chapter falls within the broader background of a growing culture of EMI in tertiary education in Europe and the world at large. There has been the anticipation in higher education across Europe and the world that the need for EFL on university campuses will drop, given the immersion space that EMI programs provide for learners. This is highly contested by these authors on grounds that English language teachers will still be needed to support teachers teaching content courses. The suggestions related to teaching time and proficiency-related policies in Bratić and Stamatović's chapter are based on the teachers' mastery of the context of work, and there is evidence that such mastery is the result of research. This begs the following questions: How many ELT teachers are involved in research? How much mastery do they have of their classrooms?

As a likely response, Ekembe in Chap. 12 assesses teacher perceptions of what would potentially count as relevant ELT policy in Cameroon. He largely reveals insensitivity to local constraints and misunderstandings among policymakers of the relationship between teacher responsibilities in the classroom and policy provisions and requirements. The study reveals that most of the commonly cited 'difficulties' of teacher work circumstances were not key concerns requiring policy innovation from teacher perspectives. In keeping with this, the chapter interrogates teachers' ability to make context-specific recommendations on relevant ELT policies in their work contexts and opens possibilities for further discussion on when teachers can provide meaningful contribution to policy recommendations in the process of policy innovation.

Conclusion

Apart from former British colonies, trending ELT policy innovations in Kachru's (1985) expanding circles have resulted in a number of issues that have affected people's lives from multiple perspectives and equally generated ideological contradictions on the spread of English in the world, the most conspicuous controversy being the intent-result confluence. The purpose for innovation is generally perceived to be beneficial in many contexts, yet with potentially unfavorable results. This begs many questions: Who makes the decision? On what grounds? What implementation provisions are made? What about teacher preparation? Oftentimes these are not placed at the center of policy innovations. Yet policy innovation is a continuing process, as the English language keeps occupying many more territories. This is where the interface between policy and practice requires much attention.

This volume offers reflections on ELT policy innovation processes across multiple contexts. The challenges generated by attempts at implementing the policies are explored, along with what practitioners think about both the process and implementation. The issues investigated include: adoption of EMI; age of starting to learn English; assessment procedures; proficiencies; exit profiles; English-only education; and use of English with other local proxy languages. All of this generates ideological complexities related to identity, social justice, inequality, proficiencies, access to resources, language maintenance, and ranges of opportunities (Simpson, 2019). These fall outs come from government policies intended to create opportunities for inter-connectedness between peoples of the world and accessibility to resources and economic empowerment. Such lofty governmental ambitions often carry different interpretations and implications that complicate the interface between English language policy and practice. The effects of these imbalances have yielded two main effects:

1. In many contexts, institutions that have developed *pragmatic, innovative solutions* to the policy-context, provide expensive 'prestigious' options. Such options are taken up by economically advantaged learners. Small, elite segments of the population in the quest for quality education exploit the situation. Quality education has been associated with high English language achievement, which in turn translates into disproportionate access to opportunities and inequality (Kuchah, 2018; Milligan, 2020).
2. Innovative implementers develop *realistic ground-level initiatives* that meet the expectations of the local population but do not receive support from policy makers despite their productive outcomes. Often, this is due to lack of awareness by policymakers, because such initiatives are often still in their infancy. It takes time and effort to develop these bottom-up dimensions and have them widely discussed as successes.

In all of these contexts, grassroots stakeholders have remained constant victims, incubating effects ranging from low levels of learner achievement, and misunderstandings of key policy targets, to multiple implementation constraints. In some other cases, the issues arising include implementers' inability to decode 'innovative' policy frameworks, which generally leads to compromised teaching and/or rejection of policy. A major consequence of this is a growing silent psychological tension between policy makers and implementers with the former claiming the primacy of policies, while the latter claim its irrelevance. The research papers in this volume contribute to the growing realization in the sphere of English language teaching and learning that for innovations in language education to work, all stakeholders must be deeply engaged in context-appropriate policy design, and implementation, with teacher support systems being key to implementation success. Without such intimate involvement, the policy is doomed to cost the nations dearly, in terms of finance, demoralized teachers, under-achieving learners and repeated systemic failure as the chapters in this volume illustrate.

References

Ayafor, I. M. (2005). Official bilingualism in Cameroon: Instrumental or integrative policy? In J. Cohen, K. T. McAlister, K. Rolstad, & J. MacSwan (Eds.), *Proceedings of the 4th international symposium on bilingualism* (pp. 123–142). Cascadilla Press.

Baldauf, R. B., Jr., & Kaplan, R. B. (2005). Language-in-education policy and planning. In E. Hinkel (Ed.), *Handbook of research in second language teaching and learning* (Vol. 1, pp. 1013–1034). Lawrence Erlbaum Associates.

Bolitho, R. (2012). Projects and programmes: Contemporary experience in ELT change management. In C. Tribble (Ed.), *Managing change in English language teaching: Lessons from experience* (pp. 33–46). British Council.

Bullock, D. (2020). *2019 International symposium on EMI for higher education in the new era: Selected proceedings*. The British Council.

Carless, D. (2013). Innovation in language teaching and learning. In C. A. Chapelle (Ed.), *The encyclopedia of applied linguistics*. Blackwell Publishing. https://doi.org/10.1002/9781405198431

Crystal, D. (2003). *English as a global language* (2nd ed.). Cambridge University Press.

Cunningham, D., & Hatoss, A. (2005). *An international perspective on language policies, practices, and proficiencies*. FIPLV.

Davis, E. K., Bishop, A. J., & Seah, W. T. (2013). "We don't understand English that is why we prefer English": Primary school students' preference for the language of instruction in Mathematics. *International Journal of Science and Mathematics Education, 13*, 583–604.

Dearden, J. (2016). *English medium instruction: A growing global phenomenon*. Accessible at www.teachingenglish.org.uk. https://doi.org/10.13140/RG.2.2.12079.94888. English to teaching through English, *CALR Journal*, 9.

Erling, E. J., Adinolfi, L., & Hultgren, K. A. (2017). *Multilingual Classrooms: Opportunities and challenges for English medium instruction in low and middle income contexts*. British Council.

Hagerman, C. (2009). English language policy and practice in Japan. *Osaka Jogakuin College Kiyo Journal, 6*, 47–64.

Holmarsdottir, H. (2005). From Policy to Practice: A study of the implementation of the Language-in-Education Policy (LiEP) in three South African Primary schools. PhD dissertation submitted to the Faculty of Education, Universitetet i Oslo.

Hu, G. (2005). English language education in China: policies, progress, and problems. *Language Policy, 5,* 5–24.
Kachru, B. (1985). Standards, codification and sociolinguistic realism: English language in the outer circle. In R. Quirk & H. Widowson (Eds.), *English in the world: Teaching and learning the language and literatures* (pp. 11–36). Cambridge University Press.
Kennedy, C. (2011). Challenges for language policy, language and development. In H. Coleman (Ed.), *Dreams and realities: Developing countries and the English language* (pp. 24–38). British Council.
Kikuchi, K., & Browne, C. (2009). English educational policy for high schools in Japan. *RELC, 40*(2), 172–191. https://doi.org/10.1177/0033688209105865
Knagg, J .(2020). English-medium instruction (EMI) in higher education: nature, benefits and risks – an introduction for non-experts. In Bullock, D (ed), 2019 International Symposium on EMI for Higher Education in the New Era: Selected Proceedings. British Council.(pp. 12–17).
Kuchah, K. (2018). Early English medium instruction in Francophone Cameroon: The injustice of equal opportunity. *System, 73*, 37–47.
Laitin, D. R., Ramachandran, R., & Walter, S. (2019). The legacy of colonial language policies and their impact on student learning: Evidence from an experimental program in Cameroon. *Economic Development and Cultural Change, 68*(1), 239–272.
Madhavan Brochier, D. (2016, May 14). Ten truths (and a lie) about EMI. *IATEFL webinar.*
Melitz, J. (2016). English as a global language. In V. Ginsburgh & S. Weber (Eds.), *The Palgrave handbook of economics and language.* Palgrave Macmillan. https://doi.org/10.1007/978-1-137-32505-1_21
Milligan, L. O. (2020). Towards a social and epistemic justice approach for exploring the injustices of English as a Medium of Instruction in basic education. *Educational Review.* https://doi.org/10.1080/00131911.2020.1819204
Milligan, L. O., & Tikly, L. (2016). English as a medium of instruction in postcolonial contexts: Moving the debate forward. *Comparative Education, 52*(2), 227–280. https://doi.org/10.1080/03050068.2016.1185251
Nomlomo, V., & Vuzo, M. (2014). Language transition and access to education: Experiences from Tanzania and South Africa. *International Journal of Educational Studies, 1*(2), 73–82.
Probyn, M .(2001). Teachers Voices: Teachers Reflections on Learning and Teaching through the Medium of English as an Additional Language in

South Africa, *International Journal of Bilingual Education and Bilingualism, 4*(4), 249–266, https://doi.org/10.1080/13670050108667731

Randall, V. (2013). The importance of teacher education: A critical discussion on policy reform relating to 2010 White Paper and its implications for preparing teachers' paper. In *Paper presented at UCET symposium*. Kings College. (Available at https://www.kcl.ac.uk/sspp/departments/education)

Richards, J. (2015). The changing face of language learning: Learning beyond the classroom. *RELC, 46*(1), 5–22.

Robayo Acuña, L. M., & Cárdenas, M. L. (2017). Inclusive education and ELT policies in Colombia: Views from some PROFILE journal authors. *PROFILE Issues in Teachers' Professional Development, 19*(1), 121–136. https://doi.org/10.15446/profile.v19n1.61075

Rose, H. (2019). The future of English in global higher education: Shifting trends from teaching.

Sah, P. K., & Li, G. (2018). English medium instruction (EMI) as linguistic capital in Nepal: Promises and realities. *International Multilingual Research Journal, 12*(2), 109–123.

Schweisfurth, M. (2013). Learner-Centred education in international perspective. *Journal of International and Comparative Education, 2*(1), 1–8.

Simpson, J. (2019). *English language and medium of instruction in basic education in low- and middle- income countries: A British Council perspective*. British Council. www.teachingenglish.org.uk/publications

Tembe, J., & Norton., B. (2008). Promoting local languages in Ugandan primary schools: The community stakeholder. *The Canadian Modern Language Review, 65*(1), 33–60. https://doi.org/10.3138/cmlr.65.1.33

Tohidian, I., & Nodooshan, S. G. (2021). Teachers' engagement within educational policies and decisions improves classroom practice: The case of Iranian ELT school teachers. *Improving Schools, 24*(1), 33–46. https://doi.org/10.1177/1365480220906625

Vavrus, F. (2009). The cultural politics of constructivist pedagogies: Teacher education reform in the United Republic of Tanzania. *International Journal of Educational Development, 29*(3), 303–311. https://doi.org/10.1016/j.ijedudev.2008.05.002

Walkinshaw, I., Fenton-Smith, B., & Humphreys, P. (2017). EMI issues and challenges in Asia-Pacific higher education: An introduction. In B. Fenton-Smith, P. Humphreys, & I. Walkinshaw (Eds.), *English medium instruction in higher education in Asia-Pacific: From policy to pedagogy. Multilingual education*

(Vol. 21, pp. 1–18). Springer, Springer Nature. https://doi.org/10.1007/978-3-319-51976-0_1

Waters, A. (2009). Managing innovation in English language education. *Language Teaching, 42*(4), 421–458. https://doi.org/10.1017/S026144480999005X

Wedell, M. (2009). *Planning for educational change: Putting people and their contexts first*. Continuum.

Yoshioda, K. (2003). Language education policy in Japan: The problem of espoused objectives versus practice. *The Modern Language Journal, 87*(2), 290–292.

Part I

Change Process in ELT Policy

2

Teaching at—Not to—the Middle in Japan: Examining How ELT Policies Aimed at Extremes Influence Mid-Tier Institutions

Giancarla Unser-Schutz, Beni Kudo, and Samuel Rose

Introduction

In the previous decade, the Japanese Ministry of Education (MEXT) made improving English language teaching and internationalization at universities major goals (Ishikawa, 2011); however, these goals have largely been unreached (MEXT, 2015). Even as MEXT has focused on raising the number of subject classes taught in English to improve internationalization and encourage foreign student enrollment (Ishikawa, 2011), remedial education has also become spotlighted as Japan's decreasing population has led to open enrollment at many universities (Mori, 2002; Yamada, 2009). Consequently, many current ELT policies focus on either top-tier or remedial institutions. Little attention, though, is given to the many universities somewhere in between, where most

G. Unser-Schutz (✉) • B. Kudo • S. Rose
Rissho University, Tokyo, Japan
e-mail: giancarlaunserschutz@ris.ac.jp

students' English proficiency levels are also in between: neither high enough to take classes taught in English, nor so low that they are required to take remedial courses. Our institution—Rissho University (RU), a small, lower mid-tier private university in Tokyo—is one such institution.

Using our institution as a case study, we examine how MEXT's policies might function at in-between universities. Following a review of MEXT policies and our institution's curriculum, we developed teacher surveys to consider how mid-tier universities may be influenced by external policies, and how aware teachers are, at least those at RU, of such policies.

Mid-Range Deviation Scores

Nearly all universities in Japan attend to a deviation score, called the *hensachi*, an important calculation in Japanese university admissions, purportedly indicating how far students' entrance exam scores deviate from the mean (Benesse Corporation, 2018). The mean is marked with the number 50, and any degree of 10 higher or lower represents one standard deviation. RU is considered an open-admission university. As with many open-admission universities, RU's *hensachi* is in the 40s, leaving its admission classes labeled as within a mid to lower range (see Yamada, 2009 for more details of how such universities are viewed).

MEXT and ELT

The Ministry of Education's focus on internationalization and ELT has changed along with the greater social and political climate, including shifts from

- internationalism to globalism (Nakane et al., 2015) and
- grammar-oriented study to speaking-oriented study (Kubota, 2002).

These changes have been crystalized recently by MEXT's focus on *gurōbaru-jinzai* (global talent), a reference to globally minded individuals ready to work in international settings. Since its establishment by the

Prime Minister's Cabinet in 2011, *gurōbaru-jinzai* has been a core concept in many competitive grants distributed by MEXT. To this end, the development of English-language degree programs was intended to increase learners' proficiencies as a way of increasing their chances to work in international environments and render Japanese universities attractive to international students (Hashimoto, 2017). The internationalization of English language education is trending globally especially in countries which originally had English as a foreign language (Rose, 2019). Sah and Li (2018) report that the EMI policy in Nepal was a response to the increasing demand for English language education by the local population, as English was seen as a prestigious language, associated with access to wealth. This is similar to the local community's perception of universities offering EMI in Turkey. Macaro et al. (2016) observe that government universities offering EMI in Turkey were perceived as prestigious and EMI policy was intended to attract international students (Dearden, 2016). English language education policies in many countries are identified with economic benefits associated with increased English language proficiencies, the need for universities to be competitive, wider job markets, and perceived prestige universities gain when they adopt English language education (see, e.g., Dearden, 2016; Rose, 2019). English language education policies innovation in many contexts are similar in scope and reveal two major controversial understandings: (1) governments' good intentions of internationalizing education, and (2) attempts at responding to local communities' demands. However good such intentions may be, the approach to designing the policies have generally been noted to be top-down (Lawrence, 2014; Dearden, 2016).

Given that most of the English language education policies are commonly designed in a non-consultative manner with direct stakeholders (Bolitho, 2012), implementation has been noted in the literature to be fraught with issues ranging from low learner proficiencies (Sah & Li, 2018), resistance to policies (Schweisfurth, 2013), policy (mis)interpretation during implementation (Galloway et al., 2020), low English language teachers' proficiencies (Dearden & Macaro, 2016) to learner achievement (Murray, 2020), and so on. These have generation more Ideological complications, as issues of inequalities and the promotion of English language hegemony over local languges. The goal is ambitious. In

2017, Japanese high school seniors, on average, scored 422 on the TOEIC IP test (Institute for International Business Communication, 2018), a remarkably modest score given that most English-medium institutions require scores in the 700s or higher. Still, the development of such programs has been crucial to universities such that MEXT funded the most recent major English and international education grant—the Top Global University Project—with ¥6.3 billion into 37 universities (Higher Education Section, International Project Office Adjustments Area of the Higher Education Department, 2018). Terasawa (2015) criticized these ambitious efforts, showing that MEXT's ELT policies have often lacked data-driven evidence to show their necessity or viability.

Remedial Education

Currently, even as MEXT has focused on raising the number of subject classes taught in English to improve internationalization and encourage foreign student enrollment (Ishikawa, 2011), remedial education has also become spotlighted as the decreasing population has led to open enrollment at many universities (Mori, 2002; Yamada, 2009). Remedial education first became relevant in Japan as the percentage of students enrolling in university increased, which led to the creation of more universities (Mori, 2002). Following Mori's prediction, in 2009 over 50% of high school students entered tertiary education following graduation.

However, universities have also been preparing for an overall decrease in Japan's population, namely a dwindling quantity of 18-year-olds (Igami, 2014). For many universities, the decrease in high school graduates has meant lowering admission standards. Consequences of doing so have included the following:

1. Increasing the number of students admitted through non-traditional means outside of the standard academic test (e.g., recommendations by high schools), has generally had a negative impact on the English skills of incoming classes (Kochiyama, 2010; Metoki, 2014).
2. The question of non-competitive, open-admission universities has become increasingly pressing (Kuzuki, 2016; Yamada, 2009).

3. Several universities have been forced to close as they were no longer able to maintain their student bodies, including Mie Chukyo University in 2013, St. Thomas University in 2015, and Tokyo Jogakkan College in 2017.

For universities feeling the need to lower admission standards in order to maintain enrollment, remedial education has come to be a way to support development of a diverse student body. Not surprisingly, though, much attention has been given to this new face of remedial education, leading to the birth of the Japan Association for Developmental Education (*Nihon Rimediaru Kyōiku Gakkai*) in 2005 (which, interestingly, uses the English loan word *rimediaru* 'remedial' in its Japanese name).

ELT in Mid-Tier Institutions

Although Japanese education policies have long been top-down—where policies are designed with the top-ranking schools in mind, which then trickle-down to lower ranking schools using these higher ranking universities as a competitive baseline (Kitagawa & Oba, 2010; Yamada, 2009)—elite-driven practices may no longer function in a diversifying system. As Tahira (2012) argues in her analysis of MEXT's push toward communicative language teaching in primary and secondary education, a major problem with MEXT's ELT policies—on all levels—has been a lack of commitment to its policies through the inclusion of support for teachers within policy planning. Indeed, given the tying in of government funding with compliance to MEXT's policies, mid-tier universities cannot afford to buck the trends; instead, they must find ways to determine how and to what degree MEXT's policies can be utilized and adapted to their own institution's needs. For many mid-tier universities, this may mean essentially feeling around in the dark, which could be a waste of the latent potential of so many students at mid-tier universities, whose abilities could be drawn out in positive and supportive programs (Kanai, 2014).

In sum, ELTs at mid-tier institutions are seemingly left to guess how to conduct their jobs satisfactorily. Thus, examining how MEXT's policies are understood, viewed, and acted upon by English language teachers at mid-tier universities is an important first step in determining (1) to what extent a gap exists between teachers' ideas about how ELT should be conducted and what is expected of them by MEXT and administrators and (2) how policies may be developed that more effectively address the needs of mid-tier universities. This contradicts the primary policy intentions of rendering education in Japanese accessible to the international community.

To this end, in 2017, our institution enacted an action research project aimed at fostering positive interfaculty connections and reassessing how we conduct English language teaching.

To analyze how ELT colleagues are responding to MEXT-driven policies, we posed the following research questions:

1. How aware are English language teachers of MEXT's current policies?
2. How have English language teachers evaluated MEXT's policies for their own faculties?

Methodology

We posed our research questions as part of the 2017 action research project. The project started with a paper survey, followed by interviews.

We conducted the study at our university. Formed in 1924, the Buddhist institution currently consists of seven liberal arts and one science faculty, with six of the faculties holding classes at its campus in central Tokyo, and two at its campus in a suburb of Saitama, the prefecture neighboring Tokyo in the north. Although all faculties have required English language classes, not all have fulltime English education teachers, meaning they are highly dependent upon adjunct professors. Thus, input from adjunct professors is crucial to understanding the impact and implementation of MEXT's policies. Nevertheless, we decided in the current project to focus specifically on fulltime faculty members as they are more centrally involved in the creation and implementation of curricula within the faculties.

The survey was given to 14 fulltime faculty members representing all the campus faculties. Descriptions of the participating colleagues are

Table 2.1 Descriptions of Participating Faculty

		Number of Teachers
Gender	Female	8
	Male	6
Tenured	Yes	7
	No	7
Background	Japanese	9
	Other	5
Education	Bachelor's	1
	Master's	9
	PhD	14
Years at RU	1–3	3
	3–6	6
	7–9	2
	10+	3

included in Table 2.1. Half of the colleagues were tenured, and seven were on contract. In Japanese universities, new teachers are hired as tenured to begin with, or on a contract. Although almost all contracts stipulate the possibility and terms of renewal, it is less common for them to formally indicate under what terms teachers could be rehired in tenured positions, if at all. Some universities have begun to utilize a more formal tenure system (Hosaka, 2014). At the time of this study, the majority of fulltime teachers at the university were Japanese (9); of the five non-Japanese teachers, one was from Canada and the other four were from the U.S. Faculty members at this time had registered an average of 5.17 years of employment at RU, not including two faculty members with over 30 years at RU. For 11 of the fulltime teachers, RU was their first fulltime university employment.

We also participated as subjects since, as a research team, we have been actively involved in all parts of the project, not only in planning and as interviewees, but also as interested, active respondents. The decision to conduct it in this way reflects the reality of our research project: Our motivations behind the project are largely fueled by our own experiences as interested parties, and as such, remaining objective outsiders is neither realistic nor necessarily desirable, given the larger project goals.

The Survey

The survey consisted of background questions, 18 five-point Likert scale questions (1 = Strongly disagree; 5 = Strongly agree), and four free answer questions. The scaled questions concerned English language teachers' (1) understanding and knowledge of national ELT policy, and (2) perceptions regarding relationships between content area faculty members and English language instructors. The survey itself was conducted in both Japanese and English.

Results and Discussion

RQ1: How Aware Are Faculty Members of MEXT's Current Policies?

Results of the survey with respect to ways RU faculty understand MEXT policies are displayed in Table 2.2.

Table 2.2 Understanding of MEXT's Policies

Policy and Curriculum Questions	M	SD
I am sufficiently familiar with MEXT's current English-education policies	3.29	0.85
RU's curricula reflect MEXT's current English-education policies	2.79	0.58
My faculty has clear English-education study goals for students at matriculation	2.71	1.14
MEXT's current English-education policies are realistic for RU	2.64	0.93
MEXT's current English-education policies are appropriate for contemporary Japan	2.36	0.93
MEXT shares enough information with English teachers	2.21	0.80
English teachers' thoughts and experiences are valued by MEXT	2.23	0.83
Preparing students to be globally minded workers is an important goal of English education	3.86	1.03
Preparing students to be globally minded workers is an important goal	3.86	1.03
Preparing students to be globally minded workers is a realistic goal for English education at RU	3.21	1.05

At an average score of 3.29 (SD = 0.85), most respondents displayed only slightly positive conviction with respect to their familiarity with MEXT's current English-education policies. However, most teachers felt a bit negative regarding how well RU's policies accurately reflect MEXT's policies (M = 2.79, SD = 0.58). Given that respondents did not respond confidently regarding their understanding of MEXT's policies, it is not surprising that they would not be able to strongly agree or disagree as to how well RU's curricula reflect those policies. The fact that they tended to score somewhat negatively in regard to how well RU's curricula reflect MEXT's policies, however, suggests several other interpretations, as well, of which two are especially worth considering:

Firstly, although most of MEXT's policies are made public in the form of government white papers and presentations, they are not systematically shared with teachers through newsletters, MEXT-led faculty development forums, or other open and accessible channels. Aside from searching on the various government websites for related documents, many teachers must seek information about MEXT's policies through secondary sources on their own, an unchecked process which may not always be accurate or current. Much of the policy information is in Japanese, thereby causing problems for non-Japanese teachers seeking out MEXT documents.

These barriers are reflected in the survey results in other ways. English language teachers responded negatively regarding how much information MEXT shares with them (M = 2.21, SD = 0.80). Thus, colleagues find it difficult to become active decision makers in policy, likely contributing to the belief amongst teachers that their feelings and experiences are not strongly valued by MEXT (M = 2.23, SD = 0.83). Tahira (2012) had found MEXT lax in terms of outreach to ELT colleagues; thus, these results are largely consistent with previous analyses.

Secondly, reforming ELT curriculum is bureaucratically daunting. Adding or changing new classes requires amending faculty bylaws *and* reporting those changes to MEXT to be in compliance with certifying requirements. Therefore, MEXT's oversight can discourage insufficiently planned changes and elongate responses to policy changes. Such administrative barriers can encourage faculties to put off making changes, creating an environment that is conservative with respect to planning within the previously existing structures and curricula. This may partially explain why the teachers responded negatively to the question of whether their faculties have clear ELT goals for students at the time of matriculation (M = 2.71, SD = 1.14).

Instead of formulating long term structural changes with clear visions reflecting current policies, faculties may be tempted to respond ad hoc or in less formal ways. As an example, one RU faculty created a curriculum map detailing the relationships between English courses and their specific goals. However, to avoid off-campus oversight, the document was kept within the department by composing it as an *oboegaki,* or memorandum. While the faculty-generated map may become a tool toward program management, as an internal memo, it cannot be officially incorporated into the faculty's bylaws, or included with the curriculum documents created by the administration for students. Such practice may become an increasingly vital policy problem given that MEXT has begun to push universities to implement their admission, curriculum, and diploma policies more transparently (Tanabe, 2019).

Additionally, teachers may also be hesitant to make changes to the curriculum because they do not have confidence in the current policies. Most respondents did not feel that MEXT's current policies were appropriate for contemporary Japan (M = 2.36, SD = 0.93), or that they were realistic for RU (M = 2.64, SD = 0.93). Interestingly, when asked specifically about ELTs' role in the fostering of globally minded individuals—which, as noted previously, is one of the centerpieces of recent ELT policy—most respondents were somewhat more positive (M = 3.86, SD = 1.03). However, as with MEXT's policies in general, they were significantly less certain of the viability of this as a goal for ELT at RU (M = 3.21, SD = 1.05); ($t(13)$ = 3.23, p = 0.007**). If one takes the fostering of globally minded individuals to be the abstract heart of MEXT's policy—as opposed to more concrete goals, such as increasing TOEIC scores—then it seems that teachers are in agreement with the heart of contemporary policies but are less certain as to how they should be implemented.

RQ2: How Have English Language Teachers Evaluated MEXT's Policies for Their Own Faculties?

One of MEXT's larger goals is for universities to offer more classes taught in English, which requires larger coordination with non-English subject specialists within each faculty beyond English language teachers. As such, it is important to consider whether each faculty's environment is receptive and open to coordinating and cooperating with English language teachers. Table 2.3 shows English language teachers' impressions regarding the interlingual environment MEXT purportedly advances.

The majority of teachers reported that they felt that there were other faculty members in the department they could talk to ($M = 4.14$, $SD = 0.95$) and that they were well-connected with the other faculty members ($M = 3.93$, $SD = 0.83$), but they did not feel as positively concerning the level of faculty support for ELT ($M = 3.00$, $SD = 1.27$) or how valued ELT was within their faculties ($M = 2.86$, $SD = 1.29$). These results may seem somewhat contradictory, but they suggest an important divide between English language teachers and subject teachers on an individual, teacher-to-teacher level versus English language teachers and subject teachers on an institutional level. As a result, although it seems that teachers feel that *individual* faculty members are supportive, English language teaching may not be well integrated into the larger curriculum,

Table 2.3 English Language Teachers and Faculty Relations

Faculty Relations Questions	M	SD
My faculty has enough fulltime English teachers now	2.86	1.35
My faculty is highly dependent upon adjunct English teachers	3.64	1.08
I am well connected with the other members of my faculty	3.93	0.83
I have people in the faculty I can confer and talk with	4.14	0.95
The other members of my faculty are interested in English education	3.07	1.27
There is support within my faculty for the development of English education	3.00	1.27
English education is valued within my faculty	2.86	1.29
I have frequent contact with fulltime English teachers from other faculties at RU	2.43	1.09
I would like more contact with other fulltime English teachers from other faculties at RU	4.21	0.80

suggesting that it may be difficult to implement some of MEXT's more ambitious plans.

These issues may be exacerbated by the fact that, to some degree, English language teachers are isolated from each other, a fact which was already clear from the number of English language teachers. Out of eight faculties, two have no fulltime English language teachers, three had one, two had three, and the one with an English literature and language program had five. Not surprisingly, many ELTs felt somewhat negative regarding the current number of English language teachers in their faculties (M = 2.86, SD = 1.35). Additionally, teachers felt that they were somewhat dependent upon part-time adjunct teachers (M = 3.64, SD = 1.08). Given that there is not much support within faculties, one might hypothesize that English language teachers receive support through English language teachers from other faculties. However, most did not report being in frequent contact with other English language teachers (M = 2.43, SD = 1.09). However, they did report a strong desire to have more contact with other RU English teachers (M = 4.21, SD = 0.80).

The isolation of English language teachers is likely one characteristic of ELT at Japanese universities, given that it is largely a result of the decentralization of English education. Following the deregulation of the University Establishment Standards in 1991, general education (GE) courses at universities were shifted to individual faculties. In turn, GE faculties, which had been responsible for university-wide first and second year general education courses, were dismantled. Many English teachers were thus shifted to other faculties, as was the case at RU in 1995. For some teachers, this meant moving to faculties well-aligned with their academic specializations. But for many others, this meant being shifted to faculties outside of their fields. As non-English-major faculties need to supply their own ELT courses, positions at such faculties continue to represent a large portion of job opportunities for English language teachers.

One positive interpretation of this would be that, given the shift toward content-based learning, having ELT specialists within each faculty can potentially lead to the development of curricula better matching the faculty's needs through the collaboration of English language and subject faculty members. However, it also means that English language specialists may not have ELT colleagues to confer with, potentially isolating them. Being in the same faculty does not necessarily mean that non-English specialist faculty members will be active and committed advocates for language education, especially as ELT teaching is often seen as being less critical than subject teaching (Byram & Risager, 1999). Improvement of these issues will require both a rehabilitation of the image of ELT teaching, particularly through expanded understanding of the importance and challenges involved in language learning, but also structural changes that encourage collaboration between faculties and create channels within faculties themselves to better incorporate English language teachers.

Conclusion

By analyzing survey data of English language teachers at the university, our study showed that teachers do not always have strong familiarity or confidence in MEXT's policies. Furthermore, implementation of MEXT's policies is made difficult by the isolation of English teachers. As this study has shown, ELT policies may not always be well understood by the people most affected by such policies; that is, teachers and learners as earlier studies (Murray, 2020, for example) have demonstrated At mid-tier universities such as RU, which are not usually the primary focus of ELT policies, English language teachers may be particularly prone to this phenomenon.

There are of course limitations to how one can apply these results. Although there are advantages to focusing on one institution—particularly, it is easier to ground the results within the institution's own practices—further cross-university research will be required to fully answer these questions.

Nevertheless, there are several reasons to think that core commonalities can be found, most important being that many of the issues touched upon here—such as the isolation of English language teachers and the sense that information is not being shared with them—result from larger systemic issues, such as the dismantling of GE faculties and MEXT's passive stance toward disseminating information. The lack of institutional support connecting English language teachers and non-English subject teachers may also be particular to mid-tier universities, as the need to provide supportive basic and intermediate English courses may muddy roles non-English subject teachers can have in developing ELT curricula. While so-called higher level universities may set ambitious goals based on robust entrance requirements, open-admission institutions are more likely to guess what evolving populations need and attempt to maneuver accordingly.

While top-down planning may be particularly problematic in Japan, it appears to be typical in the ELT policies of many countries (see Bolitho, 2012), suggesting that the process of creating policy more generally needs to be reconsidered. Our results suggest several possible ways to improve ELT policies for mid-tier universities in Japan. One point is to increase active and inclusive sharing of policy information with teachers by MEXT; this could be accomplished through creating an official ELT website with the specific goal of disseminating policy information amongst English teachers. More ambitiously, changes in ELT policy should be accompanied by funded faculty development policy workshops, which would serve the dual purpose of creating much needed English language teacher networks and offering teacher training, as well as potentially becoming a channel through which teachers could express their experiences to MEXT so that the voices of teachers at mid-tier universities can be heard and represented. Additionally, permitting more flexibility in how new curricula are created and reported may encourage universities to attempt changes which would otherwise seem risky.

Within universities themselves, there is also a clear need to both strengthen the relationships between English language teachers in different faculties and foster more ELT advocates among non-English subject teachers. Given already heavy workloads, asking for more involvement may in fact be the most difficult issue. However, open and cordial discussions involving all interested parties—Japanese and non-Japanese teachers, English-language and non-English subject teachers alike—will be crucial in determining how policies can be adapted to suit the needs of each faculty and create organic and coherent curriculum with clear visions appropriate to each individual university.

Acknowledgment This research was conducted with the support of a Rissho University Research Promotion Center Interfaculty research grant.

References

Benesse Corporation. (2018). Daigaku o shiraberu [Research about universities]. *Benesse maibijon* [Benesse my vision]. Retrieved October 22, 2018, from https://manabi.benesse.ne.jp/daigaku/school/3323/hensachi/index.html

Bolitho, R. (2012). Projects and programmes: Contemporary experience in ELT change management. In C. Tribble (Ed.), *Managing change in English language teaching: Lessons from experience* (pp. 33–46). British Council.

Byram, M., & Risager, K. (1999). *Language teachers, politics and cultures*. Multilingual Matters.

Dearden, J. (2016). *English medium instruction: A growing global phenomenon*. British Council. (Available at www.britishcouncil.org.uk)

Dearden, J., & Macaro, E. (2016). Higher education teacher' attitudes towards English medium instruction: A three-country comparison. *Studies in Second Language Learning and Teaching, 6*(3), 455–486. https://doi.org/10.14746/ssllt.2016.6.3.5

Galloway, N., Numajiri, T., & Rees, N. (2020). The 'internationalisation', or 'Englishisation', of higher education in East Asia. *Higher Education*. https://doi.org/10.1007/s10734-019-00486-1

Hashimoto, H. (2017). Government policy driving English-medium instruction at Japanese universities: Responding to a competitiveness crisis in a globalizing world. In A. Bradford & H. Brown (Eds.), *English-medium instruction in Japanese higher education* (pp. 14–31). Multilingual Matters.

Higher Education Section, International Project Office Adjustments Area of the Higher Education Department. (2018, October 3). *Sūpā gurōbaru daigaku sōsei shien* [Support for the creation of Super Global Universities]. Ministry of Education, Culture, Sports, Science and Technology-Japan (MEXT). Retrieved October 15, 2018, from http://www.mext.go.jp/a_menu/koutou/kaikaku/sekaitenkai/1360288.htm

Hosaka, M. (2014). Tenyua-torakku ni okeru mentaringu no jissen-jōkyō to nīzu: Wakate-kyōin no kanten kara [Mentoring for tenure-track faculty: Tenure-track faculty's perceptions of mentoring practices and their perceived needs]. *Tokushima daigaku kyōiku kenkyū jānaru* [Tokushima University Education Research Journal], *11*, 86–96.

Igami, K. (2014). Reform of university education for non-elite university students. *Japan Labor Review, 11*(2), 53–68.

Institute for International Business Communication. (2018, June 20). *TOEIC® Program Data & Analysis 2018: 2017nendo Jueknshaū to Heikin Sukoa*

[TOEIC® Program Data & Analysis 2018: 2017 Report Number of students and average scores]. Institute for International Business Communication. Retrieved from http://www.iibc-global.org/library/default/toeic/official_data/pdf/DAA.pdf

Ishikawa, M. (2011). Redefining internationalization in higher education: *Global 30* and the making of global universities in Japan. In D. B. Willis & R. Jeremy (Eds.), *Redefining Japanese education* (pp. 193–223). Symposium Books.

Kanai, M. (2014). Chūkensō daigaku ni okeru sūri kyōiku: Jugyō naiyō-rei to gakusei no hanō [Educational sociology of mathematics at mid-tier universities: Examples from course content and students' reactions]. *Riron to hōhō* [Sociological Theory and Methods], *29*(1), 123–130.

Kitagawa, F., & Oba, J. (2010). Managing differentiation of higher education system in Japan: Connecting excellence and diversity. *Higher Education*, *59*(4), 507–524.

Kochiyama A. (2010). Shinnyūsei no eigo nōryoku to nyūshi keitai oyobi dōkizuke ni kansuru chōsa [A study on the English ability of Wayo freshman: Focusing on their entrance exam type and motivation]. *Wayō Josei Daigaku Kiyō* [The Journal of Wayo Women's University], *50*, 93–101.

Kubota, R. (2002). The impact of globalization on language teaching in Japan. In D. Block & D. Cameron (Eds.), *Globalization and language teaching* (pp. 13–28). Routledge.

Kuzuki, K. (2016). Bōdā furii daigaku ni okeru gakusei katei kyōiku no shitsu hoshō: Gaitō daigaku kyōin no ishiki ni chakumoku shite [Quality assurance for the undergraduate programs at low-competitive universities]. *Kōbe daigaku: Daigaku kyōiku kenkyū* [Kobe University: University Education Research], *24*, 55–66.

Lawrence, A. W. (2014). Engaging elementary teachers in reform: What administrators and policy makers should know. *Education Doctoral Dissertations in Leadership*, 47. https://ir.stthomas.edu/caps_ed_lead_docdiss/47

Macaro, E., Mustafa, A., & Dearden, J. (2016). English medium instruction in universities: A collaborative experiment in Turkey. *Studies in English Language Teaching*, *4*(1), 51–76. (Available at www.scholink.org/ojs/index.php/selt)

Metoki M. (2014). T-dagaiku ni okeru nyūgaku keitai to gakusei no eigoryoku no kankei [The relationship between the types of university entrance examinations and Japanese students' English proficiency in T University]. *Tenshi Daigaku Kiyō* [Bulletin of Tenshi College], *14*(2), 53–60.

Ministry of Education, Culture, Sports, Science and Technology-Japan (MEXT). (2015, June 11). *Dai2kai gurōbaru jinzai ikusei suishin kaigi kanren shiryō/ dēta-shū* [Reference materials and data for the second meeting of the Promotion of Global Human Resources Training Meeting]. Prime Minister of Japan and His Cabinet. Retrieved May 20, 2018, from https://www.kantei.go.jp/jp/singi/global/dai2/siryou4.pdf

Mori, R. (2002). Entrance examinations and remedial education in Japanese higher education. *Higher Education, 43*(1), 27–42.

Murray, D. E. (2020). The world of English language teaching: Creating equity or inequity? *Language Teaching Research, 24*(1), 60–70. https://doi.org/10.1177/1362168818777529

Nakane, I., Otsuji, E., & Armour, W. S. (Eds.). (2015). *Languages and identities in a transitional Japan: From internationalization to globalization.* Routledge.

Rose, H. (2019). The future of English in global higher education: Shifting trends from teaching English to teaching through English. *CALR Journal.* Available at http://web.aou.edu.lb/images/stories/lebanon/Research/CALR/issue9/Article_1_by_Dr_Heath_Rose.pdf

Sah, P. K., & Li, G. (2018). English medium instruction (EMI) as linguistic capital in Nepal: Promises and realities. *International Multilingual Research Journal, 12*(2), 109–123. https://doi.org/10.1080/19313152.2017.1401448

Schweisfurth, M. (2013). Learner-centred education in international perspective. *Journal of International and Comparative Education, 2*(1), 1–8.

Tahira, M. (2012). Behind MEXT's new course of study guidelines. *The Language Teacher, 36*(3), 3–8.

Tanabe, M. (2019). Gakushi katei kyōiku no mittsu no porishī to autokamu kiban-gata kyōiku [Three policies in the baccalaureate degree program and outcome-based education]. *Igaku kyōiku* [Journal of the Japanese Society for Medical Education], *48*(4), 237–242.

Terasawa, T. (2015). *'Nihonjin to eigo' no shakaigaku* [The sociology of 'Japanese people and English']. Kenkyusha.

Yamada, H. (2009). Bōdā-furī daigaku ni okeru gakusei-chōsa no igi to kadai [The significance and the problems of student surveys at 'Border-Free University']. *Hiroshima Daigaku Daigakuin Kyōiku Kenkyūka Kiyō Daisanbu Kyōiku Ningen Kagaku Kanren Ryōiki* [Bulletin of the Graduate School of Education, Hiroshima University. Part 3, Education and Human Science], (58), 27–35.

3

The Implementation of the 4+4+4 Educational Policy in Turkey: Reflections from English Classrooms

Tuğba Birdal and Seniye Vural

The Global Status of English and the 4+4+4 Policy

Language policy refers to "the primary mechanism for organizing, managing and manipulating language behaviors as it consists of decisions made about languages and their uses in society" (Shohamy, 2006, p. 45). Undoubtedly, language policies are influenced by social and political factors (Tollefson, 2006). Similarly, ELT policies are shaped by social, economic, political, and geographical factors, among many. For example, the global status of English as a lingua franca, which led to an unprecedented spread of English, has had a considerable impact on language policies and practices in many countries (Butler, 2004; Kırkgöz, 2009;

T. Birdal
Abdullah Gül University, Kayseri, Turkey
e-mail: tugba.birdal@agu.edu.tr

S. Vural (✉)
Erciyes University, Kayseri, Turkey
e-mail: svural@erciyes.edu.tr

© The Author(s), under exclusive license to Springer Nature Switzerland AG 2022
E. E. Ekembe et al. (eds.), *Interface between English Language Education Policies and Practice*, https://doi.org/10.1007/978-3-031-14310-6_3

Kusumoto, 2008; Nunan, 2003). In this sense, many countries aim to ensure that students are adequately equipped with English skills (Tsui & Tollefson, 2007). English replaced French as the language of international diplomacy, became the lingua franca for trade, tourism, banking, popular media, science and technology, and entered the education systems and daily lives of many people, even in officially monolingual countries, including Turkey (Doğançay-Aktuna, 1998). The influence of English's global status in Turkey is evident in the incorporation of English as a compulsory subject through a planned policy, giving it more emphasis than other foreign languages (Kırkgöz, 2009).

In 2012, the Ministry of National Education (MoNE) announced a policy change in the Turkish education system, which entailed a transition from an eight-year primary and four-year high school education to a 4+4+4 system, comprising of four years of education at primary, middle, and secondary levels (MoNE, 2012). As part of this revision, in light of perceived international role of English, the starting age for English was lowered from age ten (grade 4) to eight (grade 2).

Lowering the age for when compulsory English instruction begins has been a major language policy change in many countries (Butler, 2004; Edelenbos et al., 2006; Kırkgöz, 2008; Kusumoto, 2008; Nunan, 2003). Young learners have distinct characteristics from adults (Camerun, 2003; Djigunović, 1995; Slattery & Willis, 2001). Therefore, for bolstered English instruction policies to be successful, primary school English teachers should be competent enough to teach very young learners.

Research on ELT Policy

Teachers are important because putting new legislation into practice is not easy (Çelik & Kasapoğlu, 2014). Teachers are the most powerful implementers of the policy and the curriculum (İnceçay & İnceçay, 2010), responsible for all classroom applications and influenced by the decisions directly (Haznedar, 2010). Moreover, teachers' motives for implementing a policy might be different from those of policymakers (Dearden & Macaro, 2016). Research reveals that many educational problems regarding English instruction are due to the lack of sound policies and planning (Haznedar, 2010; Suna & Durmuşçelebi, 2013) and disparities between policies and their applications (Gürsoy et al., 2013; Suna & Durmuşçelebi, 2013; Uztosun, 2016). Therefore, taking teachers' training background, competency, classroom practices, needs, and challenges into consideration during policy making and curriculum development is crucial. However, according to Nunan (2003), governments often introduce English at a younger age as a compulsory subject without adequate funding, teacher education, or materials for young learners. Unfortunately, the 2012 move to the 4+4+4 policy in Turkey was developed in a top-down manner (Kırkgöz, 2007); teachers were not involved in policymaking directly or comprehensively (Haznedar, 2010) and the policy was enacted without any pilot implementation (Gün & Atanur Başkan, 2014).

Research on ELT policy in Turkey largely comprises of historical analyses of foreign language education policies (Haznedar, 2010; Karatepe, 2005; Kırkgöz, 2007; Sarıçoban, 2012; Seyratlı Özkan et al., 2016; Suna & Durmuşçelebi, 2013) and the influence of globalization on policy changes (Hismanoğlu, 2012; Kırkgöz, 2009). On the other hand, research on the 4+4+4 policy, which is the focus of this chapter, is limited to a few studies critically analyzing the policy (Gün & Atanur Başkan, 2014) and exploring primary school administrators' perceptions (Çelik & Kasapoğlu, 2014) and teachers' opinions of the curriculum (Aksoy et al., 2018; Gürsoy et al., 2013).

Research is still needed regarding the implementation of the 4+4+4 policy, particularly regarding English. This study explores state primary school English teachers' educational backgrounds, perceived pedagogical weaknesses, needs, classroom practices, and challenges. The findings indicate the extent to which classroom practices align with policy aims and provide insights into actual classroom practices and deficiencies. To this end, this study posed the following research questions:

1. What are the state primary school English teachers' educational backgrounds regarding Teaching English to young learners (TEYL)?
2. What are their perceived pedagogical weaknesses?
3. What are their perceived needs for more effective teaching practices?
4. How do they put the policy into classroom practice with regard to

(a) the frequency of activities?
(b) achieving success in a TEYL classroom?
5. What challenges do they face in the implementation of the policy?
6. What are their perceptions regarding the 2nd-, 3rd-, and 4th-grade curricula?

English Instruction in Turkey

English was incorporated into the Turkish education system as a school subject as early as 1863 with the foundation of the first private English-medium secondary school. Since then, Turkish governments have introduced new policies based on the needs and demands of the time, including making English a compulsory school subject, increasing the duration of English instruction, and enacting new approaches to teaching English (Gürsoy et al., 2013). In the wake of the establishment of the Turkish Republic in 1923, modernization and Westernization movements led to closer connections with Europe and the United States. As a result, English became more common and dominant over other foreign languages (Kırkgöz, 2007). The 1950s were a crucial time for the spread of English education: In the 1951–1952 academic year, Turkish Education Foundation Ankara College started English instruction, followed by the establishment of the first Anatolian high school[1] in 1955, which made English the most prominent foreign language in secondary school curriculum (Kırkgöz, 2009). In the 1980s, two major language policy acts were passed: the Foreign Language Education and Teaching Act (1983), which laid the groundwork for foreign language teaching at secondary and high school education, and the Higher Education Act (1984).

The 1997 foreign language education reform was noted to be a cornerstone of English education in Turkey, aiming at promoting effective language teaching (Sarıçoban, 2012). It marks important changes in ELT policy as the introduction of English was shifted from Grade 6 to Grade 4. In line with the policy, two new courses were introduced into the curricula of teacher education departments: Teaching English to Young Learners I and II. In 2012, with the new 4+4+4 system and shift from Grade 4 to

Grade 2 for the introduction of English, no changes regarding TEYL in the curricula of teacher education departments were made (Uztosun, 2016).

Previous studies indicated need for in-service training for primary school English teachers. Gürsoy et al. (2013) explored perceptions of English teachers on age of instruction, teaching methods, and current classroom practices. Teachers reported that English instruction should start at early ages and that young learners require techniques and approaches different from those of adolescents or adults; thus, in-service training is necessary. In another study, Kusumoto (2008) found that Japanese primary school English teachers have needs relating to improving their own English proficiency and gaining language teaching knowledge and skills.

In Turkey, Mede and Işık (2016) highlighted the need for professional development, especially for teachers of young learners. Specifically, the primary school English teachers in their study reported needing training on classroom environment, adaptation of teaching methods, instructional practices, utilization of technology, materials development, and language teaching skills. In addition, Tılfarlıoğlu and Öztürk (2007) explored problems teachers and students face during implementation of the primary school English curriculum. They concluded that teachers have not been specially trained to teach students at this age, so they follow the original content of the course text, are challenged by the students' short attention span, and prefer not to test students through assignments. Moreover, many teachers found the course text difficult, which, according to the researchers, was due to lack of TEYL training.

In addition to teachers' perceptions, research was conducted to explore the perceptions of Turkish state primary school principals regarding compulsory English instruction at an earlier age (Çelik & Kasapoğlu, 2014). The findings indicated that most principals support the 4+4+4 policy since they believe that the status of English as a global language brings the necessity to learn it at early ages. There was, however, general agreement among principals that the curriculum should to be revised to address inadequacies in materials, classroom conditions, and teachers' competency.

Finally, Uztosun (2016) sought to determine pre-service and in-service English teachers' self-efficacy beliefs regarding TEYL and found that teacher education programs have deficiencies in terms of (a) the importance given to teaching practicum, (b) the number of practice-based courses, and (c) the number of courses focusing on TEYL. Other challenges included limited class hours, inefficient textbooks, characteristics of young learners, and affective issues such as short attention span, unpreparedness, lack of student motivation, and teachers' difficulties in motivating them.

Methodology

In this current study, data were collected through a questionnaire and semi-structured interviews. The questionnaire, adapted from Kusumoto (2008), consisted of three parts and aimed to explore participants' educational background regarding TEYL, their needs for more effective teaching practices, and their actual classroom practices. It included two 4-point Likert scales (1 = disagree, 4 = agree) regarding teachers' needs and classroom practices, as well as open-ended questions regarding their needs, training background, and perceived effectiveness of the training.

Means and standard deviations were calculated for the teachers' responses to questionnaire items, and Cronbach's alpha was found to be 0.83, thereby showing more than adequate internal consistency within the questionnaire.

Semi-structured interviews were then conducted with all participants. The interview comprised of seven questions, aimed at gathering in-depth insight into teachers' views of a successful TEYL classroom, pedagogical weaknesses, challenges, and applicability of the new policy at each grade. The data were transcribed, pre-coded, and coded by separating into groups and labeling the thoughts to gain extensive perspective (Creswell & Plano Clark, 2007). The data were also quantified in terms of frequency of themes and presented in percentages. The questionnaire and the interview were piloted with 10 teachers from five different schools.

Table 3.1 charts how the research questions were addressed with respect to the questionnaire and semi-structured interviews.

The participants were selected randomly in that English teachers teaching at various schools in different regions of the country were emailed about the study, and 45 teachers—30 female and 15 male—teaching

Table 3.1 Crosswalk displaying the design of the study

RQ 1: What are the state primary school English teachers' educational backgrounds regarding TEYL?	**Questionnaire Part 1** 4 open-ended questions on the training programs they have participated and their perceived effectiveness
RQ 2: What are their perceived pedagogical weaknesses?	**Semi-structured interview**
RQ 3: What are their needs for more effective teaching practices?	**Questionnaire Part 2** Likert-scale items regarding teachers' professional needs Open-ended question
RQ 4: How do the teachers put the policy into classroom practice in terms of (a) the frequency of activities? (b) achieving success in a TEYL classroom?	**Questionnaire Part 3** Likert-scale items regarding classroom practices **Semi-structured interview**
RQ 5: What challenges do they face in the implementation of the policy?	
RQ 6: What are their perceptions regarding the 2nd-, 3rd-, and 4th-grade curricula?	

English at 30 different state primary schools in Turkey volunteered for the study. The mean of their teaching experience was 9.7 years, 3.17 years of which was at primary school.

Results

RQ1: What Is the State Primary School English Teachers' Educational Backgrounds Regarding TEYL?

Eighty percent of the participants reported to have taken TEYL courses during their pre-service education. Twenty-five percent of those having taken TEYL courses felt that the courses were not useful or did not meet their needs, claiming that they were too theoretical or lacking practical ideas. On the other hand, only 31.1% of the participants participated in-in-service teacher training programs about TEYL Some teachers stated that the program content was not realistic for teaching in large classes and was difficult to apply at state schools. Nonetheless, 64.2% of those who had attended thought the training programs met their needs and were useful.

RQ2: What Are Teachers' Perceived Pedagogical Weaknesses?

Data from the semi-structured interviews indicated that finding the right material for young learners was most frequently reported as teachers' main weakness. Twenty-two percent of the teachers maintained that it is their responsibility to make class enjoyable by bringing in the right material; however, they also reported that finding, developing, and adapting age- and level-appropriate materials requires time and training.

Additionally, 15.5% of the respondents perceived themselves as lacking experience in TEYL. They stated that they have not received specific TEYL training, so they have difficulty in simplifying instruction according to students' level and age. They said they want to use English as the medium of instruction, but they do not know how to simplify teacher talk to make it comprehensible. Also, 11.1% of the teachers said they have problems maintaining younger students' attention. For example, one teacher mentioned that 2nd graders' attention span can be short; thus, they feel weak and incompetent as they struggle to maintain students' attention.

RQ3: What Are Teachers' Perceived Needs for More Effective Teaching Practices?

All teachers reported their desire to learn games to teach young learners more effectively. Other major needs, noted in Table 3.2, are songs, sources or methods for developing materials, and age-appropriate activities. On the other hand, teachers said they need less with respect to broader topics not specifically related to TEYL, such as second language acquisition,

Table 3.2 Teachers' perceived needs

Items	Mean	SD
Games	4.84	0.36
Songs	4.75	0.57
Websites for useful teaching materials	4.55	0.69
Development of materials	4.55	0.62
Useful teaching materials and how to use them	4.53	0.78
Activities suitable for young learners	4.48	0.66
The purpose of English education at primary school	4.48	0.62
Choosing materials	4.44	0.78
English language pedagogy that suits young learners	4.42	0.72
Linking units and lessons across classes	4.17	0.74
English activities suitable for the developmental stages of children	4.16	0.66
Making a one-hour lesson plan	4.15	1.01
English language pedagogy	4.08	0.76
Culture of foreign countries	4.04	0.70
Methodology of cross-cultural understanding	4.00	0.73
Curriculum development	3.97	0.86
Introduction to second language acquisition theory	3.80	0.94

methodology, curriculum development, lesson planning, and cultural issues.

Teachers' answers to the open-ended question regarding their needs in a TEYL classroom supported quantitative outcomes of the questionnaire. Just under half of the teachers (48.8%) stated that they need to learn more English games and activities to feel more competent. Additionally, 22.2% of the respondents asserted that students' attention span is too short, and that teaching them is difficult because they do not understand the importance of learning English nor do they have opportunities to use the language in their daily life.

Table 3.3 Classroom practices

Classroom practices	Mean	SD
Playing games	4.08	0.84
Singing songs	3.97	1.07
Memorizing and performing simple conversations	3.80	0.84
Role-play	3.80	0.84
Introducing language in different contexts	3.71	0.89
Introducing holidays and festivals of their country	3.44	1.03
Introducing various local and foreign foods	3.40	0.98
Playing with words	3.35	0.93
Reading English picture books	3.17	0.98
Introducing holidays and festivals of other countries	3.08	0.92

RQ4A: How Do the Teachers Put Policy into Classroom Practice in Terms of the Frequency of Activities?

Table 3.3 reveal data showing that playing games, singing songs, memorizing and performing simple conversations, role-playing, and introducing language in different contexts are classroom activities teachers report most frequently implementing. On the other hand, introducing holidays and festivals, introducing various local and foreign foods, playing with words, and reading picture books have lower mean scores. An interesting finding is that teachers introduce holidays and festivals of their country (i.e., Turkey) more than they do of other countries. In addition, teachers reported reading English picture books less frequently than directing other techniques.

RQ4B: How Do Teachers Put the Policy into Classroom Practice in Terms of Achieving Success in a TEYL Classroom?

As displayed in Table 3.4, the findings of the semi-structured interviews regarding teachers' successful classes are striking in that there exists a large overlap between the perceived sources of success in 2nd- and 3rd-grade

Table 3.4 Source of class success in 2nd, 3rd, and 4th grades

Source of success	2nd grade %	3rd grade %	Source of success	4th grade %
Audio, visual, and audio-visual materials	37.7	40	Audio, visual, and audio-visual materials	35.5
Vocabulary instruction	22.2	15.5	Speaking activities	20
Student motivation	15.5	15.5	Role-plays	11.1

classes. According to the teachers, use of audio (e.g., CDs, songs including pop music, rock music, slow music, jazz chants, and xylophone), visuals (e.g., flashcards, puppets, pictures, drawings, children's picture books, and bulletin boards), and audio-visual materials (e.g., videos) lead to successful classes. The 2nd- and 3rd-grade teachers described their second most successful classes as those where they present vocabulary via games or other fun activities.

Teachers considered motivation as a crucial construct that determines class success. One participant noted that

> 2nd graders are more enthusiastic than 3rd and 4th graders even if their attention span is too short. They enjoy learning English. They see it as a game. Motivating 2nd graders by finding and bringing the right materials to the class is very easy. (P13)

With respect to 4th grade, teachers reported speaking activities (e.g., students' introducing themselves, expressing their feelings, creating short dialogues) and role-play as second and third most important factors for success. One teacher offered this anecdote:

> While teaching health problems, I entered the classroom with a scarf and plaster on my finger. I painted my eye with black. I had a thermometer in my mouth. I acted as a sick person. By this way, they learned the words about health and health problems. I am sure that they won't forget those words. We enjoyed [class] a lot. I believe in the magic of role-plays! (P19)

RQ5: What Challenges Do Teachers Face in the Implementation of the 4+4+4 Policy?

In addition to finding the right materials, the teachers explained that they consider vocabulary instruction (8.8% of all participants) challenging, especially for 2nd graders as students do not fully know how to write and read. Teachers stated that students forget words easily, and it takes time to reiterate the same words in every class for better retention. In addition, 8.8% of the teachers reported that students' lack of interest in learning a language can present other challenges. They argued that the students do not regard learning English as a necessity; they just study to pass the course.

RQ6: What Are Teachers' Evaluations Regarding New 2nd-, 3rd-, and 4th-Grade Curricula?

The teachers asserted that the 2nd-grade curriculum could be improved, but overall, it is good, applicable, enjoyable, and realistic. They found the topics interesting, but said that two hours of weekly instruction is insufficient as students forget quickly what they have been exposed to. Instead, they recommended at least four hours a week to be effective.

However, all teachers except one stated that the 3rd-grade curriculum is far beyond the students' level, is difficult to apply, and lacks sufficient oral practices. Moreover, they lamented that the topics seem uninteresting to students and that the objectives are not realistic. In this sense, teachers report the 3rd-grade curriculum design as unsuccessful.

As for the 4th-grade curriculum, teachers did find it more applicable and realistic. They reported that topics relate to daily life, a key facet that makes learning easier. Still, they reported that the required grammar is far beyond students' proficiency and even unnecessary for that age group. With respect to content, teachers still found themes to be complex, a conclusion exacerbated by textbooks lacking sufficient pictures, audio-visual materials, or activities, leaving teachers to extend their creativity in efforts to make the content simple and comprehensible. One teacher elaborated concerns with respect to the grammar-based system for 3rd and 4th graders:

> It is not necessary to teach grammar in the way curriculum dictates, and the books are not ideal. They are so crammed with grammar and they do not have enough activities for more practice. The objectives of the book are far beyond the students' level. Target behaviors are hard for them. They should be prepared more carefully to meet the needs of young learners. (P24)

Discussion

This section seeks to situate the results of this study within relevant literature and research conversations and also to suggest next steps for supporting Turkish teachers of English to young learners. First, although in-service teacher training programs are important for successful implementation of the changes in the curriculum (Uysal, 2012), only one third of the participants in this study had attended such programs. This finding parallels Demirpolat's (2015) claim that Turkish teachers of English are not encouraged to attend in-service training or rewarded for attending them. The reason for low attendance rate might be the insufficient number of such programs (Küçüksüleymanoğlu, 2006), the lack of professional staff, a systematic in-service training model (Bayrakçı, 2009), or the fact that topics of such programs are not identified by teachers themselves (Daloğlu, 2004). Another reason might be that some teachers in the current study (22%) consider themselves competent and report not facing any challenges (31%), implying that they do not feel the need to attend in-service teacher training programs (see also Özoğlu, 2010). Moreover, 35.7% of this study's participants who have attended such programs report that they are theoretical, irrelevant to classroom practices, unrealistic, and difficult to apply in real classroom settings. Haznedar (2010) also pointed out that very few (only 8.2%) English teachers consider such programs beneficial and stress the need to reconsider their content and application.

Second, the data regarding teachers' perceived needs (see Table 3.2) reveal that the means of all the items are above 3.80 (out of 5), indicating a strong need for practical classroom applications. In addition, the standard deviations are below one, except 'making a one-hour lesson plan', showing agreement among participants. The results of the second, third, fourth, and fifth research questions reveal that teachers' most frequent classroom practices overlapped with their highly rated needs, perceived weaknesses, and challenges, showing how the teachers feel they need more support in what they are already doing (e.g., games, songs, age-appropriate materials) and more training to overcome those challenges, especially in materials adaptation and development. On the other hand, they found coursework such as SLA theory, curriculum development, or culture—elements seemingly not directly a part of their classroom practice—of secondary importance.

As the findings of the fourth research question show, teachers' most frequent classroom practices also consist of games, songs, and role-play, which are common in TEYL classes. It seems they rated techniques they are familiar with more highly. On the other hand, cultural constructs such as introducing holidays, festivals, and food of their country and other countries, and activities such as wordplay or picture books are rated low. This might be due the lack of those constructs or techniques in their learning experiences. In other words, teachers' preferences might be related to what Lortie (1975) calls *apprenticeship of observation*, or the view that student teachers have been observing and evaluating their teachers as schoolchildren for years before starting their pre-service training courses. Borg (2004) suggests this pre-program experience is so influential that, unlike many other professionals, "student teachers may fail to realize that the aspects of teaching which they perceived as students represented only a partial view of the teacher's job" (274). As a result, novice teachers may be teaching as they were taught due to the limited efficiency of teacher education courses they took and their tendency to revert to their model. For example, it is unlikely that the participants were exposed to local or foreign food or festivals, wordplay, or picture books when learning English. For one thing, they started learning English at a later age than their students. For another, the educational approach was much less communicative when they themselves were students. It might be that following their teachers' model, the participants do not consider culture a significant part of their classes, contrary to suggestions in the EU action plan (Edelenbos et al., 2006). As teachers, they took only two TEYL classes during their pre-service education. In addition, most teachers reported that they did not accomplish their practicum in a primary school, so there were few opportunities for them to observe different and novel classroom practices. Finally, for them, the English curriculum is new, so it probably fails to guide them effectively in terms of connecting their training to various new techniques.

Materials development also stands out as a crucial contributor to success but also as a major weakness. The two courses—'Instructional Technology and Materials Development' and 'Materials Adaptation and Development', mandated by the Higher Education Council and offered in all pre-service teacher education departments—seem to be insufficient for developing teachers' skills with respect to developing or adapting materials autonomously. This might be because these courses do not focus on developing or adapting materials for young learners. This being the case, courses that cover designing materials specifically for young learners should be incorporated into the curricula of teacher education programs, and teachers' skills for developing and adapting materials for young learners need to be improved via in-service teacher training programs. In addition, the course books designed for young learners and delivered to students and teachers by the government should be improved by including sufficient, balanced, and appropriate activities, as well as specific teacher guides.

Regarding the overall evaluation of the curricula of each grade, most teachers stated that they are generally happy with the 2nd- and 4th-grade curricula. However, they found the 3rd-grade curriculum neither realistic nor applicable, arguing that the transition from 2nd to 4th grade is uneven. Similarly, despite taking a positive attitude toward the 4+4+4 policy, state primary school principals are concerned about the overall instructional environment and believe that the policy change requires additional implementations (Çelik & Kasapoğlu, 2014).

In brief, based on the teachers' experiences, which is crucial in educational practices, the 2012 policy change requires some implementational modifications to achieve its goals. Kırkgöz (2009) also highlights that "Turkey needs to resolve existing incongruence between the idealized macro policy objectives and their realizations in practice at micro level teaching situations" (p. 681). Some crucial steps to overcome the problems are suggested below.

First, it is vital to establish constant cooperation between teachers, policymakers, researchers, and academics who specialize in teacher education. The changes in policy need to be investigated scientifically, and the primary school English curriculum needs to be evaluated and revised. Accordingly, the practical implications should be transferred to teachers via frequent, quality, realistic, context-specific, and practical in-service training programs based on their self-identified needs.

Second, teachers' needs and suggestions regarding policy changes and development of a new curriculum should be taken into consideration because they are the principal implementers of the curriculum, and its success largely depends on teachers' competency.

Third, although the 1997 and 2012 policies lowered the age of English instruction, not many changes in terms of TEYL have been made in the curricula of pre-service teacher education programs, except the incorporation of two TEYL courses. Teachers' needs and challenges—as Tılfarlıoğlu and Öztürk (2007) already articulated, especially in terms of methodology, classroom management, and motivation—indicate that teachers' training in TEYL is still too short in helping them ultimately feel confident when they start working with youngsters. Hence, major changes in the curricula of these programs are necessary. For one thing, the content of the theoretical and pedagogical courses should be expanded in a way that the pre-service teachers gain practical teaching skills in addition to theoretical knowledge. For another, there should be separate programs for primary (Grades 1–4) and secondary education (Grades 4–8), just like other teacher education departments (e.g., Math). In this way, future primary school English teachers will take classes specific to TEYL and accomplish their micro teaching in primary schools, meaning that they would enter TEYL classrooms feeling more self-efficacious.

Further research could include a higher number of participants and classroom observations, which could not be conducted in this study due to participant teachers' disapproval. Furthermore, a longitudinal study in which teachers keep diaries or teaching logs and reflect on their classroom practices could yield a more complete sense regarding the implementation of the new curriculum.

Conclusion

The 4+4+4 policy is multi-faceted and requires diverse elements such as teacher training for success. Teachers play a crucial role as the primary implementers of the policy; therefore, their training and competency is vital. The results of this study are important as they yield insight regarding primary school English teachers' educational backgrounds, needs, perceived weaknesses, classroom practices, and challenges, which all gain prominence when classroom practices are inconsistent with the policies. In this sense, the findings and pedagogical implications proposed in this chapter might be used in considering improvements in pre- and in-service training programs and in solving problems stemming from the 4+4+4 policy and its corresponding curriculum.

Note

1. Anatolian high schools were state schools that offered one-year intensive (i.e., 24 hours a week) English education after primary school so that most secondary and high school courses could be taught in English (Hismanoğlu, 2012).

References

Aksoy, E., Bozdoğan, D., Akbaş, U., & Seferoğlu, G. (2018). Old wine in a new bottle: Implementation of intensive language program in the 5th grade in Turkey. *Eurasian Journal of Applied Linguistics, 4*(2), 301–324.

Bayrakçı, M. (2009). In-service teacher training in Japan and Turkey: A comparative analysis of institutions and practices. *Australian Journal of Teacher Education, 34*(1), 10–22.

Borg, M. (2004). The apprenticeship of observation. *ELT Journal, 58*(3), 274–276.

Butler, Y. G. (2004). What level of English proficiency do elementary school teachers need to attain to teach EFL? Case studies from Korea, Taiwan and Japan. *TESOL Quarterly, 38*(2), 245–278.

Camerun, L. (2003). Challenges for ELT from the expansion in teaching children. *ELT Journal, 57*(2), 105–112.

Çelik, S., & Kasapoğlu, H. (2014). Implementing the recent curricular changes to English language instruction in Turkey: Opinions and concerns of elementary school administrators. *South African Journal of Education, 34*(2). Retrieved from https://www.ajol.info/index.php/saje/article/view/105556

Creswell, J., & Plano Clark, V. (2007). *Designing and conducting mixed methods research*. Sage.

Daloğlu, A. (2004). A professional development program for primary school language teachers in Turkey: Designing a materials bank. *International Journal of Educational Development, 24*, 677–690.

Dearden, J., & Macaro, E. (2016). Higher education teachers' attitudes towards English medium instruction: A three-country comparison. *Studies in Second Language Learning and Teaching, 6*(3), 455–486.

Demirpolat, B. C. (2015). *Türkiye'nin yabancı dil öğretimiyle imtihanı: Sorunlar ve çözüm önerileri*. SETA.

Djigunović, M. J. (1995). Attitudes of young foreign language learners: A follow-up study. In M. Vilke & Y. Vrhovac (Eds.), *Children and foreign languages II* (pp. 16–33). University of Zagreb, Faculty of Philosophy.

Doğançay-Aktuna, S. (1998). The spread of English in Turkey and its current sociolinguistic profile. *Journal of Multilingual and Multicultural Development, 19*(1), 24–39.

Edelenbos, P., Johnstone, R., & Kubanek, A. (2006). *The main pedagogical principles underlying the teaching of young learners*. Final Report of the EAC 89/04, Brussels.

Gün, F., & Atanur Başkan, G. (2014). New education system in Turkey (4+4+4): A critical outlook. *Procedia – Social and Behavioral Sciences, 131*, 229–235.

Gürsoy, E., Korkmaz, S. Ç., & Damar, A. E. (2013). Foreign language teaching within 4+4+4 education system in Turkey: Language teachers' voice. *Eurasian Journal of Educational Research, 53*, 59–74.

Haznedar, B. (2010). Türkiye'de yabancı dil Eğitimi: Reformlar, yönelimler ve öğretmenlerimiz. *International Conference on New Trends in Education and Their Implications*, 11–13 November. Antalya-Türkiye.

Hismanoğlu, M. (2012). The impact of globalization and information technology on language education policy in Turkey. *Procedia – Social and Behavioral Sciences, 31*, 629–633.

İnceçay, G., & İnceçay, V. (2010). A case study on needs assessment of English language teachers. *Procedia Social and Behavioral Sciences, 2*, 317–321.

Karatepe, Ç. (2005). Avrupa konseyi dil kriterleri ve Türkiye'de yabancı dil eğitimi politikalarının geliştirilmesi. *Hasan Ali Yücel Eğitim Fakültesi Dergisi, 1*, 49–61.

Kırkgöz, Y. (2007). Language planning and implementation in Turkish primary schools. *Current Issues in Language Planning, 8*(2), 174–191.

Kırkgöz, Y. (2008). A case study of teachers' implementation of curriculum innovation in English language teaching in Turkish primary education. *Teaching and Teacher Education, 24*, 1859–1875.

Kırkgöz, Y. (2009). Globalization and English language policy in Turkey. *Educational Policy, 23*(5), 663–684.

Küçüksüleymanoğlu, R. (2006). In-service training of ELT teachers in Turkey between1998–2005. *Uludağ Üniversitesi Eğitim Bilimleri Dergisi., 19*(2), 359–369.

Kusumoto, Y. (2008). Needs analysis: Developing a teacher training program for elementary school homeroom teachers in Japan. *Second Language Studies, 26*(2), 1–44.

Lortie, D. (1975). *Schoolteacher: A sociological study*. University of Chicago Press.

Mede, E., & Işık, M. (2016). The needs of primary English teachers for an in-service teacher training program. *Turkish Online Journal of Qualitative Inquiry, 7*, 1–30.

MoNE. (2012). *English curriculum for grades 2, 3, 4, 5, 6, 7 and 8*. MoNE.

Nunan, D. (2003). The impact of English as a global language on educational policies and practices in the Asia-Pacific region. *TESOL Quarterly, 37*(4), 589–613.

Özoğlu, M. (2010). *Türkiye'de öğretmen yetiştirme sisteminin sorunları*. SETA.

Sarıçoban, G. (2012). Foreign language education policies in Turkey. *Procedia – Social and Behavioral Sciences, 46*, 2643–2648.

Seyratlı Özkan, E., Karataş, İ. H., & Gülşen, C. (2016). The analysis of foreign language education policies in Turkey during 2003–2013. *Journal of Research in Education and Teaching, 5*(1), 245–254.

Shohamy, E. (2006). *Language policy: Hidden agendas and new approaches*. Routledge.

Slattery, M., & Willis, J. (2001). *English for primary teachers*. Oxford University Press.

Spolsky, B. (2004). *Language policy*. Cambridge University Press.

Suna, Y., & Durmuşçelebi, M. (2013). A compilation work about why Turkey suffers from learning and teaching English. *Türkiye Sosyal Politika ve Çalışma Hayatı Araştırmaları Dergisi, 3*(5), 7–24.

Tılfarlıoğlu, F. Y., & Öztürk, A. R. (2007). An analysis of ELT teachers' perceptions of some problems concerning the implementation of English language teaching curricula in elementary schools. *Journal of Language and Linguistic Studies, 3*(1), 202–217.

Tollefson, J. W. (2006). Critical theory in language policy. In T. Ricento (Ed.), *An introduction to language policy: Theory and method* (pp. 42–59). Blackwell Publishing.

Tsui, A. B. M., & Tollefson, J. W. (2007). Language policy and the construction of national cultural identity. In A. Tsui & J. W. Tollefson (Eds.), *Language policy, culture, and identity in Asian contexts* (pp. 1–21). Erlbaum.

Uysal, H. H. (2012). Evaluation of an in-service training program for primary school teachers in Turkey. *Australian Journal of Teacher Education, 37*(7), 14–29.

Uztosun, M. S. (2016). Pre-service and in-service English teachers' efficacy beliefs about teaching English at primary schools. *Elementary Education Online, 15*(4), 1191–1205.

4

Teachers' Appreciation of ELT Policies and Practices in Egypt

Islam M. Farag and Mohamed Yacoub

Introduction

Egypt exerts enormous efforts to provide children with English education. However, Egyptians' desire to speak fluent English is underwritten by the inconsistency between policies and practices. While educational policies regarding English exist within The National English Language Curriculum Framework Grades 1–12, henceforth known as The Framework (El-Araby et al., 2012), actual practices of ELT enforce a "product" model of English best manifested in the Thanaweya Amma,[1] the series of high stakes examinations taken at the end of secondary school (Gebril & Brown, 2014; Hargreaves, 2001).

I. M. Farag (✉)
University of Pittsburgh, Pittsburgh, PA, USA
e-mail: imf12@pitt.edu

M. Yacoub
Florida International University, Miami, FL, USA
e-mail: myacoub@fiu.edu

Hoping to narrow gaps between policies and practices, most newly appointed Ministers of Education introduce new policies (Bakr, 2003; Zaid, 2017)—ranging in degrees of harmony with previous policies but always forced on students, teachers, and parents. The hodgepodge of these approaches supports Walker and Dimmock's (2000) argument that policy-makers believe "that policies and practices designed in one context can be unproblematically transported elsewhere" (p. 157), likely reducing education quality. To investigate these conflicts, particularly as they apply to Egypt, this chapter explores teachers' appreciation, or lack thereof, of the interplay between ELT policies and practices.

Background

A Retrospective of Egyptian History and Its Ministry of Education

Education in Egypt has been considered a key factor for political stability and ideological domination. Therefore, the Egyptian government, regardless of who has been in power, has considered that "[formulating] educational policies, the organization, administration and supervision of education is in the first place an obligation of the Egyptian State" (Stopikowska & El-Deabes, 2012, pp. 131–2).

During the Ottoman Empire in Egypt (1517–1867), the European educational system was introduced to Egyptian schools in an effort to nurture those carefully chosen by the government—an act accomplished not for elevating education but for building the army (Loveluck, 2012). During British occupation (1882 to 1952), out of concern that students might revolt one day, officials downsized education quality, aiming to keep Egyptians at a level of knowledge just good enough to do minimal office work.

After independence from Britain in 1956, revolution leader and ultimately president Gamal Abdel-Nasser made changes in the education system with the purpose of "[disseminating] the [revolution's] ideals of socialism, Arabism and nationalism" (Hargreaves, 2001, p. 249). Before the revolution, schools were available for economically privileged students; however, the revolutionary government composed this statement into the 1956 constitution:

> [E]ducation is a right for all Egyptians, guaranteed by the government … Education is compulsory and should be free of charge in state schools … The state oversees public education and regulates its fairs. ("1956 Constitution of Egypt," 1965, pp. 5–6)

Since then, public schools have been open and free to all students, including those in higher education.

Following the legacy of Abdel-Nasser's policies, the Egyptian president and the People's Assembly, in coordination with its education committee, have been responsible for composing educational legislation. The Ministry of Education (MoE) has the authority to make new policies and decrees, petition for a change or a cancelation of an existing policy, select curricula, and submit proposals to the People's Assembly (Stopikowska & El-Deabes, 2012).

Other governmental bodies may oversee the implementation of education policies enacted by the MoE; however, they have no authority to make decisions. Instead, "the structure of the legislative, executive, and administrative system of education observes the principle of centralization and decentralization [while] most of the prerogatives in this regard are still highly centralized" (Stopikowska & El-Deabes, 2012, p. 133). Explaining the rationale behind the centralization of policy-making decisions, the 2003 Minister of Education, Hussein Kamel Bahaeddin, said that "education falls under the direct supervision of the state so that it would ensure the minimum common level of enculturation and socialization … This, he argued, would enhance national unity and the cohesion of the social fabric" (cited in Loveluck, 2012, p. 7).

English Language Policies

The MoE acknowledges the importance of English and stresses teaching it to students from an early age. According to the Framework (2012),

English should be taught to help students "develop the confidence to communicate effectively in speaking, listening, reading, and writing English that will enable them to participate actively in a global society" (El-Araby et al., 2012, p. 4). The Framework emphasizes that learning English should not be reduced to memorizing grammar and vocabulary. Rather, teaching should use the communicative approach to help students from grades 10 to 12 (a) confidently collaborate in groups and (b) formally and informally communicate complex ideas (El-Araby et al., 2012, p. 7).

In promoting the communicative approach in policy, the MoE has underscored the use of technology, current research assessment, and student-centered activities. However, in practice, education in Egypt faces different challenges. With control centralized in the hands of the minister of education, almost every minister has come up with reform. Most reforms have had one goal: making education and English teaching less dependent on rote learning and more dependent on technology and critical thinking (Loveluck, 2012; Stopikowska & El-Deabes, 2012), as outlined in Table 4.1.

As seen in Table 4.1, some decisions have shifted back and forth, depending on the minister (Bakr, 2003), including whether elementary education should be five or six years or how Thanaweya Amma can be less stressful. In Table 4.2, we review the ministers' policies regarding using technology in schools.

School Types, MoE Authority, and ELT in Egypt

As mentioned earlier, so-called free public education is offered throughout Egypt. Side effects of this include overcrowding and poor teaching. Resultantly, in the 1990s, the private sector emerged "as a way of addressing the pitfalls of the public system and taking the load off government schools" (El-Fiki, 2012, p. 21). These schools purportedly offer modern facilities, smaller classes, cutting-edge materials and technology, transportation, and advanced communication with families. Private Arabic schools teach all subjects in Arabic. The minimum private school fee is around 2000 Egyptian pounds (L.E.), or 110 US dollars (USD) per year

4 Teachers' Appreciation of ELT Policies and Practices in Egypt 63

Table 4.1 Timeline of key MoE mandates regarding ELT

Year	Minister	Policy
2011	Ahmed Zaki Badr	Stopped the practice of sending teachers abroad
2012	Ibrahim Ghounim	Issued The National English Language Curriculum Framework Grades 1–12 (The Framework). Curricula were changed in hopes of helping students cope with technological advancement
2014	Mahmoud Abo Al-Nasr	Changed the start year of teaching English in public schools to the second grade (from the fourth grade)
2014		Issued a strategic plan for three years to create a path and a foundation for the 2030 vision
2014		Announced that an overhaul of the curricula, in tandem with the European Union, would be implemented gradually such that it could regularly be reviewed with respect to reducing reliance on memorization and encouraging critical thinking
		Reopened scholarships for teachers studying abroad, believing that teacher-scholars would add value to the quality and advancement of education in Egypt when they return
2015		Confirmed that 30% of the curriculum had been improved
2017	Al-Hilaly Al-Shirbiny	Deleted 25% of curricula based on the recommendation of a committee of curricular design consultants
2017	Tarek Shawky	English becomes a mandatory school subject from kindergarten
		Launched a new campaign targeting comprehensive education reforms related to the re-use of tablets at schools, new curricula, teaching math and science in Arabic, a unified English textbook in public and experimental schools, and cancelation of final exams until the fourth year

Contributing sources: Abdulaal (2018); Alam (2014); Badwy (2014); El-Shaarawi (2015); Hamdi (2016); Omar (2018); Salama (2017)

(Al-Ganzouri, 2019), while in public schools, elementary students pay almost 145 L.E. or approximately 9 USD per year (Mohamed, 2019). Table 4.3 shows tuition rates for the varying kinds of schools within the country.

The MoE has full authority over public and experimental schools. Its administration hires and pays teachers while mandating

Table 4.2 Timeline of key MoE mandates regarding technology

Year	Minister	Policy
2012	Ibrahim Ghounim	Initiated a new vision of using tablets instead of paperback textbooks
2013	Mahmoud Abo Al-Nasr	Applied Ghounim's vision, distributing tablets in six governorates
		After less than a month and after spending 400 million Egyptian pounds, the initiative failed, and schools demanded that the ministry send them paperback textbooks
2017	Al-Hilaly Al-Shirbiny	Announced his intention to give tablets to students and digitalize curricula, yearning to rid schools of unnecessary information and make students use technology more. However, as a result of public outcry against the proposal, largely due to the 2014 fiasco, he did not impose it
2017	Tarek Shawky	Announced that he, too, would experiment with the use of tablets, but this time only on an experimental basis with first-year high schoolers (Grade 10)

Contributing sources: Badran (2017); Zaid (2017)

Table 4.3 School tuition

	Run and owned by	Primary language	Tuition
Public schools	Government	Arabic	Propagated as free (fees are about 9 USD)
Experimental language schools	Government	English	Around 60 USD
Private Arabic schools	Individuals	Arabic	Around 110 USD
English private schools	Individuals	English	From 150 USD to 600 USD
International schools	Individuals; accredited by international countries	English	Starts from 1500 USD
Azharian schools	Al-Azhar religious institution	Arabic	Around 9 USD

the implementation of every decision it imposes. The MoE's authority, however, on other schools is diminished, especially when it comes to

ELT. MoE supervision over ELT in private language schools is limited to administrative paperwork, notably supervisory checks, to see if the number of sessions, exam dates, standardized tests, and curriculum mapping are in accordance with government-set criteria.

To illustrate the power of the MoE, minister Tarek Shawky announced in 2018 in his educational reform that

(a) there would be a new English curriculum, named *Connect*, to be taught in all schools.
(b) there would not be an advanced level of English to be taught in Experimental schools.
(c) Arabic would be the medium of instruction in these Experimental language schools; and
(d) math and science would be taught in Arabic until grade 6, whereupon these subjects would be taught in English. (Omar, 2018)

This policy was obligatory in governmental schools, including experimental language schools; however, international schools and private language schools were exempted (Omar, 2018). This decision caused an uproar, especially from those with children enrolled in experimental language schools, to which the Minister said that "the experimental language school curriculum will be *in Arabic*," as the cost of translating curricula from Arabic to English was too high and those wishing to study a foreign language could travel abroad (Ali, 2018). Ultimately, due to public pressure, it was announced that math and English would also be taught in English in experimental language schools. Since teachers are those implementing educational policies, and since literature regarding teachers' perspectives on decision-making policies and practices is lacking, there is a need to examine teachers' perspectives regarding the interplay between ELT policies and practices in Egypt by interrogating how teachers of English perceive the quality, policies, problems, and solutions of teaching English in Egypt.

Methodology

MoE Process and Practice: A Proposal for a Critical Lens

Given the historic policy rollercoaster unleashed by MoE leadership, we asked nine Egyptian teachers of English about these policies, what they think of the challenges of teaching English in Egypt, and possible solutions. We were particularly interested in exploring their opinions toward professional development training courses, how policies affect the Egyptian educational context, how policies work in relation to assessment that focuses on product, and how portfolios work. Thus, to answer our research question, we developed—through exploring literature and through our own expertise as ELT teachers, as explained below—a seven-pronged critical lens to be able to examine both ELT policies and practices:

I. **Context**

Importing reforms and policies from a context (or country) without paying attention to how historical, political, and cultural factors play significant roles in a successful implementation of these policies can cause problems (Whitty et al., 1998). In particular, Dimmock and Walker (1998) emphasize the significant role culture plays in the formation, adaptation, and implementation of policies because the acceptance of such adaptation "largely depends on the receptivity" (p. 564) of the host context. In fact, they warn that socio-political-economic contexts may be so dissimilar that cloning and adaptation of policies may be inappropriate, later warning that focus on "surface similarities" (Walker & Dimmock, 2000, p. 157) between two contexts can lead to failure in implementation.

II. **Process, not Product**

Learning any language is, indeed, a process not a product, especially the development of writing and speaking. This process cannot be measured in one sitting of an exam; in fact, the Conference on College Composition and Communication (2014) posed that

> Writing ability must be assessed by more than one piece of writing, in more than one genre, written on different occasions, for different audiences, and responded to and evaluated by multiple readers as part of a substantial and sustained writing process. (Para. 11)

III. Portfolios

Portfolios have been implemented successfully in many countries; however, when they were first mandated in Egypt in grades 5 and 6 in 2008 and later in all grades in 2010–2011, Yousri AlGamal, the minister of education, hoped to help students focus more on academic achievement than test scores. He applied the following grading criteria: 50% for portfolio (15% for written exams, 15% for oral participation, 15% for experiment and class activities, and 5% for behavior), and the other 50% for extra-curricular activities. This new assessment process went into immediate effect in 2008 (Hassanen, 2009).

IV. Professional Development

Professional development (PD) is important because high-quality workshops positively influence teaching skills, advance use of technological tools, and update teachers' subject-matter knowledge (Yin, 2013). PD helps teachers set lifelong learning goals that, in turn, encourage students to view learning as a lifelong journey (Armour & Makopoulou, 2012; James et al., 2007). DeMonte (2013) believes that PD should be ongoing, suggesting that teachers engage in at least 14 hours of training each semester in order to uphold high standards.

V. Teacher Voice

An employee voice is "the discretionary communication of ideas, suggestions, concerns, or opinions about work-related issues with the intent to improve organizational or unit functioning" (Morrison et al., 2011,

p. 138). More specifically, teacher voice is meant to "amplify the views, experience, and perspective of teachers on educational policy and practice" (Frost, 2008, p. 347). Heneveld (2007) and Gozali et al. (2017) reasoned that teacher voice is critical because teachers know the most about schools, their systems, and their problems, and thus can come up with the most practical solutions. Therefore, their voice signifies knowledge, power, and resistance (Kahlenberg & Potter, 2015). However, Llorens (1994) noted that their voice has generally been neglected in the policy-making process.

VI. View of Reform

Seemingly little has changed since Llorens's 1994 comment, at least in Egypt. Loveluck (2012) wrote that

> as a result of such tight central control, teachers have little freedom to structure the progress of their classes or to cover material that is not included in the day's lesson plan. Government inspectors frequently attend class lessons, increasing pressure on teachers to adhere strictly to the given Curriculum. (p. 8)

Therefore, it is crucial to consider teachers' views on how to reform Egyptian education.

VII. Teacher Pay

According to the Committee for Economic Development of the Conference Board (2009), no reform policy can be effective without considering a competitive income for teachers which helps attract and retains high-quality teachers who can help students reach high levels of academic performance. The opposite is also true: If teachers are not paid well, qualified teachers may not be retained (*Teacher compensation*, 2009). According to the World Bank (2018), the poverty line for lower-middle-income countries such as Egypt was 3.20 USD per day per person in 2015 (*Poverty*, 2018). Resultantly, teachers making only 100 USD per month are likely seeking supplemental work.

With these seven lenses/concepts in mind, we laid out a semi-structured interview style with the following seven main questions, shown in Table 4.4.

Participants

We interviewed nine Egyptian English teachers. Table 4.5 illustrates the demographic information of the participants. The participants represent a variety of teaching experiences, ranging from 2 to 11 years, and a variety of school types. Also, all participants had two years of pre-service training in public schools, as a part of their undergraduate degrees. Participants were recruited through a snowballing technique. Since we, the researchers, were ELT teachers ourselves, we started by contacting three participants we knew (Dina, Rashad, and Ismail); the rest of the participants were reached through these three participants. All of the participants were ELT teachers. To protect participants' privacy, we use pseudonyms.

Table 4.4 Interview questions

Lens category	Interview question
Context	To what degree do you see the degree to which MoE pays attention to their current teaching conditions?
Process (not product)	How do you regard the interface between MoE policies and their practice?
Portfolios	What are your reactions to MoE's instructions regarding portfolio assessment?
Professional development	Discuss professional development, particularly as it relates to PD provided or requested by MoE
Teacher voice	To what extent do you feel you can comment on current teaching conditions?
View of reform	If asked, what advice might you have for reforming ELT in Egypt with better policies fostering harmony with actual practices?
Teacher pay	In what ways does your current salary affect your teaching and your livelihood?

Table 4.5 Demographic information of the participants

Name	Gender	Years of experience	Current location of teaching	Types of schools (participant has worked at)
Dina	Female	9	Cairo	Public, language schools, and international schools
Ismail	Male	10	Cairo	Experimental public school
Iyad	Male	5	Giza	Public, Arabic private, and international schools
Rashad	Male	10	Giza	Private language schools
Reem	Female	9	Giza	Public schools
Alaa	Male	11	Cairo	Private language schools
Ramzy	Male	2	Cairo	Private language and Arabic schools
Yaseen	Male	4	Giza	Public, Azharian, and private language schools
Dawood	Male	9	Cairo	Private language schools, experimental, international schools

Interviews and Data Analysis

Interviews were conducted and recorded via Facebook Messenger's video chat feature. Each interview took between 40 and 60 minutes and was conducted in Arabic and English. All nine interviewees code-switched between the two languages, Arabic and English. We transcribed the interviews and translated Arabic commentary into English (Slembrouck, 2007). We used NVivo software to perform thematic analysis by creating line-by-line inductive coding (Joffe & Yardley, 2004). Transcripts were coded with urgent and emerging themes highlighted (Creswell & Poth. 2016). After an initial examination, transcripts, findings, and discussion were sent to the participants for a member check (Koelsch, 2013; Lincoln & Guba, 1985). Finally, data analysis and discussion were double-visited and peer-checked by researchers as part of investigator triangulation (Carter et al., 2014).

Results

The interviews yielded several key themes: issues pertaining to teaching to the test, context, portfolios, professional development, teacher voice, low salary, and views of reforms.

Teaching to the Test

Six participants underscored discord between MoE policies and actual teaching practices. While policies encourage the communicative approach, participants felt the urge to teach for the Thanaweya Amma. Dina explains further:

> There is a common culture among parents enforced by school practices; that is, students learn to get perfect scores on the final exams. Parents, students, and the school system prioritized test scores over actual education and learning. Students from grade 1 are driven to score perfectly on exams, and parents don't care about anything but their children's final scores. Such an understanding … [starts] from Grade 1.

Because the MoE has used final test scores as principal assessment criteria since the 1970s, success is measured in terms of final scores and students' rank, thereby fostering competition as a key feature of Egyptian education. Iyad further explains:

> Everything is tied to students' scores in grade 12. A student's scores on the final exams at the end of Thanaweya Amma decide what college this student can join and, hence, decides the student's whole life career.

To this end, participants expressed concern that the focus on students' final accumulative scores inhibits learning as a process and perpetuates learning as a product. Accordingly, Rashad believes that teaching for the test has created criteria that define good teachers:

> We [teachers] just teach for the exams … Parents, students, and schools evaluate teachers' performance based on students' scores in the final exams.

> A good teacher is the one who can help his students memorize the curriculum to get the full mark. Teachers don't care about what teaching method they use; they are more concerned with how to makes students memorize the curriculum … Exams always test students' knowledge of grammar, spelling, reading, and writing questions to which we provide students memorized answers; so why I should use the communicative approach, task-based, or theme-based activities? I use very traditional teaching techniques to make students memorize the information and use drills, exercises, and past exams to make them practice for the final test.

So embedded is the accountability of exam scores to the MoE that even the supervisors, at least as expressed by the participants, became more concerned with paperwork than the actual effectiveness of teaching. Dina's observations regarding governmental supervisors showcase this sentiment: "The supervisor's job is just to make sure the lesson plans are there, so he/she can see, but nothing beyond that."

As an effort toward minimizing learning for tests, the current minister, Tarek Shawky, decreed that students from Grade 1 to Grade 4 would *not* have summative assessments—only formative assessments. Students were to advance automatically to the following grade. Ismail disagreed with this policy:

> [Hmmmm] [silence] I don't think this is the right decision. Not testing students at the middle and end of the year will make students care less about learning and encourage them to play more inside and outside the class. In addition, I don't know how to assess my students. I don't think using formative assessment, which is not specified in the decree, would be enough for evaluating each student's performance … [silence] I don't know why the minister issued such a policy; it does not seem right. But he is the minister and knows more than us.

Reem, however, said, "The new ministers' idea of not having any tests from Grade 1 to Grade 4, gives hope as students, parents, and teachers may focus on actual learning, not the final grade." Reem thinks that not having final exams and not stressing students' final scores from Grade 1 to 4 is a crucial introductory move toward the deconstruction of exam culture such that parents and teachers evaluate students on what students learn, not what they memorize to pass the test.

Context

When asked about how the MoE attends to the adaptation of imported policies to Egyptian contexts, all nine participants concord that a successful strategy in another country does not necessarily mean that such would be successful in Egypt. For example, Ismail argued that public classrooms lack even the minimum educational equipment:

> I bring my personal speakers and laptop to play the conversations in the class … We just have a chalkboard and desks that hardly encompass all the students.

When participants were asked to provide examples of how policies were enacted without reference to Egyptian contexts, participants referred to the historical examples of the tablets and portfolios. Ismail complained:

> How can this [use of tablets] be successful while there are not enough seats in classrooms for students to sit on … I have more than 70 students in my class and students are crammed together.

As did Iyad:

> The issue is not about the distribution of tablets to students. The main problem is that summative assessment is still traditional; Thanaweya Amma is still the same.

The teachers saw little value in distributing tablets to Grade 10 students. Instead, they indicated that there are more urgent issues, such as classroom capacity and assessment. Reem, however, was highly critical, posing that tablet distribution was merely to show off: "The idea of using tablets may be just to show the world that education in Egypt is up-to-date." When asked why policies are not studied well before they can be applied in Egypt, Dina referred directly to the revolving door that is the office of the Minister of Education:

> The problem of regular change of ministers of education created a show-off situation. Every minister wants to show off by what he has brought to Egypt, but unfortunately what he has brought is not working and always fails.

This lack of articulation has, at least from the perspectives of Egyptian English teachers, prevented a clear long vision coming from the MoE where each newly appointed minister contributes to the implementation of such vision.

Portfolios

When asked about the portfolio assessment initiated in 2008, participants argued that it was imposed without fully taking into account the Egyptian context. Reem offered these comments:

> The overall idea of the portfolio seems amazing and wonderful. But the first time we were requested to follow it, all of us, I remember, were very upset because we knew it won't work … not because the portfolio is not an effective assessment method, but because it is almost impossible to implement [portfolio assessment] correctly as it should be or envisioned. Let me give you an example, in 2010, I had taught three classes, each 50 students. How do you expect a teacher with such a load to create portfolios for 150 students in a semester?

Ismail maintained that portfolios were not replacing exams:

> If we [as Educators] want the portfolio to succeed, the policy of the exams and the exam formats themselves should change, as well. Most importantly, [the] Thanaweya Amma system should completely change.

Issues such as classroom overcrowding, lack of resources, too much pressure on students, teacher salaries, private tutoring, and using the same format of Thanaweya Amma examination were also mentioned.

Professional Development

When asked about MoE-mandated professional development training, participants pointed out the disparity between what they learn at the workshops and the actual practices in crowded classes. Iyad offered this critique:

> Teachers in public schools are forced to go to attend such training … because they find it fruitless and much of what is being said is impractical … Trainers and supervisors put too much pressure on teachers: [Teachers] are required to use proper classroom management, use group work and active learning strategies, focus on communication in teaching.

Dawood added:

> It would be better if trainers came to our cramped classes and showed us how to teach 70 students using active learning and group work activities with no equipment, or teaching assistants. In my classroom, there is no room for me to move around desks at which four to six students sit.

Teacher Voice

When participants were asked how their concerns are taken into consideration in policy-making, they indicated that teacher voice is nonexistent. Yaseen suggested that teachers may not

> even come to a realization that they should have a voice; they do not even know that. And if they know, they don't have time to express their voices. Teachers work almost 18 hours a day.

Seven participants suggested that even if teachers pondered expressing opinions, they would likely conclude that doing so would be a waste of time. Rashad explained that

> Teachers are de-empowered ... and usually are portrayed by the Media as one of the reasons for the policies' failure because teachers give private tutoring.

Dina agreed, saying that teachers have to follow orders:

> We need to make a living; we don't possess the privilege or the luxury to object or ask for change ... The over-centralization control over policy making transforms teachers to just robots who are required to deliver the curriculum.

Meanwhile, Reem said the positions of teachers has not changed in quite some time:

> During the last 10 years, there came three different curricula that were imposed on teachers, students, and parents. All of them were supposed to make students perform better in English. Yet, when [the curriculum] failed, nobody listened to the teachers.

Still, embedded in these comments is teachers' recalcitrance, as mentioned by Ismail, for not being consulted:

> The ministry of education should empower teacher voice and involve them in the decision-making process ... The authoritative power that the ministry of education practices creates more problems than it solves.

Low Salary

Our participants collectively complained about their low salaries, especially in public schools. Rashad described his salary as unreflective of his contribution to the community: "I receive what equals 40 dollars a month, and this is considered to be too low for one of the most important jobs in the country." Iyad compared his salary to that of others: "My salary is about 150 dollars, but I know friends who work in international schools whose salary is almost 400 dollars." Meanwhile, Dina lamented that her current pay was insufficient toward paying bills, and she had no choice but to give private tutoring. Dawood concurred, commenting that, "My salary is barely enough to cover my transportation." Both Dina and Dawood tutor students on the side.

Additionally, teachers worried that pay scales adversely affected their quality of teaching. Yaseen explained how she distributes lesson plans across a day:

> I don't have time to teach students communication. All we focus on is how to make students ace the exam which assesses students traditionally. So, all that I care about is how to make students understand the grammar rule and memorize the vocabulary and answer the questions in the private lesson [tutoring] which is about an hour weekly.

Rashad concurred, stating that "low salaries lead to low quality" for two reasons: (1) obliging students to ask for tutoring and (2) saving energy so he might tutor from 4:00 pm to midnight.

Views of Reforms

When asked about ELT reform and how colleagues might come up with better policies, our participants shared practical views for educational reformation. Two participants expressed how media has a role in portraying teachers. Dina said that teachers are not treated favorably:

> You see teachers not being respected in the movies or soap operas. They are depicted as people who have no knowledge and people who are greedy. This is not ethical.

Dawood, however, said that

solving the problem of teaching English in Egypt starts with the collaboration of the whole society … Media, for instance, is important in upholding the status of teaching in Egypt.

Meanwhile, Yaseen pointed out:

Education has been commercialized … The government should provide equity in education and give educational rights to everyone regardless of their background because it depends on how much money you [parents'] have. The more money you [parents] have, the better education quality you [parents] can get for your [their] children.

Discussion

The English teachers were clear in their consternation with the over-centralization of MoE decision-making. They were worried about borrowing methods from another country and enacting them without fully considering how they might problematically interact with an established system. To this end, the teachers found that the MoE made rash financial decisions regarding tablets. They registered substantial criticism regarding professional development, which seems unleashed without concern for teachers' and students' actual experiences. The participants were particularly troubled by portfolios in that they felt their classes were too crowded for appropriate implementation.

Gozali et al. (2017) and Binder (2012) argue that policy-making is thought of as the job of non-practicing researchers and administrators who underestimate the contributions teachers can make to reform education. Indeed, the participants appear generally miffed that they are not even consulted by MoE officials with respect to any of these decisions. Since they felt they might have assistive input into such decisions, they concluded that the MoE centralization demonstrates greater concern for showing off. From their reasoning, this does not fit the Egyptian context, including students' culture, beliefs, classroom logistic issues, state funding, and the overall economy. Hargreaves and Shirley (2008) speculated that teachers are the endpoint of educational reform; the last to hear, the last to know, and the last to speak. They are mainly the objects of reform, not its participants. (p. 1)

Feeling disempowered and robotic with respect to doing what they are told, the teachers feel not only disappointed and pessimistic, as Dina mentioned, but also angry for being blamed for everything. They feel they are seen as the "villains" who cause "poor performance" (Samuel, 2014, p. 611).

There is a discrepancy between ELT policies and actual teaching practices in Egypt. One reason for this conflict seems to be over-centralized control on policy-making. Orders come from above, and schools have to abide by them, causing inconsistency between policies and practices. At the practice levels, many issues are discussed: parents and students are concerned about final test scores; exams reinforce rote memorization; teachers must consider tutoring to make a living; classrooms suffer from overcrowding, and different types of schools offer different qualities of ELT.

In conclusion, we point to Yaseen, who highlighted that government should consider children as humans who need to be empowered through good education. Empowering students comes as a result of humanizing teaching that values children and helps them co-construct what they learn. If a government considers all students as humans with the right to be empowered regardless of what they are able to pay, the desired outcomes of English teaching policies in Egypt should change from mastering something to empowering students. As a result, "students can develop a healthy body and mind and become better citizens in the future" (Shih, 2018, p. 197). But this can't happen unless education policy development involves all stakeholders to ensure that reforms stem from the Egyptian context itself. There are, of course, limitations to the study. We only interviewed teachers in large cities, more specifically in Greater Cairo—not a full representation throughout Egypt. Having teachers from other parts of the country and a wider range of participants' years of experience could lead to additional considerations. Finally, with the wide range of school types in Egypt, the focus of the reported viewpoints was concerned with governmental schools. Nonetheless much of what is mentioned is likely applicable to all other schools.

Note

1. At the end of Thanaweya Amma (grade 12) academic year, students are usually required to take final tests in seven subjects, including English. Students' percentage of the sum of their test scores in all subjects determines which major students can pursue.

References

1956 Constitution of Egypt. (1965, January 16). *Alwaqa'a Almasryeh* (pp. 1–15). Retrieved from https://constitutionnet.org/sites/default/files/constitution_of_1956-arabic.pdf

Abdulaal, M. (2018, September 11). English language to be taught in Egyptian kindergarten for the first time. *Egyptian Streets* [Cairo]. Retrieved from https://egyptianstreets.com/2018/09/11/english-language-to-be-taught-in-egyptian-kindergarten-for-the-first-time/

Alam, S. (2014, January 4). The Minister of Education: "Teaching English starts from the second grade." *Alyoum AlSabeh* [Cairo]. Retrieved from https://www.youm7.com/story/2014/1/4/1434564/وزير-التعليم-تدريس-الإنجليزية-من-الثاني-الابتدائي-العام-المقبل

Al-Ganzouri. (2019, June 16). Private schools Tuition for 2019–2020 and Increase in the school bus fees. *KalamSaleem* [Cairo]. Retrieved from https://kalamsaleem.com/

Ali, W. (2018, May 5). Lawsuit demanding cancellation of the Arabized curriculum postponed on 3 June. *Egypt Today*. Retrieved from https://www.egypttoday.com/Article/1/49386/Lawsuit-demanding-cancellation-of-Arabized-curriculum-postponed-on-3-June

Armour, K. M., & Makopoulou, K. (2012). Great expectations: Teacher learning in a national professional development program. *Teaching and Teacher Education, 28*(3), 336–346.

Badran, A. (2017, September 29). Tablets threaten the ministry of education and student to be in jail. *Al-Nabaa* [Cairo]. Retrieved from https://www.elnabaa.net/665718

Badwy, Y. (2014, March 05). The return of teaching sending abroad to the US and England after a long period of suspension. *El-Balad* [Cairo]. Retrieved from https://www.elbalad.news/841162

Bakr, A. (2003). *Education policies and decision-making* (1st ed.). Alwaffaa House Publisher.

Binder, M. (2012). Teacher as researcher: Teaching as lived research. *Childhood Education, 88*(2), 118–120. https://doi.org/10.1080/00094056.2012.662132

Carter, N., Bryant-Lukosius, D., DiCenso, A., Blythe, J., & Neville, A. J. (2014). The use of triangulation in qualitative research. *Oncology Nursing Forum, 41*(5), 545–547. https://doi.org/10.1188/14.ONF.545-547

CCCC Committee on Assessment. (2014). *Writing assessment: A position statement.* Retrieved from College Composition and Communication website: https://ncte.org/statement/writingassessment/

Creswell, J. W., & Poth, C. N. (2016). *Qualitative inquiry & research design: Choosing among five approaches.* Sage.

DeMonte, J. (2013). *High-quality professional development for teachers: Supporting teacher training to improve student learning.* Center for American Progress.

Dimmock, C., & Walker, A. (1998). Comparative educational administration: Developing a cross-cultural conceptual framework. *Educational Administration Quarterly, 34*(4), 558–595.

El-Araby, S. A., Al-Naggar, Z. A., Gheith, A. G., El-Dib, A. A., Mostafa, A. A., El-Said, M. F., et al. (2012). *The National curriculum framework for English as a foreign language: Grade 1–12.* Ministry of Education.

El-Fiki, H. (2012). *Teaching English as a foreign language and using English as a medium of instruction in Egypt: Teachers' perceptions of teaching approaches and sources of change.* Doctoral dissertation. Retrieved from https://tspace.library.utoronto.ca/handle/1807/32705

El-Shaarawi, S. (2015, January 25). Egypt's generation lost: Why fixing a broken education system is one of the biggest challenges facing president Sisi. *Foreign Policy* [Washington, DC]. Retrieved from https://foreignpolicy.com/2015/01/23/egypts-generation-lost/

Frost, D. (2008). "Teacher leadership": Values and voice. *School Leadership and Management, 28*(4), 337–352.

Gebril, A., & Brown, G. T. (2014). The effect of high-stakes examination systems on teacher beliefs: Egyptian teachers' conceptions of assessment. *Assessment in Education: Principles, Policy & Practice, 21*(1), 16–33.

Gozali, C., Claassen Thrush, E., Soto-Peña, M., Whang, C., & Luschei, T. F. (2017). Teacher Voice in global conversations around education access, equity, and quality. *FIRE: Forum for International Research in Education, 4*(1), 32–51.

Hamdi, W. (2016, November 24). Al-Hilaly Al-Shirbiny: Some students graduate illiterate. *Elfagr* [Cairo]. Retrieved from https://www.elfagr.com/2363021

Hargreaves, E. (2001). Assessment in Egypt. *Assessment in Education: Principles, Policy & Practice, 8*(2), 247–260.

Hargreaves, A., & Shirley, D. (2008). The fourth way. *Educational Leadership, 66*(2), 56–61.

Hassanen, O. (2009, August 22). The agreement to implement a portfolio as comprehensive assessment tools. *Al-bashaeer* [Cairo]. Retrieved from https://elbashayer.com/118033/2009/08/22/60762/

Hayes, D. (2012). Planning for success: Culture, engagement and power in English language education innovation. In C. Tripple (Ed.), *Managing change in English language teaching: Lessons from experience* (pp. 47–60).

Heneveld, W. (2007). Whose reality counts? Local educators as researchers on the quality of primary education. *International Review of Education, 53*(5–6), 639–663.

James, M., McCormick, R., Black, P., Carmichael, P., Fox, A., Drummond, M. J., et al. (2007). *Improving learning how to learn: Classrooms, schools, and networks*. Routledge.

Joffe, H., & Yardley, L. (2004). Content and thematic analysis. In *Research methods for clinical and health psychology* (pp. 56–68). Sage.

Kahlenberg, R. D., & Potter, H. (2015). Restoring Shanker's vision for charter schools. *American Educator, 38*(4), 4.

Koelsch, L. (2013). Reconceptualizing the member check interview. *International Journal of Qualitative Methods, 12*, 168–179. https://doi.org/10.1177/160940691301200105

Lincoln, Y., & Guba, E. G. (1985). *Naturalistic inquiry*. Sage.

Llorens, M. B. (1994). Action research: Are teachers finding their voice? *The Elementary School Journal, 95*(1), 3. https://doi.org/10.1086/461784

Loveluck, L. (2012). *Education in Egypt: Key challenges*. Universitäts-und Landesbibliothek Sachsen-Anhalt.

Mohamed, Y. (2019, September 11). Prices start from 140 L.E … Ministry of Education announces public schools' tuition. *Masrawy* [Cairo] Retrieved from https://www.masrawy.com/news/education-school education/details/2019/9/11/1632699/المدار-ومصروفات-تعلن-التعليم-ا-جنيه145--من-أتبدaمية-الحكو-س-

Morrison, E. W., Wheeler-Smith, S. L., & Kamdar, D. (2011). Speaking up in groups: A cross-level study of group voice climate and voice. *Journal of Applied Psychology, 96*(1), 183.

Omar, I. (2018, May 5). Questions and answers about the new education system. *Sout Alomma* [Cairo]. Retrieved from http://www.soutalomma.com/Article/

Poverty and equity brief: Arab Republic of Egypt. (2018). Retrieved from World Bank website: https://databank.worldbank.org/data/download/poverty/33EF03BB-9722-4AE2-ABC7-AA2972D68AFE/Global_POVEQ_EGY.pdf

Salama, S. (2017, November 14). Seven mistakes will lead to the resignation of Al-Hilaly. Retrieved from *Alyoum AlSabeh* [Cairo]. Retrieved from http://mobileparlmany.youm7.com/News/

Samuel, M. (2014). South African teacher voices: Recurring resistances and reconstructions for teacher education and development. *Journal of Education for Teaching: International Research and Pedagogy, 40*(5), 610–621. https://doi.org/10.1080/02607476.2014.956546

Shih, Y. H. (2018). Towards a pedagogy of humanizing child education in terms of teacher-student interaction. *Journal of Education and Learning, 7*(3), 197–202.

Slembrouck, S. (2007). Transcription – The extended directions of data histories: A response to M. Bucholtz's "Variation in Transcription.". *Discourse Studies, 9*(6), 822–827. https://doi.org/10.1177/1461445607082582

Stopikowska, M., & El-Deabes, Y. M. (2012). The education system of Egypt: Contexts, frames, and structures. *Problems of Education in the 21st Century, 40*, 129.

Teacher compensation and teacher quality. (2009). Retrieved from the Committee for Economic Development of the Conference Board (CED) website: https://www.ced.org/pdf/Teacher-Compensation-and-Teacher-Quality.pdf

Walker, A., & Dimmock, C. (2000). One size fits all? Teacher appraisal in a Chinese culture. *Journal of Personnel Evaluation in Education, 14*(2), 155–178.

Whitty, G., Power, S., & Halpin, D. (1998). *Devolution and choice in Education: The School, the State and the Market.* Open University Press.

Yin, C. L. (2013). The impact of an in-service professional development course on writing teacher attitudes and pedagogy. *Journal of Pedagogic Development, 3*(1), 12–18.

Zaid, A. (2017, January 2). Tablet instead of a paperback textbook. *Al Wafd* [Cairo]. Retrieved from https://alwafd.news/تحقيقات-وحـوارات-/1435969«التابلت»-بديلًا-عن-الكتاب-المدرسي

5

ELT Policies in Multilingual Contexts: An Analysis of Rural-Urban Experience in Ghana

Raymond Karikari Owusu and Andrea Sterzuk

Introduction

Ghana was a British colony for almost 100 years, from the mid-nineteenth century until it gained independence in 1957 (Owu-Ewie, 2006). Today, English is the sole official language of Ghana, even though another 49 languages are spoken across the country (Anyidoho & Dakubu, 2008; Davis & Agbenyega, 2012).[1] The introduction and spread of English began when the British started to train Ghanaians as interpreters and later opened formal schools under missionaries. The inception of formal education in Ghana paved the way for the use of English as the medium of instruction, and indigenous languages became "inadequate" for teaching (Bamgbose, 2000; Owu-Ewie, 2006). So strong was this attitude that accounts of literacy were measured and reported only with respect to students' ability in English (Ministry of Education Ghana, 2008). Under British rule, English cemented its place in the Ghanaian society as the

R. K. Owusu (✉) • A. Sterzuk
University of Regina, Regina, SK, Canada
e-mail: raymond.owusu@uregina.ca; andrea.sterzuk@uregina.ca

© The Author(s), under exclusive license to Springer Nature Switzerland AG 2022
E. E. Ekembe et al. (eds.), *Interface between English Language Education Policies and Practice*, https://doi.org/10.1007/978-3-031-14310-6_5

language of trade, education, governance, and a cross-ethnic lingua franca (Adika, 2012).

Today, English occupies a central role in most official places and is used in schools as the medium of instruction. Nine other languages are approved as subjects of study in Ghanaian schools and have written literature: Akan (Twi, Fante, and Akuapem), Dagaare/Wale, Dagbane, Dangme, Ewe, Ga, Gonja, Kasem and Nzema (Anyidoho & Dakubu, 2008; Opoku-Amankwa, 2009). These languages are also used in other spheres. For example, Akan, Dagbane, Ewe, Ga, and Nzema are spoken on national radio and television (Ansah, 2008). While not every language in Ghana is used in media or education, every ethnic group speaks their local language in their communities. Due to inter-ethnic marriages and migration, certain communities are identified as multilingual. Because of the many local languages spoken in the country by various ethnic groups, English serves as the lingua franca. However, Ghana remains a multilingual context.

Despite the multilingual realities of most Ghanaian people, English remains the privileged language of teaching and learning throughout most of Ghana's education system. But is English the best medium of instruction to provide Ghanaian students with the best academic experiences? Using comparative case study methodology, this chapter examines the effects of implementing official English language-in-education policy in rural and urban Akan (Twi) contexts in Ghana. We begin with a brief review of relevant literature, which is useful for understanding decision-making processes, language policy implementation, and current realities of classrooms in Ghana. Next, the chapter turns to findings from the study in response to the following research questions: (1) How does ELT impact students? (2) What are the distinguishing effects of ELT in two different contexts in Ghana? Data sources for the study include classroom observations and one-on-one interviews with teachers regarding ELT policy in Ghana.

Language-in-Education Policy Reform and Implementation in Africa and Ghana

Colonial and postcolonial language policies in some African countries share similarities due mainly to political, cultural, and linguistic repertoire (Heugh, 2008). Due to difference in political ideologies, multiplicity of ethnic groups and language, some African countries continue to use colonial languages as official language of administration and education. The multiplicity of African languages meant that, choosing one ethnic language over others as the official language could be a potential source of disunity and ethnic tension (Bamgbose, 2000). African languages tend to be used as the medium of instruction at lower levels of education. In contrast, English has been adopted for high-status functions in English-speaking African countries (Heugh, 2008; Mfum-Mensah, 2005). Early exit programs,[2] or transitional bilingual programs, encompass the language model used in South Africa and other countries in sub-Sahara Africa (Heugh, 2008). In Mozambique, Zambia, and Malawi there have been concerns since the mid-1990s over low achievement in literacy and general education. This has led to suggestions for a language policy that emphasizes the extension of use of African languages and additive bilingual principles in schools (Heugh, 2008).

Over the years, language policies across most African countries have undergone a number of revisions. In most cases, revisions take place to alter language policies that favor the development and use of indigenous languages for instruction. Arguably policymakers occupy elite positions in the country. As a result, educational policies are formulated based on the ideals and aspirations of the elite who prefer to educate their children in English because doing so guarantees social mobility. Recognizing English as panacea for social mobility is one of the root causes of a lack of commitment to the promotion mother tongue education.

Like other African countries, Ghana has a history of educational reforms, dating back from the colonial era and continuing to the present. The Ministry of Education undertakes all educational reforms in Ghana. The Ghana Education Service (GES), a subsidiary of the Ministry which oversees all activities of pre-tertiary institutions, implements policies from the Ministry. Some of the basis for the reforms is to ensure that the education sector is structured along current local and international demands, as well as modern trends of development. Changes in government often lead to educational reform. In 1974, for instance, Ghana reverted to a former policy of using Ghanaian languages as the medium of instruction at the lower primary level with English being studied as a subject (Davis & Agbenyega, 2012). This policy was aimed at giving currency to the use of local languages.

However in 2002, there was a dramatic turn to the implementation of an English-only language-in-education policy following the transition to a new government in 2000. According to the 2002 policy, the medium of instruction from primary one should be English-only, with a Ghanaian language studied as a compulsory subject up to senior secondary (Owu-Ewie, 2006). The most recent educational reform occurred in 2007 (Ansah, 2014; Carter et al., 2020). This change allowed for the medium of instruction in kindergarten and lower primary to be both a Ghanaian language and English. The 2007 reform did not completely eliminate the use of English for instruction in the early primary years. Rather, it left it up to educators to adopt the best medium of instruction under the prevailing circumstances. In all grades after kindergarten and lower primary, English is the sole language of instruction and Ghanaian languages are permitted as subjects only.

The belief in English as a vehicle for social mobility persists in many African contexts, including within schools (Heugh, 2008; Mfum-Mensah, 2005). Mfum-Mensah (2005) examined the impact of colonial and postcolonial Ghanaian language policies in two northern Ghanaian schools. Interviews with community members, parents, school children, and school authorities revealed that English proficiency largely accounts for achieving success academically, socially, politically, and economically—a viewpoint akin to those observed by Pennycook (2016) and Rapatahana and Bunce (2012).

But is using English as the medium of instruction in Ghanaian schools the best thing for learning? There is evidence to suggest that the majority of children in Ghanaian schools do not attain proper numeracy and literacy: Casely-Hayford and Hartwell (2010) provide results from a 2008 National Education Assessment (NEA) report that shows that "in Ghana, 75% of sixth graders are not able to read and write in any language, and 90% do not achieve basic numeracy skills." Based on this finding, a program aimed at supplementing students' education with mother tongue instruction at schools was introduced in the rural northern parts of Ghana. This program, known as *Education for Life*, is an initiative of a non-profit private organization to support children's education with their mother tongue (Casely-Hayford & Hartwell, 2010). Casely-Hayford and Hartwell performed an impact assessment and revealed that a complementary education program facilitates students' rapid acquisition of basic literacy skills in their mother tongue compared with what formal state primary schools can achieve. These findings suggest that English-only education in a multilingual society may not work well for all children. Indeed, the results illustrate how incorporating children's mother tongue can positively affect students' literacy skills and point to policymakers ensuring that curriculum is designed to meet the needs of the target community, including languages.

Language policies implemented in Ghana over the years have used a top-down approach, with one government after another determining the suitability of various language policies for Ghanaians. Yet, efforts to implement one single educational language policy for all, with little regard for individual differences in terms of exposure to official languages, can create issues for both students and teachers in Ghana (Ambatchew, 2010). In reality, educators can be seen as policymakers rather than simply implementers of policies (Garcia & Menken, 2010). From this perspective, "good educators do not blindly follow a prescribed text or march to an imposed ELT policy but instead draw on their own knowledge and understandings in order to teach" (p. 258). Educators often resist top-down approaches to language policy in schools because these policies are not viewed as representing the socio-economic and academic wellbeing of students. As policymakers introduce policy, practitioners use their agency to make their own decisions in the classroom.

Given the series of reforms in Ghanaian language-in-education policy over the past decades and in light of differences between rural and urban communities' social, economic, and infrastructural circumstances, this study addresses the real need to examine how one national language-in-education policy affects classroom realities of students and their teachers and offers research-informed recommendations for future language-in-education planning and policy.

Methodology

This chapter presents a comparative case study (Yin, 2013) of two school contexts in Ghana. The design of this research draws on critical ethnography (Dutta, 2014) to attempt explanation to the following questions:

1. How do students whose mother tongue is not English respond to English-only instruction?
2. What are the distinguishing effects of the policy on rural and urban students?

Purposive sampling (Creswell, 2014) was used to select participants, who consisted of students and educators in two different primary schools in Ghana: one rural and one urban. The locations of the two schools raise the issue of equal access to English, inside and outside of the classroom, as well as the impact of English-only instruction on students' content acquisition. Students were included in the study because they are supposed to be the beneficiaries of the policy. Students who participated in the study were between seven and eight years old and were in class 4 (grade 4). This grade was chosen because class 4 is the transition point from indigenous language instruction to English-only instruction under both current and previous language policies. Teachers, on the other hand, were chosen because they are the implementers of the language policy and curriculum. Six teachers from each school were selected for the study. Data from both teachers and students were valuable in understanding how the language of instruction is negotiated in the classroom. Data from teachers were important for their roles as interpreters and implementers of the language policy in the classroom.

In our writing, we refer to the two participant schools in this study, using the following pseudonyms: Adom Rural Primary School (RPS) and Asempa Urban Primary School (UPS). Both schools are located in Twi-dominant communities in Ghana. Adom RPS is situated in a farming community where the inhabitants are mostly cocoa farmers. There is no electricity in this village and inhabitants do not speak English. In contrast, Asempa UPS is found in the heart of Kumasi, the second largest city of Ghana. Although the school provides education to a Twi-dominant community, most people in Kumasi speak English and are literate in the language. Asempa UPS is a well-constructed building with internet connection.

Data for this study were collected from classroom observations of interactions between teachers and students (not recorded but captured with field notes), one-on-one interviews with teachers (audio-recorded), and analysis of official educational documents. All six teachers participated in semi-structured one-on-one interviews. During observations of classroom lessons, particular attention was paid to students' level of participation in lessons and teacher instruction choices around language. Data from observations and interviews were triangulated (Stake, 2010) with examination of official documents on education language policy in the country.

Findings

English and Twi in the Classroom

Interactions between teachers and students show interesting similarities in both schools. Data from our observations revealed switching from English to Twi and sometimes mixing the two languages in lessons. For instance, during a mathematics lessons at Asempa UPS, where the class teacher was teaching the topic of fractions, the teacher and students were using both Twi and English in their exchanges, despite state policy which plans for English as the sole language of instruction. Twi is the community's language and every person in the community speaks the language. The fieldnote extract below summarizes one interaction between a teacher (Akoto) and a student (Adwoa) at Asempa UPS:

Akoto(Twi/English):	*24 aseɛ ne sɛn wɔ fraction mu?*
Translation:	*What does* 24 *stand for in fraction?*
Adwoa (Twi):	*Sɛ nnipa nnan rekyɛ adeɛ mmienu a obiara bɛnya sɛn?*
Translation:	*If four people share two kinds of an item, how much would each of them get?*

The interactions observed in the classroom highlight the usefulness of the mother tongue to teachers and students. Mathematics, Science, and Information and Communication Technology (ICT) are subjects that have been described as technical, with terminologies that are missing in native language vocabularies. Yet, in the example above, the teacher and students were using the local language to learn the concepts of fractions. Admittedly, apart from numbers and alphabets in the Twi language there were no symbols to represent some mathematics concepts. Still, for the most part, students contributed meaningfully in their mother tongue during the lesson. Some students also responded to teacher's questions in Twi when uttering long sentences but in English for short mathematical answers. The students' demonstration of understanding of the mathematical concept in Twi suggests that it could be less difficult and more beneficial to the students' learning to teach students math with a language familiar to them.

Similarly, code-switching and code-mixing were common in all the lessons we observed at Adom RPS. The mixing of languages is common in bilingual and multilingual communities but has not always been positively framed by education systems or language researchers. In the past, researchers and educators tended to view multilinguals' knowledge of each language as separate systems (García, 2009). Indeed, the term *code-switching* reflects this perspective; speakers are understood to be switching between separate languages or codes. However, there has been a shift toward the idea of translanguaging, or strategically employing a full array of linguistic options for communication. Translanguaging as an instructional strategy is common to classrooms in other formerly colonized parts of the world, including Malaysia (Martin, 2005), The Gambia (McGlynn & Martin, 2009), South Africa (Brock-Utne & Holmarsdottir, 2004), Tanzania (Brock-Utne & Holmarsdottir, 2004; Vavrus, 2002), and Hong Kong (Lin, 1999). In the Malaysian example, teachers often used local language of the students to explain content and code-switched between English and local languages to facilitate understanding and encourage students' participation (Martin, 2005). Many of the exchanges in Asempa UPS align with this understanding of multilingual communication. Despite official language-in-education policies which dictate an English-only approach, teachers and students make use of the full array of resources at their disposition.

The teacher's use of Twi in the following excerpt from an English lesson highlights the usefulness of Twi in classroom discussion. It also raises issues as to how teachers interpret educational policies. Apart from English being the officially sanctioned language of instruction, it is also one of the subjects that students study. This lesson is reading and comprehension concept. In this lesson, Osei (the teacher) begins by assuring learners that he is going to read in English and translate into Twi so that they can understand. Osei reads a passage about types of stoves from the students' textbook. Speaking English, Osei provides examples of different types of stoves but the students were only familiar with one of them, the particular stove used in their homes. Some key points emerged in the course of reading. Using Twi to verify comprehension, Osei wants to know if the students understand these words:

Osei (Twi):   *Sɛ yɛka "advantage" a aseɛ ne sɛn?* (*Said in Twi*)
Translation: *What is the meaning of the word "advantage"?*

No student was able to respond to the teacher's question. Osei had no option other than to provide the meaning of the word in Twi. He went on to ask for the meaning of *disadvantage*. Osei is hopeful that students would be able to see a connection between the two words. But the students have difficulty in making this connection. We were expecting this English class to be delivered in English but apart from the reading from the textbook by the teacher, everything else was in Twi. The students did not get the opportunity to read the passage, meaning that only the teacher used English. In the same lesson, Osei asked the students to provide the meaning of the word "expensive" in Twi. After waiting for a while without a response, the teacher decided to put the word in context by coming up with the following sentences in English:

Osei: 1. *My mother bought an expensive car.*
           2. *The book is expensive.*

Students attempted to respond, however, none of them was able to give the correct meaning of the word in Twi. The lesson then entered the evaluation stage. Below is how the interaction between the teacher and the students ensued:

Osei: ***What makes cooking pots black?*** This question is translated into Twi by Osei as:

                ɛdeɛn na ɛma nkyɛnsen a yɛde noa aduane ho yɛ tuntum?
Students: Enwusie (smoke). This is chorus response.
Osei: So how can you say "enwusie" in English?

There were no students who could say "*enwusie*" in English. The teacher therefore said it to them in English. Osei continued the discussion with this question:

Osei: Why do some families not use modern cookers?

In this case the teacher is expecting the students to use the word "expensive" to respond to the above question. No students are able to construct a sentence in English or Twi to respond to this question.

The teacher had indicated earlier in the lesson that students were going to read the passage after all reading and translations were done by him. We were curious to see how the students were going to read the passage but that did not happen. When asked after the lesson why he didn't allow the students to read as indicated in his introduction, he replied that it is difficult for the students to read English.

The two teachers in these particular instances had to choose between the mandated English-only instruction and imparting knowledge to students in both English and a language they understand. Both teachers chose to revert to Twi when students were unable to comprehend in English. Although attempting hybrid language practices (Makoe & McKinney, 2009, 2014), the teachers and students relied heavily on the mother tongue of the students, an act in contradiction to the English-only language policy in place, but in accordance with the realities of their classrooms and the needs of their students.

Mode of Enforcing English Speaking

The environment in which students in both schools learn and speak English contributes to the success or challenges of the English-only policy. Teachers apply all manner of strategies to enforce English use. For example, teachers use punishment to ensure that students learn and speak English. Although corporal punishment is still present in Ghanaian schools, the severity is less than in the past. Punishment takes the form of flogging, cleaning of classrooms, and kneeling down and raising the two hands. In our discussions with educators, it emerged that students in both Adom RPS and Asempa UPS often refuse to speak at all when the English-only policy is enforced. Madam Afriyie, a teacher at Adom RPS Primary 5, shared this experience:

> One day I told the students that this week nobody should speak Twi. That week even some of the students didn't speak throughout the week, but the child has a problem, but he won't talk. For him to speak Twi to be beaten (punished by teacher), he would keep the problem to himself.

In this case, by denying the students at Adom RPS the opportunity to communicate in their mother tongue, active learning becomes difficult or impossible. In an attempt to enforce English speaking at Adom RPS, the teacher ended up denying some students the opportunity to take part in interaction in the school.

Similarly, Haruna, a primary 6 teacher at Asempa UPS, shared his experiences about how English speaking is enforced in his class: "Because I force them to speak English, they are good. And sometimes I use punishment." We have not found any research study that suggests that punishment is appropriate for ensuring that students learn English. Nonetheless, the teacher's statement suggests that he believes the students are good at English because punishment is productively applied in the classroom.

Adherence/Resistance to English-Only Policy

Teachers in both schools demonstrate their resistance to English-only instruction on a daily basis. Teachers' ideologies, standpoints, and personal experiences influence decisions they make in classroom regarding languages of instruction. According to the teachers in both schools, students would not understand anything if English was used as the sole medium of instruction and interaction. The teachers believe that lesson objectives cannot be achieved if they only use English. The frustrations experienced by teachers when implementing English-only instruction is expressed by Adom RPS primary 5 teacher, Afriyie:

> I observed in my first time in this school, looking through our curriculum I realized that upper primary we need to use English solely. So, I decided to use English. I realized when I asked them "do you understand?" They said, "Yes madam." But I gave them an exercise, and none was able to score three out of five. So, I realized they didn't understand everything I was teaching so I changed everything to solely Twi on that day. I realized five persons were able to score five out of five.

The resistance exhibited by the teacher may be borne out of the prevailing circumstances in the classroom, which the language policy fails to address. Possible consequences of implementing the policy without adaptation could be poor class performance, whereupon students might be perceived as less-academically skilled. Top-down ELT policies are often resisted and negotiated by teachers (Menken & Garcia, 2010) whose beliefs and experiences are at odds with the officially prescribed program.

Likewise in Asempa UPS, the teachers do not strictly adhere to the English-only instruction. For example, a lower primary 2 teacher Agyeiwaa, explained:

> Because if you use the English language alone, you know some pupils they speak their local languages home. So, you have to bring in the local language so they would understand you and answer questions.

It is not surprising that lower primary students struggle to understand English as their counterparts in upper primary encounter the same problem. While this school is located in a city where many inhabitants have some English language knowledge or abilities, the teacher acknowledges that some students come to school with no English proficiency. Out of frustration over students' limited proficiency, teachers may adopt suitable strategies, even if doing so violates official policy. In the excerpt, the teacher shows knowledge of linguistic situations in the community where the school is located. From one angle, it could be seen as the teacher undermining policy by negotiating it, but it is also possible to understand her instructional strategies as teaching according to the experiences she has had over the years.

English for Inter-ethnic and Global Interaction

Although the teachers in the respective schools underscore the importance of teaching with students' mother tongue, they do not discount the role played by English in Ghanaian society. For instance, the English syllabus for upper primary (primary 4 to 6) emphasizes the role English plays as the official language in national life in Ghana. It is stated explicitly in the document that the rationale for learning English in Ghana is that English is the language of government and administration, the language of commerce, the learned professions, and the media. It adds that "success in education at all levels depends, to a very large extent, on the individual's proficiency in the language." In other words, English is being used as a benchmark for academic progression.

Indeed, teachers in both schools, when considering the multilingual nature of Ghana, view the necessity of English in students' lives. Their point is that when one travels to another part of the country where their mother tongue is not spoken, a common language is required for communication. Some teachers further indicated that English is necessary because it is widely spoken globally so it is necessary for students to learn it for international communication. In fact, for some teachers, the power of English as both a common language in Ghana and a worldwide communication tool demonstrates that one's local language may actually be downplayed. Afriyie, an Adom RPS primary 5 teacher, speaks of the role of the home language:

> To me I don't think it will help. Let's take for instance you want to travel out of your country how can you talk to people with your dialect? But majority of people outside Ghana can understand you when you speak English. I went to SRC meeting in north where Twi is not spoken but I was able to communicate with them in English.

Akoto, a Primary 4 teacher at Asempa UPS concurred:

> To the best of my knowledge I think it won't help. The best thing is to combine the two languages when teaching or communicating with the children. Using only local language, though other countries are practicing

that—for example, China—they use their language in everything they do. But in our country, we don't have one particular language. We have different languages and people would be moving from one place to the other it would be very difficult.

In sum, the teachers of this study believe that Ghanaians need English for international purposes and for inter-ethnic purposes.

Discussion and Conclusion

Our study suggests that there is an overemphasis on English in the two schools. Regardless of students' proficiency in a Ghanaian language, if students are unable to read and write in English, they are not considered literate. This situation creates inequality in a society where public formal spaces are dominated, dictated, and led by those who have superior command of English. Those who have rich knowledge in indigenous languages, traditions, and culture are relegated to the background, leading to a waste of valuable human resources. Furthermore, an overemphasis on English for education and formal administrative and official businesses in Ghana and other postcolonial Africa countries renders indigenous languages as underutilized and seemingly inferior.

Classroom discussions in English in the two schools do not encourage students' participation. Students find it difficult to respond to questions posed in English. Drawing on all the linguistic resources at their disposition, they respond in Twi to questions that were framed in English. Teachers speak Twi and briefly engage in code-switching and code-mixing with English in the classroom. The teachers in both schools reported that when they speak English only in a lesson, students do not understand. The teachers also indicated that students are unable to achieve lesson outcomes when lessons are delivered in English only. They, therefore speak almost entirely in Twi with brief insertion of English words to facilitate teaching and learning.

It is problematic to use punishment to enforce English speaking since most students in the rural school cannot communicate in English. Students who are unable to speak English fluently may remain silent in class even if they have ideas to contribute to class discussions. Moreover, students have difficulty in retaining vocabulary because classroom teaching practices do not offer opportunities for repeated or contextualized practice. Many students' English linguistic resources in both schools are inadequate to understand content taught in English only. Thus, it is an infringement on the rights of students to be compelled to speak English through punishment. Any attempt to use punishment to implement a language policy is an admission that the policy falls short of addressing the academic challenges of students.

In addition, the English-only language policy does not work equally for students in both schools. Although students in the Asempa UPS have challenges with the policy, students in the Adom RPS are comparatively more disadvantaged. Unlike some students in Asempa UPS who can speak, read, and comprehend some English, almost all the students in Adom RPS do not possess those crucial skills for English-only instruction. The students' inability to speak, read, and comprehend English in Adom RPS means they do not perform as their urban school counterparts during district or national standardized examinations. An unequal playing field is created for students to negotiate the path of education. As a result, general expectations of quality, quantity, and equality in terms of knowledge expected to be acquired by students across the country are a mirage. There is no equality as it stands now in Ghana with respect to quality education. Ghanaian students do not have equal opportunity to advance because not every student has quality and equal access to the official language of instruction. This situation hampers students' social mobility as they cannot then gain admission into secondary school.

Overall, this study has revealed challenges faced by students under English-only instruction in the two respective schools we observed. While this study does not seek to make generalizations, we believe the phenomenon observed is not peculiar to just the two schools studied. For instance, a study of language practices in Tanzanian and South African pre-tertiary classrooms (Brock-Utne & Holmarsdottir, 2004) revealed that teachers practiced code-mixing and code-switching contrary to the official language policy. According to the authors, the teachers switched to a familiar language any time they found it challenging to use the official language, English. Similar findings can be found in Maluleke (2019), Bose and

Choudhury (2010) and Ndlangamandla (2010) in South Africa, Salehmohamed and Rowland (2014) in Mauritius, and Marungudzi (2014) in Zimbabwe. In light of differences in social, economic, and infrastructural circumstances, this study comparing a rural school and an urban school provides insight to how a monolingual national language-in-education policy affects different contexts with different constraints. Findings from the study demonstrate that the English-only language policy is negotiated and resisted by teachers. We recommend that Ghanaian policymakers consider multilingual education with both English and indigenous languages to address linguistic and academic imbalances in the education system. Lastly, we recommend that education and literacy in Ghana not be defined as only people who can read, write, and communicate fluently in English. Literacy in Indigenous languages should equally be valued and recognized.

Notes

1. Davis and Agbenyega do not describe how distinctions are conceptualized between languages and dialects.
2. An early exit program is an early switch from L1 to English (i.e., mother tongue instruction from primary 1 to 3, after which only English is used).

References

Adika, G. S. K. (2012). English in Ghana: Growth, tensions, and trends. *International Journal of Language, Translation and Intercultural Communication, 1*, 151–166.

Ambatchew, M. (2010). Traversing the linguistic quicksand in Ethiopia. In L. M. Gutstein (Ed.), *Negotiating language policies in schools: Educators as policymakers* (pp. 198–210). Routledge.

Ansah, G. N. (2008). Linguistic diversity in the modern world: Practicalities and paradoxes. *International Journal of Language Society and Culture, 26*.

Ansah, G. N. (2014). Re-examining the fluctuations in language in-education policies in post-independence Ghana. *Multilingual Education, 4*(1), 12.

Anyidoho, A., & Dakubu, M. K. (2008). Ghana: Indigenous languages, English, and an emerging national identity. *Language and National Identity in Africa*, 141–157.

Bamgbose, A. A. (2000). *Language and exclusion: The consequences of language policies in Africa* (Vol. 12). LIT Verlag Münster.

Bose, A., & Choudhury, M. (2010). Language negotiation in a multilingual mathematics classroom: An analysis. In *Mathematics education research group of Australasia*.

Brock-Utne, B., & Holmarsdottir, H. B. (2004). Language policies and practices in Tanzania and South Africa: Problems and challenges. *International Journal of Educational Development, 24*(1), 67–83.

Carter, E., Sabates, R., Rose, P., & Akyeampong, K. (2020). Sustaining literacy from mother tongue instruction in complementary education into official language of instruction in government schools in Ghana. *International Journal of Educational Development, 76*, 102195.

Casely-Hayford, L., & Hartwell, A. (2010). Reaching the underserved with complementary education: Lessons from Ghana's state and non-state sectors. *Development in Practice, 20*(4–5), 527–539.

Creswell, J. W. (2014). *Research design: Qualitative, quantitative, and mixed methods approaches* (4th ed.). Sage.

Davis, E., & Agbenyega, J. S. (2012). Language policy and instructional practice dichotomy: The case of primary schools in Ghana. *International Journal of Educational Research, 53*, 341–347.

Dutta, U. (2014). Critical ethnography. In J. Mills & M. Birks (Eds.), *Qualitative methodology: A practical guide* (pp. 89–105). Sage.

García, O. (2009). Education, multilingualism and translanguaging in the 21st century. *Social Justice Through Multilingual Education*, 140–158.

Garcia, O., & Menken, K. (2010). Stirring the onion: Educators and the dynamics of language education policies (looking ahead). In L. M. Gutstein (Ed.), *Negotiating language policies in schools: Educators as policymakers* (pp. 249–261). Routledge.

Heugh, K. (2008). *Language policy and education in Southern Africa* (pp. 355–367). Springer.

Lin, A. M. (1999). Doing-English-lessons in the reproduction or transformation of social worlds? *Tesol Quarterly, 33*(3), 393–412.

Makoe, P., & Mckinney, C. (2009). Hybrid discursive practices in a South African multilingual primary classroom: A case study. *English Teaching, 8*(2), 80.

Makoe, P., & Mckinney, C. (2014). Linguistic ideologies in multilingual South African suburban schools. *Journal of Multilingual and Multicultural Development, 35*(7), 658–673.

Maluleke, M. J. (2019). Using code-switching as an empowerment strategy in teaching mathematics to learners with limited proficiency in English in South African schools. *South African Journal of Education, 39*(3).

Martin, P. (2005). "Safe" language practices in two rural schools in Malaysia: Tensions between language policy and practice. In A. Lin & P. W. Martin (Eds.), *Decolonisation, globalisation: Language-in-education policy and practice* (Vol. 3). Multilingual Matters.

Marungudzi, T. (2014). Deploying a sense of plausibility in language choice: The role of English-Shona code switching in Zimbabwean classrooms. *International Journal of English and Education. ISSN: 2278, 4012.*

Mcglynn, C., & Martin, P. (2009). "No vernacular": Tensions in language choice in a sexual health lesson in the Gambia. *International Journal of Bilingual Education and Bilingualism, 12*(2), 137–155.

Menken, K., & García, O. (Eds.). (2010). *Negotiating language education policies: Educators as policymakers*. Routledge.

Mfum-Mensah, O. (2005). The impact of colonial and postcolonial Ghanaian language policies on vernacular use in schools in two Northern Ghanaian communities. *Comparative Education, 41*(1), 71–85.

Ministry of Education, Ghana (2008). *2007 National Education Assessment Report.*

Ndlangamandla, S. C. (2010). (Unofficial) multilingualism in desegregated schools: Learners' use of and views towards African languages. *Southern African Linguistics and Applied Language Studies, 28*(1), 61–73.

Opoku-Amankwa, K. (2009). English-only language-in-education policy in multilingual classrooms in Ghana. *Language, Culture and Curriculum, 22*(2), 121–135.

Owu-Ewie, C. (2006, April). The language policy of education in Ghana: A critical look at the English-only language policy of education. In *Selected proceedings of the 35th annual conference on African linguistics* (pp. 76–85). Cascadilla Proceedings Project.

Pennycook, A. (2016). Politics, power relationships and ELT. In *The Routledge handbook of English language teaching* (pp. 44–55). Routledge.

Rapatahana, V., & Bunce, P. (Eds.). (2012). *English language as hydra: Its impacts on Non-English language cultures* (Vol. 9). Multilingual Matters.

Salehmohamed, A., & Rowland, T. (2014). whole-class interactions and code-switching in secondary mathematics teaching in Mauritius. *Mathematics Education Research Journal, 26*(3), 555–577.

Sey, K.A. (1978). Ghanaian English, an Exploratory Survey. London and Basingstoke: Macmillan Education Limited.

Stake, R. E. (2010). Qualitative research: Studying how things work. New York: Guilford Press.

Vavrus, F. (2002). Postcoloniality and English: Exploring language policy and the politics of development in Tanzania. *Tesol Quarterly, 36*(3), 373–397.

Yin, R. K. (2013). *Case study research: Design and methods*. Sage.

Part II

Practice Steering the Wheel

6

Integrating Communicative Language Teaching Activities in Overcrowded Classrooms: Policy and Practice Issues in South Sudan Secondary Schools

Alex D. D. Morjakole

Teaching and Learning in Overcrowded Classrooms

Scholars and teachers have not agreed on what number of learners can qualify a particular class to be regarded as a "large one" (Khurram, 2018; Shamim & Coleman, 2018). West (1960) coined the term *difficult circumstance* as denoting classrooms of 30 or more students, with students squeezed on benches, under instruction by teachers with low English proficiency, and harsh climatic conditions like heat. Kuchah (2016), however, contends that difficult circumstances are constructed by the person experiencing them, entailing "those circumstances that are outside the control of teachers and learners, but which affect their daily experiences of teaching and learning significantly" (151). Shamim and Coleman (2018) posit that classes may be deemed large based on several considerations: (a) class size seen either in terms of the classroom dimensions or the number of learners, (b) teacher-pupil ratio (TPR), (c) classroom

---

A. D. D. Morjakole (✉)
University of Warwick, Coventry, UK

density or "number of learners per square meter," and (d) crowding, or the perception that there are too many people in the room.

In some Western contexts, a class of 20 can be seen as large and challenging, whereas in many parts of the world (in most African countries) a class of 20 or 30 is a luxury (Kuchah, 2018). In this chapter, we rely, as Kuchah suggests, upon teachers' opinions. The chapter mainly examines the perceptions of English language teachers about the implementation of Communicative Language Teaching (CLT) approaches in large classes in South Sudan. Specifically, I draw attention to teachers' "thought" about class size, challenges faced, and their perceptions about the success of the strategies they use to address the challenges faced. Scholars such as Khurram (2018) have also argued that the perception of large classes is not merely restricted to the number of learners per classroom, but also extended to skills taught and the classroom setting (Locastro, 1989), workload and stress (Shamim, 1993), and the content taught (Todd, 2006).

It is vexing that policy makers who purportedly aim for quality in education continue to create circumstances leading to large and overcrowded classrooms (Kuchah & Shamim, 2018). A persistent practice among policymakers that directly and/or indirectly leads to the creation of large classrooms is the reliance on Pupil Teacher Ratios (TPRs). Coleman (2018) warns that TPR is not an appropriate formula to match number of learners with that of the teachers, thereby producing rather than mitigating large classes. Instead, he suggests that enrolment be based on numbers of classes available in the school and how many are enrolled for each grade. Other factors that give rise to large classes are economic such as the desire by private institutions to make profit (Trang, 2015; Todd, 2006), and societal as indicated by the increasing importance of education and the fact that access to education has become a basic right in a democratic society (Locastro, 2001).

The prevalence of large classrooms in English as a Foreign Language (EFL) contexts—whatever the factors that have created them—has concerned teachers and educationists for ages. Studies investigating issues of large classes show that novice teachers well-trained on Western well-resourced and comfortably small-size classes find it difficult to implement their textbook pedagogies in crowded, poorly resourced classrooms (Kuchah, 2018). In order to address this, Tchombe (2013) recommends that teachers in large classes be *transformative* in their pedagogy if they are to deal with unexpected difficult circumstances.

Studies (e.g., Shamim et al., 2007; Trang, 2015) have shown that the key problems of teaching in large classes concern classroom management, evaluation and giving feedback, difficulty in organizing group/pair work, affective/emotional challenges and disruptive behavior during. Large classes affect both teachers who find it difficult to provide "sustained interaction and differentiated attention" and students whose "ability to concentrate on a task" may be diminished (Day, 1999: 73). Given this environment, Coleman (2018) unsurprisingly observed that large classes are "associated in teachers' minds with emotional stress, physical exhaustion and professional frustration" (29)—attributes that ultimately affect student achievement.

Todd (2006) observed that large classes are particularly challenging for EFL teachers because conditions do not allow even the most experienced teacher to apply a variety of teaching activities. Therefore, even though a teacher may have a toolbox of strategies at hand, there is an inversely proportional relationship with class size. Consequently, the larger the class, the greater the need for the teacher to revise her already established teaching methods. For example, a large classroom makes it practically difficult to employ learner-centered approaches, and even more difficult—if not impossible—to get every learner to participate (Shamim et al., 2007).

Large Classes and Communicative Language Teaching

Communicative interaction and negotiation among students is believed to foster learning (Lee, 2004). Thus, central to Communicative Language Teaching (CLT), where focused interaction can be so vital, is the creation of situations that involve practice of the target language. In order to encourage L2 learners to produce more target language, communicative tasks are seen as "[stretching] learners beyond their limited linguistic resources" (Lee, 2004: 10). These interactions include *oral activities:* reaching a consensus, relaying instructions, story construction, communication games, problem solving, interpersonal exchange story construction;

and

written activities: exchanging letters, story construction, writing games, relaying instructions, fluency writing and writing reports. (Harmer, 1987: 113–140)

Large class size has been perceived as a major drawback in the implementation of CLT because "when CLT was first introduced across Europe, the English as a foreign language (EFL) context in which it would inevitably be applied was not considered" (Chowdhury, 2003: 283). This makes the approach impractical outside the countries for which it was developed (Ramanathan, 1999). The incompatibility, Chowdhury (2003) argued, is that there are differences in culture, teaching resources, classroom context such as large class size, language proficiency of learners and teachers' capabilities in the non-native speaker contexts. In many ESL/EFL contexts, large classes make it difficult to engage learners, manage the class and, above all, control the noise level that comes with student interaction.

Scholars have raised alarm over the enactment of policies that in effect, do not reflect realities of educational contexts. Gorsuch (2000), for example, pointed out that government policies on education tend to address content at the expense of instructional methods. Investigating government promotion of CLT in Egypt, Ibrahim and Ibrahim (2017) found CLT implementation painful, noting "if students talk at the same time or become over-enthusiastic, the class becomes raucous" (299–300). Anderson (2016), however, argued that classroom noise signifies that communicative exchanges are taking place— that students are working together, helping each other and discussing with the teacher; nevertheless, he demurs that it is reasonable to respect neighboring classes.

The Purpose of the Study

The purpose of this study was to explore how EFL teachers in South Sudan secondary schools integrate communicative strategies into their large classes and how they conceptualize the success of their strategies within their classroom context. Research into the phenomenon of large classes has been concerned with examining the nature of challenges, and the effects of the challenges on teaching and learning. Moreover, some scholars (e.g., Anderson, 2016; Hess, 2001; Shamim et al., 2007; Smith et al., 2017) have shown some strategies for teaching English in large classes. Studies that have investigated teachers' perceptions about the success of their classroom strategies in large classrooms and how the strategies might be operating within the policy dictates—that is, the use of communicative language teaching approaches. Thus, my study sought answers to these research questions:

1. What challenges do English language teachers face in incorporating communicative language teaching strategies in crowded classrooms? How do they conceptualize overcrowded classrooms?
2. What communicative strategies do they employ to counter these challenges?
3. How do teachers perceive the success (or lack thereof) of their adopted strategies in their teaching context?

Methodology

The research was conducted with six English language teachers in secondary schools in South Sudan over a two-month period of intermittent interactions via phone calls, social media chats, document sharing, and ultimately two interviews. Each interview lasted 30–40 minutes.

Two semi-structured interview guides, presented in Table 6.1, were constructed. Open-ended guiding questions were prepared and delivered in an exploratory manner (Dörnyei, 2007), thereby providing freedom to clarify issues raised by the participants (Mackey et al., 2005). The first interview explored teachers' perception of their classes in terms of size

Table 6.1 Semi-structured interview question guides

Questions in the first interview:
How many students are in your class? How would you describe your class?
What are the major problems you face in your teaching situation / classroom—what is problematic and why?
Please describe anything you have done to address (some of) these problems. Was this successful? Why/Why not?
Please mention some of the strategies you use to encourage communication during your lesson in the class
Final comment?
Questions in the post-lesson interview:
What were the lesson objectives you developed for this lesson?
Briefly describe the steps of the lesson
What activities did the learners do?
Why did you choose those activities? Did you include those activities during your lesson planning?
Please explain how successful those activities were
Were there any problems with your preselected activities?
Please describe the best/worst moments during your lesson
If you have any other comment, please share now

and how class size impacted their teaching. The second interview was a post-lesson exploration of how challenges identified in the first interviews were reflected in lessons taught during the time of the research.

Data analysis began with the transcription of the recorded interviews (Erlingsson & Byrsiewicz, 2017). The "transitional process" (Saldana, 2013: 5) of coding was used in which salient features of the talk were identified in the transcript. While performing the thematic coding, key themes were generated from the first transcript by identifying responses that answered parts of the research questions (Atkinson, 2017; Elliott, 2018) which were then mapped into Shamim and Coleman's (2018) conceptual framework for studying class size.

Results and Discussion

RQ1: Teachers' Perception of Class Size and Challenges Faced

Before each interview, class size information was obtained for reference to the interview questions. Teachers' perceptions of the sizes of their classes were obtained by asking teachers to describe their classes using three adjectives: Small, Normal and overcrowded. Table 6.2 shows class statistics, participants' description of their classes and their preferred class size.

Table 6.2 shows that most classes start with 70 students with exception of Paulina's class of 37 students. Participants were also asked about the factors responsible for the class sizes that they taught. Paulina thought her class of 37 was exceptional, reasoning that few upper secondary students enjoy sciences. While Jake and Yasia described their classes—87 and 81 respectively—as overcrowded, a class of 85 was normal for Jose. Darius, David and Jake all described their classes as overcrowded, while for Jose, since all his classes were uniformly fixed, through a new school policy, he only had "normal" classes. Teachers mostly agreed with respect to maximum class size of 45 to 50. Still, Dario warned that "any class that exceeds the teacher pupil ratio is already overcrowded and problematic."

When participants were asked what factors led to large classes, two sets of factors—categorized into *pull factors* and *push factors*—were mentioned.

Pull factors involved a range of extra-value adding characteristics of schools and activities that offer more opportunities for student learning.

Table 6.2 Participants' description of their classes and their preferred class size

Participant	Number of classes taught	Smallest	Description	Largest	Description	Preferred class size
David	4	96	Overcrowded	122	Overcrowded	45
Darius	3	105	Overcrowded	120	Overcrowded	40–45
Jake	3	87	Overcrowded	95	Overcrowded	45–50
Jose	3	85	Normal	85	Normal	40–45
Paulina	3	37	Normal	80	Overcrowded	40–50
Yasia	2	70	Normal	81	Overcrowded	45–50

According to Jose, these include extra teaching and coaching—for instance, during weekends which tend to attract students to a school. Another pull factor was the presence of qualified teachers in a school. Jose reported his school has "teachers with good quality, [and] education; they even do coach on the weekends." These extra services were found, particularly in Juba, to draw more students to schools, thereby leading to increased enrolment, especially among financially fit families (Longfield & Tooley, 2013).

Push factors include characteristics within a school or region that pose challenges to student education, including political instability and insecurity. Jose reiterated this when he mentioned, "conflict in other states: the students will not be in a stable situation so that they can learn." In such communities, safety takes precedence over education. According to the United States Agency for International Development (2019), one third of schools were either destroyed, damaged, or under occupation by armed forces. Students in these areas seek education, especially in Juba, since it is relatively safer than rural areas.

Push factors also include absence of qualified teachers as "all the teachers are running to organizations and working with other NGOs" (Jose interview 1). According to the South Sudan NGO forum (2018), South Sudan has a total of 330 NGOs, thereby making them huge employers with better pay (Maxwell et al., 2012). Consequently, this has resulted in internal brain drain (Sherr et al. 2012) as they attract qualified workers, especially when teachers can move to relatively peaceful environments.

These findings point to the observation by Bahanshal (2013) that, in developing countries, large classes "tend to be obligatory rather than exceptional" (49), an unsurprising phenomenon given Anderson's (2016) observation that large classes often occur in low-income countries, especially in sub-Sahara Africa.

Challenges Faced

Shamim and Coleman's (2018) model for understanding class size includes—among others—the following categories: physical factors, classroom processes, and assessment and feedback. These factors influence the teaching and learning process in varied ways.

Physical Factors

Physical factors involve those classroom conditions that impose difficulties such as intra-class movement by both teachers and learners, student physical comfort such as seating arrangement, and physical flexibility such as reaching out to a fellow student. In Shamim and Coleman's (2018) framework, this could be understood in terms of "class density," the understanding that there are too many students occupying a small space.

All participants expressed physical challenges in their classrooms differently. In Paulina's words, "The main problem in my classroom is the number of the students in the class." The effect results in inadequate classroom space. All participants expressed the need for teachers to move about the class to monitor learners as part of classroom management. Emphasizing this need, Yasia noted:

> Classroom management is always what can make teaching to be successful when the seats are arranged well. You can move from one point of the class to another.

Consequently, his comment reflects Hayes's (1997) observation that congested space negatively affects classroom processes such as grouping learners and monitoring student work, but promotes the danger of actually stepping on learners. David described his class:

> Once the classrooms are overcrowded, that means some of the students will be uncomfortable and as a result of this, they may not be able to participate in any interaction with the teacher.

David's observation reflects Moghal, Kazi, and Bukhari's (2019) findings that crowded, uncomfortable learners have low response to the teacher's questions during lessons. This scenario reveals effectively a *triple discomfort*: firstly, that students are squeezed in their seating leading to physical discomfort; secondly, when teachers ask questions, students may feel uncomfortable (possibly because they may be caught unawares as they could have been psychologically attending to their physical discomfort); and, thirdly, that the combination of the physical discomfort and the discomfort caused by the question may lead to affective discomfort.

In Paulina's class, five students share a desk instead of the three the bench was built for. She reported that sometimes others sit on the tops of the desks or simply stand during the lesson because

> [t]he seats are not enough. Students are squeezed in the benches and so they are not comfortable.

However, despite this challenge, the participants showed they value staying in close contact with learners because "to be a successful teacher, a teacher must attend to what students do, what they say and how they perform" (Ochoma, 2013: 28).

Climatic conditions are another variable that affect work conditions. Paulina reported that her student numbers dropped considerably when it rained heavily in the morning. According to Jose, when classes were hot, he moved toward the door to feel relief from the heat.

Another challenge reported was the lack of books for English language teaching. According to the teachers, the new curriculum had no books developed for it; thus, they inadequately relied on Kenyan books.

Classroom Processes

Classroom processes involve those aspects of the classroom interaction such as "teacher and pupil behaviour and relationships, relationships between pupils, pupil engagement and involvement" (Blatchford et al., 2009: 779). In this sense, while classroom processes are limited to the acquisition of knowledge by the learner, the limitation somehow seems to create rapport between the teacher and the learners. By creating interaction in the classroom, the teacher also creates a conducive environment sharing and, as a consequence, relationship building.

Participants cited encouragement of interactive activities as their most difficult challenge. Jake explained:

> When you want to form groups you need to mix them. Others face the other side. But if you look at the sitting arrangement, there is not space for the teacher to move around. Even the chalkboard, when you are writing, it is very difficult for you to move and step backward. If you move backward, then you will be hitting a learner.

The participant in the extract describes the difficulty experienced by the teacher in the context of a very crowded classroom. While the teacher could have the *best intention*—involving every learner in classroom activity—in attempts to reach out to all learners in his class, he is still constrained by the fixed space.

According to Ochoma (2015) teaching interactively means engaging student-student collaboration in which students are "[using] inquiry methods to ask questions, [investigating] a topic, and [using] a variety of resources to find solutions and answers" (34). According to David and Paulina, it is difficult to involve every learner in a congested classroom. Yasia emphasized this point, noting that students at the back of the class "will just remain behind there," implying that students are likely to be passive, only listening to the teacher.

Still, Dario indicated:

> The teaching of English is very good, very enjoyable. Generally, there is active learning—have active participation by learners. I really enjoy it. The more the learners are, the more the lesson is enjoyable. I enjoy it when there is interaction between the learners and me. Learning becomes competitive when learners are more. You have variety of choice to make.

According to Dario, the teacher in a large class is not restricted to a few active individuals and instead has a range of students to choose from when soliciting responses to a question. Still, it appears that emphasis is placed on teacher-student interaction, and, conversely, learner-to-learner interaction is less utilized. Importantly, how teachers use the term *interaction* seems to suggest less language practice by the learners, meaning "the teacher decides who the next speaker is going to be, the next speaker responds to the call, and then the teacher takes over again, automatically" (Lier, 1984: 163).

Participants also underscored the shortage of time for classroom activities. Jose emphasized that "one hour is not enough for comprehension and giving other things like composition, summary writing." One reason for this lack of time during classroom activity, as explained by Yasia, is that other learners also had factors which required more input from the teacher, so the teacher "must spend a lot of time explaining … to the students" with thinner educational orientation. David observed that shy students and slow learners who may need more "special attention" are disadvantaged, a comment resonating with Bahanshal's (2013) findings that "students in large classes receive less individual attention than their peers in small classes, [leading] to dissatisfaction among students, especially weak ones who will feel marginalized" (54).

Assessment and Feedback

Three teachers—Dario, Paulina and David—all pointed out that assessment and feedback are challenges. David explained that marking student work is "time consuming and sometimes delayed." Dario reported that "There are very many books, [and] by the end of the day you become very tired." This particular point raises a concern over the quality of teaching going on in the classroom. It is apparent here that the teacher, limited by time to finish checking student work for areas of improvement, leaves a majority of the students without feedback on their work.

RQs 2 and 3: Strategies and Success

During interviews, research questions 2 and 3—which focused on strategies for addressing overcrowded classes and how teachers perceive strategies as successful—were often addressed simultaneously. Strategies reported here addressed four key challenges: (1) managing limited space and time, (2) engaging learners, (3) encouraging interaction and language practice, and (4) dealing with lack of books.

Managing Limited Classroom Space and Time

The most widely reported strategy involved creating situations to enable interaction and movement, including seating re-arrangements, as suggested by Yasia:

> If [benches] are arranged, you will be able to make a square … and it can accommodate 15.

Paulina, meanwhile, talked of taking groups outside to "work under the trees while others remain." Both participants' comments refer directly to the role of learners' responsibilities in such classrooms, a point explained by Dario regarding the importance of involving students remedying challenges they face:

> They treat their own classes. They are already experts. They know how to do it.

Dario's comment reflects Kuchah and Smith's (2011) class of 230 where they found involving students in eliciting solutions to in-class challenges absolutely indispensable.

Engaging Learners

Parsons and Taylor (2011) urged teachers to have a wealth of strategies to get their learners engaged beyond classroom contexts. The participants highlighted their range of strategies. One method repeatedly mentioned by Jake, Paulina and Jose was the use of *student sampling*. *Student sampling* emerges as a practice in which the teacher, constrained by the large number of students, picks a few representative students to take active part in an educational activity. For example, Jose reported:

> I will choose two in the first row next to the blackboard. Then I take other two in the middle, then other two at the other end.

Indeed, since getting every learner to participate simultaneously is difficult, participants indicated the importance of rows and placement of representative student leaders within these rows because sampling depends on these strategically placed leaders. Still, Paulina was skeptical of sampling fully enhancing learning among non-participating individuals, citing that after picking a few leaders, she felt unable to assess "whether they have understood [or learnt] or not."

Encouraging Interaction and Language Practice

Student engagement, from the participants' viewpoint, is multifaceted. It could mean getting students to talk among themselves, or tasking students to organize themselves in independent units with students playing defined roles for accomplishing common tasks. Dario explained how to encourage group work:

> You can also go further to choose the leader. One can volunteer as a leader. Another one can volunteer as a writer or secretary and another one volunteer as the presenter. By doing this, you are encouraging communication; you are encouraging participation; you are encouraging students how they can (unclear) on their own and choose leaders.

Yasia used grouping to enable students to share printed text during reading exercises, establishing collaboration where students work together to understand the section of a text. Paulina, however, contended that "grouping happens when they are not reading," implying that reading is an individual activity.

Two participants commented on how they try to take care of less prominent students. Paulina emphasized that she liked "picking up those ones who are not showing their hands or not putting up their hands so that they can show what they have not understood." Jose similarly explained how he tried to track quieter students:

Those ones who did not do the pair work I will give them seven numbers for individual work … I give three to people who raised their hands. Then the four I give to those who do not want to raise up their hands, they are just seated.

While the teaching pedagogy described in the extract is aimed at reaching out to every student, and to ensure that students have had a "touch" on a learning activity by the end of the lesson, the teachers could not describe the outcomes expressed shown through student performance.

Interaction and Language Practice

In terms of how teachers incorporate communicative strategies in their overcrowded classrooms Dario and Jose specifically reported the use of classroom debates to encourage speaking among learners. One advantage, according to Dario, for using debates is that learners understand topics more deeply as learners are encouraged to think critically. Jose agreed:

> We do this in the class so that some of these students will stand up and talk gently. Other students are listening to them seriously. This means it will encourage them and the rest of the students.

Jose enumerated key uses of debate: (1) language practice, (2) development of presentation skills, and (3) encouragement of shy students. Still, Jose admitted that debate depended on availability of time.

Dealing with Lack of Teaching Materials

All six participants expressed inadequacy and, in some instances, total lack of materials for teaching English. Yasia, Dario and Jose explicitly explained how they navigated this challenge. Jose explained that textbooks serve to (1) help learners follow lessons, (2) enable learners to answer classroom exercises, and (3) help learners develop reading skills.

Thus, while planning lessons without such material, Jose and Dario offered this advice:

> You will look for the topic in the syllabus content, and then look for the textbooks. Then you come and check. You select and then you prepare yourself the notes and a lesson plan.

It is surprising that, given the absence of teaching/learning materials at the disposal of the teacher, teachers still struggle to bring knowledge to the learners using whatever resources they could find even if the schools cannot avail them. Furthermore, despite the demands on the use of the language teaching policy which could imply provision of teaching materials for the teacher to facilitate the CLT approach, teachers are left on their own, using their own resources, including their own credibility, to ensure that the students at their disposal continue to receive education.

Finally, to expose learners to written text, Yasia implemented Richards's (2006) communicative jigsaw activities, photocopying pages of a passage:

> I gave them the printed story. One group would work on one paragraph and the other group deals with the second paragraph and the other with the other paragraphs.

Conclusion

This chapter provides insights into the under-researched South Sudan English Language Teaching (ELT) context. The study sheds light onto issues of praxis, where policy implementation can be effectively assessed. Participants' responses demonstrate that their classes are overcrowded where employing engaging teaching methods—particularly language practice activities such as speaking—is difficult. Due to the constraints imposed by limited classroom space and large number of students per class, teachers adopt strategies to suit their teaching context. Strategies such as student sampling and the difficulty of giving feedback to all students on their classroom work call for further inquiry on their implications on language learning in particular.

Two major limitations warrant mention. First, no wider survey was conducted, which could reveal more generalizable information. Second, there exists a dearth of contextually specific academic studies on ELT in South Sudan secondary schools upon which to build. This chapter is one of the few, if not the first, systematic inquiry into classroom practices in a South Sudan ELT context. Hopefully, school managers (head teachers, directors of studies, supervisors, and inspectors), education policy makers, teacher training institutions, and education-supporting agencies might find the phenomena relayed in this chapter relevant to their practices.

References

Anderson, J. (2016). *Teaching English in Africa: A guide to the practice of English language teaching for teachers and trainee teachers*. East African Educational Publishers Ltd.

Atkinson, J. D. (2017). *Journey into Social Activism: Qualitative Approaches*. Fordham University.

Bahanshal, D. A. (2013). The effect of large classes on English teaching and learning in Saudi secondary schools. *English Language Teaching, 6*(11), 49–59.

Blatchford, P., Russell, A., & Brown, P. (2009). Teaching in large and small classes. In L. J. Saha & A. G. Dworkin (Eds.), *International handbook of research on teachers and teaching* (pp. 779–790). Springer.

Chowdhury, M. R. (2003). International TESOL training and EFL context: The cultural disillusionment factor. *Australian Journal of Education, 47*(3), 283–303.

Coleman, H. (2018). An almost invisible "Difficult Circumstance": The large class. In K. Kuchah & F. Shamim (Eds.), *International perspectives on teaching English in difficult circumstances, international perspectives on English language teaching*. Palgrave Macmillan.

Day, C. (1999). *Developing teachers: The challenges of lifelong learning*. RoutledgeFalmer.

Elliott, V. (2018). Thinking about the coding process in qualitative data analysis. *The Qualitative Report, 23*(11), 2850–2861.

Erlingsson, C., & Brysiewicz, P. (2017). A hands-on guide to doing content analysis. *African Journal of Emergency Medicine, 7*(3), 93–99.

Dörnyei, Z. (2007). *Research methods in applied linguistics*. Oxford University Press.

Gorsuch, G. J. (2000). EFL educational policies and educational cultures: Influences on teachers' approval of communicative activities. *TESOL Quarterly, 34*(4).

Harmer, J. (1987). *The Practice of English Language Teaching*. London and New York: Longman.

Hayes, D. (1997). Helping teachers to cope with large classes. *ELT Journal, 51*(2), 106–116.

Hess, N. (2001). *Teaching Large Multilevel Classes*. Cambridge University Press.

Ibrahim, M. K., & Ibrahim, Y. A. (2017). Communicative English language teaching in Egypt: Classroom practice and challenges. *Issues in Educational Research, 27*(2).

Kuchah, K. (2016). ELT in difficult circumstances: Challenges, possibilities and future directions. In T. Pattison (Ed.), *IATEFL 2015 Manchester Conference Selections* (pp. 149–160). IATEFL.

Kuchah, K. H. (2018). Teaching English in Difficult Circumstances: Setting the Scene. In Kuchah, K.H & Shamim, F (Eds.), *International Perspectives on Teaching English in Difficult Circumstances: Contexts, Challenges and possibilities* (pp.1–25). Palgrave Macmillan. https://doi.org/10.1057/978-1-137-53104-9

Kuchah, K., & Shamim, F. (2018). *International perspectives on teaching English in difficult circumstances, international perspectives on English language teaching*. Palgrave Macmillan.

Kuchah, K., & Smith, R. (2011). Pedagogy of autonomy for difficult circumstances: From practice to principles. *Innovation in Language Learning and Teaching, 5*(2), 119–140.

Lee, C. (2004). *Language output, communication strategies and communicative tasks*. University Press of America.

Lier, L. V. (1984). Analysing interaction in second language classrooms. *ELT Journal, 38*(3), 160–169.

LoCastro, V. (1989) Large size classes: The situation in Japan. *Lancaster-Leeds Language Learning in Large Classes Research Project Report No. 5.*

LoCastro, V. (2001). Teaching English to large classes: Large classes and student learning. *TESOL Quarterly, 35*(3).

Longfield, D., & Tooley, J. (2013). *A survey of Schools in Juba*. Newcastle University: EG West Centre.

Mackey, A. et al. (2005). *Second language research: Methodology and Design*. Tylor and Francis.

Maxwell, D., Gelsdorf, K., & Santschi, M. (2012). *Livelihoods, basic services and social protection in South Sudan*. Secure Livelihoods Research Consortium.

Retrieved from https://fic.tufts.edu/wp-content/uploads/SS_EvidencePaper_final-published_July2012.pdf

Moghal, S., Kazi, A. S., & Bukhari, A. (2019). Large classes and English language teaching and learning in public sector secondary schools of Pakistan. *Indonesian TESOL Journal, 1*(1), 1–8.

Ochoma, M. U. (2015). Classroom processes, student learning and development. *International Journal of Scientific Research in Education, 8*(1), 27–36.

Parsons, J., & Taylor, L. (2011). Improving student engagement. *Current Issues in Education, 14*(1).

Ramanathan, V. (1999). "English Is Here to Stay": A critical look at institutional and educational practices in India. *TESOL Quarterly, 33*(2), 211–231.

Richards, J. C. (2006). *Communicative language teaching today*. Cambridge University Press.

Saldana, J. (2013). *The coding manual for qualitative researchers.* (Second edition): SAGE publications.

Shamim, F., Negash, N., Chuku, C., & Demewoz, N. (2007). *Maximizing learning in large classes: Issues and options*. British Council.

Shamim, F., & Coleman, H. (2018). Large-sized classes. The TESOL Encyclopedia of English language teaching, 1–15.

Sherr, K., Mussa, A., Chilundo, B., Gimbel, S., Pfeiffer, J., Hagopian, A., & Gloyd, S. (2012, April 27). *Brain drain and health workforce distortions in Mozambique*. PLOS ONE. Retrieved from: https://journals.plos.org/plosone/article?id=10.1371/journal.pone.0035840#s3

Smith, R., Padwad, A., & Bullock, D. (2017). *Teaching in low-resource classrooms: Voices of experience*. British Council.

South Sudan NGO Forum. (2018). *3W data visualization for international NGOs at county level*. Retrieved from https://southsudanngoforum.org

South Sudan's New National Curriculum. (2015). Retrieved from: http://ssmogei.org/curriculum/

Tchombe, T. M. S. (2013). *Promoting the learning process in English language teaching: Pedagogic challenges*. Retrieved from: https://camelta-cameroon.weebly.com/camelta-2013-conference.html

Todd, R. W. (2006). Why investigate large classes? *Reflection Journal*. Retrieved from http://arts.kmutt.ac.th/sola/rEFL/Vol9_Reflections_Large_Classes.pdf

Trang, N. M. (2015). Large classes: Universal teaching and management strategies. *LangLit, 2*(1). Retrieved from: www.langlit.org

UNICEF. (2015). *South Sudan: First-ever comprehensive national curriculum launched*. Retrieved from https://www.unicef.org/

West, M. (1960). *Teaching English in difficult circumstances*. Longmans, Green.

7

ELT Policies and Practices in Superdiverse Central Ohio: From "Flexible" to "English-Centric"

Brian Seilstad

Introduction

The United States has a long and tortured history with non-European, non-English-speaking populations, that is, first peoples, enslaved peoples, and immigrants. Indeed, the primary theme through its history has been the dominance of White supremacy and English-only policies and practices. More specifically, historical educational language policies and practices have vacillated between efforts to eradicate, restrict, tolerate, or support the languages people use privately and publicly (Crawford, 2004, Chapter 3; García, 2008, Chapter 8).

However, many oppressed and minoritized communities have insisted on their rights to equitable education. For example, the US Supreme Court's 1974 *Lau v. Nichols* decision demanded that students speaking languages other than English not be subjected to English-only education but rather be provided adequate linguistic support to learn English and

---

B. Seilstad (✉)
Al Akhawayn University, Ifrane, Morocco
e-mail: b.seilstad@aui.ma

therefore be able to participate in mainstream schools. More specifically, the Supreme Court's 1981 *Castañeda v. Pickard* decision required that

1. programs be based on (a) a sound educational theory that is (b) supported by some qualified experts;
2. programs be provided with sufficient resources and personnel to be implemented effectively; and
3. after a trial period, students be actually learning English and, to some extent, subject matter content. (de Jong, 2011; Haas & Gort, 2009).

While a positive step in many ways for English language learners (ELLs), this decision does not mandate languages of instruction. This leeway perpetuates debate between those promoting bilingual education (García, 2008, p. 5; García et al., 2008) and those centering English-language acquisition with little or no institutional concern for the students' home language (Porter, 1996, 1998) or, more fully, their languaculture (Agar, 1996), meaning the full combination of students' linguistic and cultural backgrounds that they bring to educational contexts. Moreover, these decisions obscure the "mono" orientation toward language, culture, literacy, and nationalism at the root of the challenges for minoritized communities (Auerbach, 1993; Babino & Stewart, 2020; Cummins, 2007). Absent clear policies backed by firm leadership, these gaps allow actors—from states to individual teachers—to make decisions that may or may not be commensurate with learning theory or aligned with the interests of the minoritized communities. Ohio, the focal state for this chapter, is a clear case study in that, despite the empirical support for bilingual education (Collier & Thomas, 2004; Umansky & Reardon, 2014; Valentino & Reardon, 2015), it has opted for a policy position of "flexibility" by offering districts five program models:

- Bilingual education
- The immersion approach
- Pull-out English as a Second Language (ESL) classes
- In-class or inclusion instruction
- Individual tutoring. (Ohio Department of Education, 2014)

This chapter explores these interrelated phenomena of language policy and pedagogical practices by focusing on an adolescent newcomer program in a superdiverse Central Ohio school district where nearly 15% of the student population is labeled *Limited English Proficient*. Superdiversity (Vertovec, 2016) is a demographic condition coined to both highlight, on the one hand, that the modern world has created novel conditions for the acceleration and expansion of global movement and the complexity of local diversity and, on the other hand, that this is a positive phenomenon with the potential to create greater opportunities for interaction and dialogue among the world's peoples. Of course, the forces of xenophobia and populism may push back on these demographic trends, but the hope of superdiversity scholars and many others is that peaceful coexistence will emerge.

Based on a year-long institutional ethnographic and discourse analytic study, this chapter focuses on teachers' attitudes and instructional practices reflecting their commitments toward bilingual and languaculturally sustaining approaches. As these approaches consistently show stronger outcomes for ELLs in addition to a concern for the high dropout rate of adolescent newcomers nationally (Fry, 2005), these attitudes and practices are important for indexing and clarifying shifts in ELT in this local context, which may resonate with other regions of the United States and even globally.

Radically Languaculturally Sustaining Theory and Practice

Theoretical and practical understanding of learning and teaching have evolved across time from individualistic approaches that focus on the one-way transfer of knowledge from teacher to student to more sociocultural and dialogic approaches that center the iterative co-construction of knowledge in and beyond formal educational contexts. Understanding these broader developments sheds light on the factors at play when working with ELLs, particularly in the United States and Ohio context, the focus of this chapter.

The behaviorist perspective centers the individual as the learner and the mind as a rational/quasi-mechanical machine that can/should receive information from external sources, store it, and recall it when necessary

(Atkinson, 2012; Castagnaro, 2006). This view of learning and teaching has been criticized, justly or not (Moore, 2006), as creating stultifying and "banking" practices where students are forced to memorize material without developing a personal or social connection to it (Freire, 2000; hooks, 1994; Scribner & Cole, 1973). In language acquisition, this framework aligns with cognitive approaches interested in how the mind receives and processes language information, drawing on theoretical concepts such as attention, long-term and working memory, and controlled/automatic language performances (Ortega, 2008, Chapter 5). Thus, pedagogies that flow from this method, such as the direct method or audio-lingual/visual method, rely heavily on repetition and corrective feedback to develop proficient language users (Castagnaro, 2006).

The sociocultural approach to learning draws on the work of Vygotsky and responds to behaviorism by emphasizing the social and recursive nature of learning (Kelly & Green, 1998; Lave, 1996). In this framework, information is not something fixed that can simply be acquired, and the learner is understood not as a blank slate but rather a social creature with developed and developing understandings of the world informed by the learner's culture, prior experiences, and personality. Thus, learning itself becomes a social act as people co-construct knowledge through activities such as discussions, play, and competitions. In language acquisition studies that draw on conversation analysis of the actual practices in these contexts (Ortega, 2008, pp. 227–233), this perspective emphasizes that teachers and learners communicate together by drawing on the learners' wide range of knowledge, including the home language (Auerbach, 1993; Lantolf, 2000; Lantolf & Poehner, 2014; Lucas & Katz, 1994). Indeed, this prior knowledge—especially the first, native, or home language—is not seen as impeding to learning as sometimes cross-linguistic influences are described (Ortega, 2008, pp. 31–54) but rather essential to developing new ways of understanding language and expressing oneself socially.

Cultural-historical theory resists the universalist tendencies in sociocultural learning that suggest that people in groups will often learn following predictable rates or patterns. Cultural-historical theory, connected to and drawing inspiration from a range of scholars such as Edward Said (1979), Franz Fanon (2008), Linda Tuhiwai Smith (2012), Luis Moll (1992), Paolo Freire (2000), or Bell Hooks (1994), point out that non-dominant groups have many assets that are submerged by dominant policies and practices in a vast array of fields, including politics, art, and education. Pedagogies formed around these theories, especially those focused on critical approaches to race, gender, or sexuality (e.g., Anderson, 1995; Collins, 2008; Dixson & Rousseau, 2006; Misawa, 2010) encourage the questioning and challenging of those norms (Gutiérrez, 2008; Gutiérrez & Rogoff, 2003; Meacham, 2001; Picower, 2009; Roth & Lee, 2007). With language acquisition, cultural-historical theory helps teachers and learners understand that language, especially that taught in schools, is not neutral or natural but rather a social construction that promotes, often quite invisibly, certain varieties of language over others (Hirvela & Belcher, 2001). Resisting this in language learning leads to an embrace of translanguaging, which challenges many of the nationalist norms around languages and, in terms of classroom practice, supports multiple voices and perspectives that teachers and learners make meaning together, often in spaces explicitly designed to challenge society's or school's status quo (Canagarajah, 2013; García & Wei, 2014; Orellana, 2016; Otheguy et al., 2015).

Just as there is a risk of universalism in sociocultural theory, there is a risk of essentialism and sedimentation in cultural-historical theory built on the inaccurate but popular view that culture and history are static facts of life rather than a collection of social and shared activities (McDermott, 1999; Street, 1993). This can be particularly challenging with some critical perspectives that take oppression to be a constant in human life rather than something that can be resisted, negotiated, and indeed eradicated under the right conditions. Thus, a modification to cultural-historical theory is necessary, dialogic approaches. This body of work, drawing on the works of Bakhtin (1982) and Volosinov (1986), argues that human social life, much like a good novel or play, is filled with multiple perspectives, each worth exploring (Edmiston & Enciso, 2003). The connections here to language learning processes have been taken up by a number of scholars (Ball & Freedman, 2004; Hall et al., 2013), and there even seems to be a connection with the field of emergentist and chaos/complexity theories. These theories stress that language learning is associative and probabilistic, and that learners draw on rational contingency strategies to use language in various communicative and social situations. This leads to a dynamic system where patterns of language use form and dissolve repeatedly rather then become inherently stable and mature (Ellis & Larsen-Freeman, 2006; Larsen-Freeman, 1997; Ortega, 2008, pp. 102–105). In short, these theories may help explain how humans engage with and are attracted by such complex dialogue with each other, as well as the texts they encounter and create in everyday life.

In sum, learning combines a broad spectrum of issues that includes and contrasts notions of the individual mind and its ability to process new information with the power of the social world and the ever-evolving set of understandings and knowledge that people must engage with and make meaning of across time and space. However, this chapter argues that ELT teachers in superdiverse contexts must take a radical stand for languaculturally sustaining policies and pedagogies. In theoretical terms, this involves challenging the centrality of English and monolingual assumptions about language and learning. In practical terms, this invokes the question of how much home languages are incorporated into ELT classrooms. Thus, this chapter draws on a continuum proposed by Pérez & Enciso (2017)—cushioned, contextualized, extensive, and radical—to explore this phenomenon in the context of an Ohio adolescent newcomer program. *Cushioned* is defined as limited and marked with instant translation, *contextualized* is somewhat more extended but still readily understandable, *extensive* is embedded and may not be understood by all, and *radical* includes multiple languages and challenges the context's underlying power structure. In ELT contexts this includes, at a minimum, the centrality of English and the role of the teacher as ultimate expert and arbiter of meaning.

Methodology

This chapter draws on institutional ethnographic and discourse analytic data collected during the 2016–2017 academic year at an adolescent newcomer program in Central Ohio. The pairing of these two methods allows for, on the one hand, a broad perspective connected to "studying up" (Nader, 1974) and committed to "*discovering* 'how things are actually put together,' 'how it works'" (D. E. Smith, 2006, p. 1, italics in original), and, on the other hand, detailed studies of language-in-use in schools (Bloome et al., 2005). This approach has, to my knowledge, never been applied to newcomer programs, although other studies exist documenting common program features, critical issues, and student narratives at newcomer programs (Hauser, 2012; Hertzberg, 1998; Short & Boyson, 2012). However, this approach has been used in a range of similar educational contexts and communities to highlight the individual and structural challenges and opportunities that exist for newcomers in specific ELL contexts in the United States (Allard, 2015, 2016, 2017).

Pairing institutional ethnography and discourse analysis requires a long-term focus on both an institution and a focal educational context that can provide rich opportunities to explore macro-micro connections related to central issues such as neoliberalism (Nespor, 1997) or, this chapter's focus, the evolving nature of languaculturally sustaining approaches to English language learning and teaching.

Throughout the year of fieldwork, I was able to develop the following data corpus:

- approximately 145 hours of classroom audio-video recordings following one cohort of adolescent newcomers, aged 15–21, across four subject areas—English, Social Studies, Math, and Science—as well as a small-group Reading program for beginning level students;
- interviews with relevant program actors from the director to students;
- regular observation/field-notes; and
- artifacts.

The focal adolescent newcomer program has been in operation in different forms for about 20 years and has developed a certain amount of local and national attention (Short & Boyson, 2004, 2012). The main research question for this study was the degree to which the program offered a languaculturally sustaining program to the learners.

The program itself arose due to the superdiverse demographics of the region, as Ms. Sharp, one of the program's most senior members, narrated:

> Ms. Sharp: I would say about '97 we started getting Somali students. In Spring, I remember we had one family. The next year we had more families, and the following year I had 116 students and 65 of them were Somali … So it was a growing community. (Personal communication, April 27, 2017)

These trends continued, reflected in the enrollment predictions of Mr. Samuelson, a new school counselor and school scheduler:

> Mr. Samuelson: I'm thinking if we grow just like we did this year with the 400 who will be back, we could be at 800 [by the end of the year]. I don't know what we could handle … I don't know how many kids are going to leave. You don't know how many are really going to give, with Trump in the office and things are changing. You don't know, you can't bet, you can't prepare. You just know that they're coming. (Personal communication, June 5, 2017)

However, today the focal program continues to evolve, particularly to address shortcomings regarding graduation rates, which the director's comments underline:

> Brian: What would be like, what's your guesstimate of kids [in a four-year cohort] who come into the program pre-functional, and then they make it all the way to graduation?
> Mr. Smith: If I had to guess, and I bet I'm pretty close, less than 20%. 15–20%. (Personal communication, November 17, 2016)

Throughout the year, I followed one cohort of newly arrived, high-school aged students considered new English language learners across their main subject areas using discourse analysis of the video records and also engaged in the broader institutional ethnography primarily through interviews and artifact collection. Table 7.1 summarizes the study's main actors.

Table 7.1 Program actors

Name	Role	Gender	Ethnicity	Time in program	Linguistic repertoire
Mr. Smith	ESL/School Director	Male	African-American	10 years	English
Ms. Johnson	Assistant Principal	Female	African-American	5 years	English
Ms. Lincoln	Assistant Principal	Female	African-American	3 years	English
Ms. Sharp	Instructional Assistant coordinator	Female	African-American	30 years	English, some Cambodian
Mr. Samuelson	School counselor	Male	White American	2 years	English, Spanish
Ms. Cabot	Teacher: English	Female	White American	15 years	English, some learning of Latin, German, French, and Spanish
Mr. Barre	Teacher: Math	Male	Somali	16 years	English and Somali with advanced proficiency in Italian
Mr. Shahiya	Teacher: Science	Male	Somali	16 years	English, Somali, Arabic
Ms. Popov	Teacher: Social studies	Female	Russian	17 years	English, Russian, Spanish

Findings

Following on the literature review and the evolving trends in English language learner education, what emerged is much less a picture of an institution with a clear and radical level of languacultural support for the students but rather a more English-centric program with the program actors, including the focal teachers, expressing differential levels of support for the students' home languacultures and commitments to centering the home languacultures pedagogically.

This is certainly due to the fact that the current staff includes a wide range of individuals in terms of previous experiences, bilingual abilities, and perspectives on bilingual education. The administrators all started as teachers in the mid-2000s and moved to administration through accelerated training programs. Although no administrators were bilingual, they developed ad hoc understandings of language acquisition and bilingualism that nevertheless led to English-centric positions:

Mr. Smith:	We got to get them first in English because this is where they're going to be. We need to get them ready ... though in the future is probably leading to learning and teaching in his language because if he can count to 10 in his language, there's a merit to that. (Personal communication, November 17, 2016)
Ms. Johnson:	I don't want to have to make [the students] turn on two lights, because you think about it, if you're in a living room and you want to turn on the light in the kitchen you can't reach both of them. (Personal communication, March 29, 2017)

Ms. Lincoln, a relative newcomer, may be more accommodating of bilingual approaches but is admittedly less experienced:

Brian:	The school could provide a space for that [bilingual programming], I'm just curious what you think about it.
Ms. Lincoln:	Well to be honest with you, ... if it was me I would want to know how to speak my own language well, ... if they have the academic piece of English and the academic piece of their own language, then maybe they could transfer their language to the English language piece and ... make them stronger as a student.
Brian:	That's been shown in the research.
Ms. Lincoln:	Oh really?
Brian:	Oh yeah, for sure. Yeah.
Ms. Lincoln:	Right, I'm smart! (personal communication, April 17, 2016)

The teachers are more languaculturally diverse, and their attitudes toward bilingualism represent this continuum:

Mr. Shahiya:	I think bilingual should be like an assistant and understanding doing that way. I think the main lesson, instructional medium should be English. (Personal communication, December 20, 2016)
Mr. Barre:	To educate [the students] in a language then what is the problem is when they're going to learn the language, the English, so when they are going to learn if they're just taught everything in Somali? (Personal communication, December 20, 2016)
Ms. Cabot:	I don't understand why we can't create a heritage Spanish class, get these kids working on their reading skills, in their native language. (Personal communication, October 28, 2016)
Ms. Popov:	I like using their language … when the people are with different languages in the same class, it enriches them. They learn from each other and like this interaction. (Personal communication, November 22, 2016)

Mr. Shahiya and Mr. Barre express an opinion commensurate with Mr. Smith's above. Ms. Cabot's view might be more radical, orienting toward support of the home language as a goal per se, and Ms. Popov's view straddles the two, seeking home language in interactions to help students learn (English) from each other.

However, the analysis of the videos focused on teacher-class or teacher-student talk (Bloome, 1989). The videos showed moments when the teachers engaged students' languacultural backgrounds. Following Pérez & Enciso, these moments can be demonstrated on the continuum of cushioned, contextualized, extensive, and radical.

Cushioned talk generally included short glosses of individual vocabulary items. Ms. Cabot, for example, drew on her linguistic repertoire to translate numbers from English into Spanish or use Google Translate on her overhead projector to translate words into the various classroom languages. While this is often useful, it has limitations and the locus of power remains with the teacher.

Contextualized moments included longer stretches of talk requiring some more complex translation or glossing. For example, Ms. Popov, who understood Spanish, would often listen carefully to the

Spanish-speaking students and interject when appropriate to make interpersonal connection or help students understand a task or text. These interjections might be in English or Spanish. One day she counseled students complaining in Spanish about the cold room to zip up their jackets and breathe deeply. She also frequently would sit individually with students and discuss concepts such as birthdays and how they are written month/day/year in the United States. rather than day/month/year as in other contexts. Again, this is a positive step to support students but the power structure remains clear.

A telling moment happened with Mr. Shahiya and one of the Arabic-speaking students named Omar. Mr. Shahiya frequently would instruct science to Omar using Arabic, but Omar had been having trouble with Mr. Barre who, in Omar's reading of the situation, was not teaching the math class well by simply giving worksheets and telling students to work individually. Thus, Omar would complain in Arabic to Mr. Shahiya about Mr. Barre. Mr. Shahiya did his best to allay Omar's concerns and even mediate with Mr. Barre. Although the situation may not have dramatically improved for Omar with Mr. Barre, Mr. Shahiya's extensive engagement subverted the power relations slightly and opened space for more complex discussions of students' and teachers' rights and responsibilities at school.

Radical engagement is perhaps best exemplified by Ms. Popov's practice as she displayed the most robust efforts by a teacher to make connections between the home and target languages. Ms. Popov's statement above shows her predilection for engaging students' home language. Among Ms. Popov's methods include a home language assessment, pictured in Fig. 7.1.

Although this was not a formal school assessment, it shows Ms. Popov's commitment to home language and provided her a view into the students' previous education and home language literacy. In fact, Ms. Popov was the only teacher to design a resource, as shown in Fig. 7.2, to help students learn target vocabulary through their home language.

Crucially and in contrast to her peers or the institution generally, Ms. Popov used this tool throughout the year, dedicating extended class time to it. For example, on March 9, Ms. Popov, as shown in the transcript presented in Table 7.2, oriented students to the sheet with the focal words

L1 Writing Sample

Name:_____
Age:_____
Date:_____
Language literate in:_____

Ask the student to write a story in their L1.

Story Prompters:
- What did you like to do in your home country?
- Retell a story that you know.
- What is your favourite thing to do? Why?

[blank box for writing]

Note: Obtain a foreign language literacy sample from a newly arrived non-English speaking student, if that student has had previous schooling. Ask the family translator/a student translator to tell the child that you would like a sample of their writing. Remember that some students' literacy skills are in a language other than their mother tongue. Upon completion have the student read the story to the translator so you can write the English version below. This sample will enable you, the teacher, to observe, in a general way, the student's fluency, thought processes and story-writing abilities.

Fig. 7.1 Ms. Popov's home language test

Vocabulary-	Name		Class	Date
WORD and VISUAL:	WORD IN MY NATIVE LANGUAGE:	WHAT IT ACTUALLY MEANS:	CONNECTION: (Text-text, text-world, text-self)
right			
freedom			
speech			
law			
vote			

Fig. 7.2 Ms. Popov's vocabulary building sheet

Table 7.2 Transcript of Ms. Popov and six students discussing a vocabulary building sheet

#	Speaker	Message unit (paralinguistic information)
1	Ms. Popov	I can show you some examples from my other groups, ok
2		alright (goes to computer at front of room)
3		so, we have five words
4		say together
5		conquistador
6	Students	conquistador
7	Ms. Popov	(continues with 'to sail, trade, route, to suffer' and students repeat)
8		definitions are here
9		and on the backside
10		on this side there are some definitions
11		on this side, ok
12		and let me show you examples
13		a lot of students finished in my period 1 2 3
14		I have different languages, let's see, please this,
15		Somali language

(continued)

Table 7.2 (continued)

#	Speaker	Message unit (paralinguistic information)
16		do we have Somali speakers, yes, like 4 students, let me show Somali
17		this is Spanish speaking
18		nice picture, look at this picture
19		(puts it on the overhead) funny pictures (moves other papers out of the way)
20		check, translation, oh you don't see very well (makes projection larger)
21		this is, Fatima, this is good, I think it is good Somali language
22		check the translation in Somali, do you understand?
23		Mohammed, do you understand, is it correct?
24	Mohammed	(doesn't respond)
25	Ms. Popov	yes no
26	Mohammed	some are wrong
27	Ms. Popov	some are wrong
28		this is Nepali language, check your
29		guys and you can come and take the paper and look what other students do
30		and check your translation
31		French, no French
32		that's, this student should be good in Somali
33		she's always, she's usually very good
34		check translation, Mohammed, is it good
35	Mohammed	yeah, that's correct
36	Ms. Popov	this is good to sail, how do you say
37	Mohammed	fi3a
38	Ms. Popov	to trade
39	Mohammed	garna
40	Fatima	gana3siga
41	Ms. Popov	right?
42	Mohammed	yeah, gana3siga
43	Ms. Popov	route
44	Fatima	waddo
45	Ms. Popov	waddo
46		to suffer
47	Fatima	(reads, hard to hear on recording)
48	Ms. Popov	good
49		so you are welcome to take what language if you need or you do by yourself
50	Fatima	I need Miss
51	Ms. Popov	you need Somali?

(continued)

Table 7.2 (continued)

#	Speaker	Message unit (paralinguistic information)
52	Dhan	I need Nepali
53	Ms. Popov	ok, I'll give you, but try not to copy, just look, make up your own sentence
54		you, Nepali
55	Puspa	yeah
56	Ms. Popov	(passes paper to Puspa)
57		Nepali, she's (indicating name of other student) usually good
58		and these are nice pictures (puts copy on the overhead)
59		ha! look at the conquistador
60		he's (with arms up like flexing)
61	Maria	(laughs)
62	Ms. Popov	ok, Nepali language, examples
63		I find more, more Somali, do you want Somali language, yeah
64		you are good, Mohammed, you have it, do you need Somali
65	Mohammed	yeah, I need Somali
66	Ms. Popov	pass to him (passes paper to Gabriela)
67		she's (the student's name from other class) good, good pictures, I like the pictures
68		(laughs a bit) I like this train, you see this is a modern train, like plane, people trade, do business by plane
69		trade routes
70		so (looks at some papers, laughs)
71		oh my, look at this, these are interesting
72		to suffer
73		trade by car, you can do trading by car
74		and the conquistador (laughs)
75		ok
76		ok, you understand right?
77		go ahead do it your way, you can copy a little bit
78		but if you copy, understand what you're copying
79		you learn it
80		ok
81		good
82		I'm going to remove
83		do it your way please

conquistador, *sail*, *trade*, *route*, and *suffer*. Ms. Popov held up the sheet and said, "So show me who finished at home. If you finished, you go to the next step." As most students had not completed it, Ms. Popov began the following section of talk, lasting approximately five minutes. The students mentioned from the class of 25 are Mohammed and Fatima (two

Somali students), Dhan and Puspa (two Nepali-speaking Bhutanese students), Maria (a Spanish-speaking student from El Salvador), and Gabriela (a Brazilian student).

This extended section demonstrates Ms. Popov's radical commitment to the home languacultures through her openness to creating space for multiple linguistic repertoires to exist and to decenter her own knowledge, punctuating the activity with "do it your way please." Although there are individual and behaviorist elements to this activity in that the ultimate goal is the students' acquisition of five key vocabulary items, the focus is clearly on the sociocultural through the interactions between the teachers, Ms. Popov, and even the other classes. Although cultural-historical knowledge or clearly dialogic approaches do not emerge directly in this transcript, later classes, both led by Ms. Popov and other teachers, did take up the history of colonialism and migration and created opportunities for critical reflection.

Discussion and Conclusion

This chapter began with presenting the broad picture in the United States that, due to Supreme Court decree, students' home languacultures could not be removed or ignored in schools. However, there remains a lack of clarity about how to incorporate or center students' home languacultures, and Ohio perhaps is a good case study for how a "flexible" policy may lead to somewhat confusing pedagogies and experiences for learners. This study's findings show that, despite the possibility of creating radical languaculturally sustaining programming for adolescent newcomers, the focal program is "English-centric" because

> English is the medium of instruction due to not only official language policy, but through the dominance of English as the language of verbal exchanges, the curriculum, instructional materials, and classroom resources like textbooks or storybooks. I use English-centric rather than *English-only* with an understanding that students and teachers in these environments are often multilingual, and thus, the negotiated and constructed contexts

in which they participate reflect aspects of this multilingualism. (Pacheco, 2016, pp. 3–4)

Although it is certainly attractive for policymakers to promote flexibility for program actors to help students meet state or national language goals, there is a significant gap between both the stated and practiced policy and what research shows would be most equitable and efficient for languaculturally diverse students—namely a strong bilingual approach in which the students' home languacultures are centered and infused throughout all aspects of program policy, design, and instruction. Although the example from Ms. Popov's class points in this direction, it is important to point out that she was a relative outlier in her pedagogical approach and, moreover, the ultimate goal of her pedagogy was English language acquisition, not strong bilingual abilities for the students.

These frictions were perceived by the various program actors, and Ms. Cabot perhaps put the challenges and opportunities most directly by saying:

> Ms. Cabot: To me, I think it's a structure thing and I think that's something that we at [the program] can fix. The problem is getting everybody on board with the same idea and it's like too many cooks in the kitchen. (Personal communication, June 29, 2017)

This quote dovetails with Mr. Smith's final interview when he said that the program "isn't there yet" in terms of program organization or outcomes. Although this focus on program improvement is laudable, I worry that the program, Ohio, and even the United States as a whole will continue to fall short in its support of minoritized and newcomer communities especially without a much more robust commitment to creating (public) school policies and pedagogies that directly challenge White hegemony and monolingualism and create extensive and radical spaces and curricula that affirm and accredit these students' languacultural repertoires.

References

Agar, M. H. (1996). *Language shock: Understanding the culture of conversation.* Harper Paperbacks.

Allard, E. C. (2015). Undocumented status and schooling for newcomer teens. *Harvard Educational Review, 85*(3), 478–501. https://doi.org/10.17763/0017-8055.85.3.478

Allard, E. C. (2016). Latecomers: The sources and impacts of late arrival among adolescent immigrant students. *Anthropology & Education Quarterly, 47*(4), 366–384. https://doi.org/10.1111/aeq.12166

Allard, E. C. (2017). Re-examining teacher translanguaging: An ecological perspective. *Bilingual Research Journal, 40*(2), 116–130. https://doi.org/10.1080/15235882.2017.1306597

Anderson, E. (1995). Feminist epistemology: An interpretation and a defense. *Hypatia, 10*(3), 50–84.

Atkinson, D. (2012). Cognitivism, adaptive intelligence, and second language acquisition. *Applied Linguistics Review, 3*(2), 211–232. https://doi.org/10.1515/applirev-2012-0010

Auerbach, E. R. (1993). Reexamining English only in the ESL classroom. *TESOL Quarterly, 27*(1), 9–32.

Babino, A., & Stewart, M. A. (2020). *Radicalizing literacies and languaging: A framework toward dismantling the mono-mainstream assumption* (1st ed. 2020 edition). Palgrave Macmillan.

Bakhtin, M. M. (1982). *The dialogic imagination: Four essays* (M. Holquist, Ed.; C. Emerson, Trans.). University of Texas Press.

Ball, A. F., & Freedman, S. W. (Eds.). (2004). *Bakhtinian perspectives on language, literacy, and learning.* Cambridge University Press.

Bloome, D. (1989). Beyond access: An ethnographic study of reading and writing in a seventh grade classroom. In D. Bloome (Ed.), *Classrooms and literacy.* Praeger.

Bloome, D., Carter, S. P., Christian, B. M., Otto, S., & Shuart-Faris, N. (2005). *Discourse analysis and the study of classroom language and literacy events: A microethnographic perspective.* Routledge.

Canagarajah, S. (2013). *Translingual practice: Global Englishes and cosmopolitan relations.* Routledge.

Castagnaro, P. J. (2006). Audiolingual method and behaviorism: From misunderstanding to myth. *Applied Linguistics, 27*(3), 519–526. https://doi.org/10.1093/applin/aml023

Collier, V. P., & Thomas, W. P. (2004). The astounding effectiveness of dual language education for all. *NABE Journal of Research and Practice, 2*(1), 1–20.

Collins, P. H. (2008). *Black feminist thought: Knowledge, consciousness, and the politics of empowerment* (1st ed.). Routledge.

Crawford, J. (2004). *Educating English learners: Language diversity in the classroom* (5th ed.). Bilingual Education Services, Inc.

Cummins, J. (2007). Rethinking monolingual instructional strategies in multilingual classrooms. *Canadian Journal of Applied Linguistics, 10*(2), 221–240.

de Jong, E. J. (2011). *Foundations for multilingualism in education: From principles to practice.* Caslon Publishing.

Dixson, A. D., & Rousseau, C. K. (2006). *Critical race theory in education: All God's children got a song.* Routledge. http://site.ebrary.com/lib/alltitles/docDetail.action?docID=10172130

Edmiston, B., & Enciso, P. (2003). Reflections and refractions of meaning: Dialogic approaches to reading with classroom drama. In J. Flood, D. Lapp, J. Squire, & J. Jenson (Eds.), *Handbook of research on teaching the English language arts* (2nd ed., pp. 868–880). Lawrence Erlbaum Associates.

Ellis, N. C., & Larsen-Freeman, D. (2006). Language emergence: Implications for applied linguistics--Introduction to the special issue. *Applied Linguistics, 27*(4), 558–589. https://doi.org/10.1093/applin/aml028

Fanon, F. (2008). *Black skin, white masks* (R. Philcox, Trans.; Revised edition). Grove Press.

Freire, P. (2000). *Pedagogy of the oppressed.* Continuum.

Fry, R. (2005, November 1). The higher drop-out rate of foreign-born teens. *Pew Research Center's Hispanic Trends Project.* http://www.pewhispanic.org/2005/11/01/the-higher-drop-out-rate-of-foreign-born-teens/

García, O. (2008). *Bilingual education in the 21st century: A global perspective.* Wiley-Blackwell.

García, O., & Wei, L. (2014). *Translanguaging: Language, bilingualism, and education.* Palgrave Pivot.

García, O., Kleifgen, J. A., & Falchi, L. (2008). From English language learners to emergent bilinguals. *Equity Matters, 1.*

Gutiérrez, K. D. (2008). Developing a sociocritical literacy in the third space. *Reading Research Quarterly, 43*(2), 148–164. https://doi.org/10.1598/RRQ.43.2.3

Gutiérrez, K. D., & Rogoff, B. (2003). Cultural ways of learning: Individual traits or repertoires of practice. *Educational Researcher, 32*(5), 19–25. https://doi.org/10.3102/0013189X032005019

Haas, E., & Gort, M. (2009). Demanding more: Legal standards and best practices for English language learners. *Bilingual Research Journal, 32*(2), 115–135. https://doi.org/10.1080/15235880903169951

Hall, J. K., Vitanova, G., & Marchenkova, L. A. (Eds.). (2013). *Dialogue with Bakhtin on second and foreign language learning: New perspectives* (Reprint edition). Routledge.

Hauser, B. (2012). *The new kids: Big dreams and brave journeys at a high school for immigrant teens*. Atria Books.

Hertzberg, M. (1998). Having arrived: Dimensions of educational success in a transitional newcomer school. *Anthropology & Education Quarterly, 29*(4), 391–418. https://doi.org/10.1525/aeq.1998.29.4.391

Hirvela, A., & Belcher, D. (2001). Coming back to voice: The multiple voices and identities of mature multilingual writers. *Journal of Second Language Writing, 10*(1), 83–106.

hooks, bell. (1994). *Teaching to transgress: Education as the practice of freedom.* Routledge.

Kelly, G. J., & Green, J. (1998). The social nature of knowing: Toward a sociocultural perspective on conceptual change and knowledge construction. In B. J. Guzzetti & C. R. Hynd (Eds.), *Perspectives on conceptual change: Multiple ways to understand knowing and learning in a complex world* (pp. 145–181). Routledge.

Lantolf, J. P. (2000). *Sociocultural theory and second language learning*. Oxford University Press.

Lantolf, J. P., & Poehner, M. E. (2014). *Sociocultural theory and the pedagogical imperative in L2 education: Vygotskian praxis and the research/practice divide* (1st ed.). Routledge.

Larsen-Freeman, D. (1997). Chaos/complexity science and second language acquisition. *Applied Linguistics, 18*(2), 141–165.

Lave, J. (1996). Teaching, as learning, in practice. *Mind, Culture, and Activity, 3*(3), 149–164. https://doi.org/10.1207/s15327884mca0303_2

Lucas, T., & Katz, A. (1994). Reframing the debate: The roles of native languages in English-only programs for language minority students. *TESOL Quarterly, 28*(3), 537–561. https://doi.org/10.2307/3587307

McDermott, R. (1999). Culture is not an environment of the mind. *The Journal of the Learning Sciences, 8*(1), 157–169.

Meacham, S. J. (2001). Vygotsky and the blues: Re-reading cultural connections and conceptual development. *Theory Into Practice, 40*(3), 190–197.

Misawa, M. (2010). Queer race pedagogy for educators in higher education: Dealing with power dynamics and positionality of LGBTQ students of color. *The International Journal of Critical Pedagogy, 3*(1), 26.

Moll, L. C. (1992). Bilingual Classroom Studies and Community Analysis: Some Recent Trends. *Educational Researcher, 21*(2), 20. https://doi.org/10.2307/1176576

Moore, L. C. (2006). Learning by heart in Qur'anic and public schools in northern Cameroon. *Social Analysis, 50*(3), 109–126.

Nader, L. (1974). Up the anthropologist: Perspectives gained from studying up. In D. H. Hymes (Ed.), *Reinventing anthropology* (pp. 285–311). Vintage Books. http://eric.ed.gov/?id=ED065375

Nespor, J. (1997). *Tangled up in school: Politics, space, bodies, and signs in the educational process*. L. Erlbaum Associates.

Ohio Department of Education. (2014). *Characteristics of programs serving LEP students in Ohio*. https://education.ohio.gov/Topics/Other-Resources/Limited-English-Proficiency/ELL-Guidelines/Characteristics-of-Programs-Serving-LEP-Students-i

Orellana, M. F. (2016). *Immigrant children in transcultural spaces: Language, learning, and love*. Taylor & Francis.

Ortega, L. (2008). *Understanding second language acquisition*. Routledge.

Otheguy, R., García, O., & Reid, W. (2015). Clarifying translanguaging and deconstructing named languages: A perspective from linguistics. *Applied Linguistics Review, 6*(3), 281–307. https://doi.org/10.1515/applirev-2015-0014

Pacheco, M. B. (2016). *Translanguaging in the English-centric classroom: A communities of practice perspective*. Vanderbilt University.

Pérez, A. H., & Enciso, P. (2017). Decentering whiteness and monolingualism in the reception of Latinx YA literature. *Bilingual Review/Revista Bilingüe, 33*(5). http://bilingualreview.utsa.edu/index.php/br/article/view/182

Picower, B. (2009). The unexamined Whiteness of teaching: How White teachers maintain and enact dominant racial ideologies. *Race Ethnicity and Education, 12*(2), 197–215. https://doi.org/10.1080/13613320902995475

Porter, R. P. (1996). *Forked tongue: The politics of bilingual education* (2nd ed.). Transaction Publishers.

Porter, R. P. (1998, May). The case against bilingual education. *The Atlantic*. http://www.theatlantic.com/magazine/archive/1998/05/the-case-against-bilingual-education/305426/

Roth, W.-M., & Lee, Y.-J. (2007). "Vygotsky's neglected legacy": Cultural-historical activity theory. *Review of Educational Research, 77*(2), 186–232. https://doi.org/10.3102/0034654306298273

Said, E. W. (1979). *Orientalism* (1st ed.). Vintage.

Scribner, S., & Cole, M. (1973). Cognitive consequences of formal and informal education. *Science, 182*(4112), 553–559.

Short, D. J., & Boyson, B. A. (2004). *Creating access: Language and academic programs for secondary school newcomers*. Delta Systems Co..

Short, D. J., & Boyson, B. A. (2012). *Helping newcomer students succeed in secondary schools and beyond* (p. 78). Center for Applied Linguistics.

Smith, D. E. (Ed.). (2006). Institutional ethnography as practice. Rowman & Littlefield Publishers.

Smith, L. T. (2012). *Decolonizing methodologies: Research and indigenous peoples* (2nd ed.). Zed Books.

Street, B. V. (1993). Culture is a verb: Anthropological aspect of language and cultural process. In D. Graddol (Ed.), *Language and culture: Papers from the annual meeting of the British Association of Applied Linguistics held at Trevelyan College, University of Durham, September 1991* (pp. 23–43). Multilingual Matters.

Umansky, I. M., & Reardon, S. F. (2014). Reclassification patterns among Latino English learner students in bilingual, dual immersion, and English immersion classrooms. *American Educational Research Journal, 51*(5), 879–912. https://doi.org/10.3102/0002831214545110

Valentino, R. A., & Reardon, S. F. (2015). Effectiveness of four instructional programs designed to serve English learners: Variation by ethnicity and initial English proficiency. *Educational Evaluation and Policy Analysis, 37*(4), 612–637.

Vertovec, S. (2016). *Super-diversity*. Routledge.

Volosinov, V. N. (1986). *Marxism and the philosophy of language*. Harvard University Press.

8

English Language Teaching in Colombia: From Policy to Reality

Daniel Ramírez Lamus

We indulge in the revery that our history won't look like the Colombia we live in, but instead that Colombia will end up resembling its written history. Therefore, our conformist and repressive education seems to have been conceived to adapt children by force to a country that wasn't thought for them, instead of bringing the country within their reach so they can transform it and enhance it. (Gabriel García Márquez; my translation)

Prelude

Escuela Nueva

In the 1970s, a small-scale experiment in rural schools of Colombia called the *Escuela Nueva*[1] got underway. *Escuela Nueva* began as a community education model when schools in the countryside brought students of different ages and levels together and their teachers started developing their own approaches to teaching. Teachers created "learning guides"

D. R. Lamus (✉)
Universidad de los Andes, Bogotá, Colombia
e-mail: da.ramirezl1@uniandes.edu.co

(*guías de aprendizaje*) that offered students guidelines into what they were supposed to do or explore, while the teacher—usually one for all students—circulated, monitored, and assessed each student. This idea seemed to work and, due to its organic growth, the model was declared by the government as the standard model of schooling in rural areas of Colombia: one that grew from 500 schools in the 1970s to 24,000 in 1987. Farrell's (2008) report regarding community education in Colombia highlighted the case of *Escuela Nueva* as an example of "the quiet revolution in schooling."

Although there were efforts in 1987 by the Foundation *Escuela Nueva Volvamos a la Gente* (FEN) to adapt the *Escuela Nueva* model to urban contexts under the name of *Escuela Activa Urbana*, the model remained in place primarily in rural areas. The *Escuela Nueva*, nevertheless, became an important model of education in and outside Colombia (*Fundación Escuela Nueva Volvamos a la Gente,* 2020). In 1989, it was selected by the World Bank as one of the most successful reforms to impact public policy in the developing world. In 1992, it became one of the five pillars of Colombia's National Development Plan to eradicate poverty. From 1994—with the help of agencies such as UNICEF, USAID, the World Bank, and the Inter-American Bank Development Bank—the *Escuela Nueva* started a process of internationalization. The model has since been taken to countries throughout Latin America, Southeast Asia and Africa, where it has adopted different names and has reached more than five million children.

In 2001 the FEN created *Círculos de Aprendizaje—Escuela Nueva Activa* to assist the needs of displaced children and become the national educational policy for displaced children by the FEN in 2008. In 2012 the FEN was included in the top 100 best world non-governmental organizations by Switzerland's *Global Journal*. In 2017, 2018, and 2019 the FEN was recognized by the non-profit organization HundrED as one of the top 100 innovative educational projects in the world (*Fundación Escuela Nueva Volvamos a la Gente,* 2020). In international standardized tests of subjects such as Spanish language and mathematics, *Escuela Nueva* students have scored higher than students in traditional schools. *Escuela Nueva* students have also shown lower repetition and dropout rates and usually have higher levels of self-esteem and more developed civic values (Farrell, 2008).

The *Escuela Nueva* has continued its process of organic growth throughout the country and the Escuela Activa Urbana has been enacted in cities like Manizales, where students experiencing this model now make up 62% of the public-school population (Fundación LUKER, 2020).

Programa Nacional de Bilingüismo

In 2004, in anticipation of the 200th anniversary of Colombian independence to be commemorated a decade and a half later, the *Ministerio de Educación Nacional* (MEN) established several objectives in a document called *Visión Colombia II Centenario: 2019* (DNP Dirección de Desarrollo Empresarial, 2006). Among these was a proposal—the *Programa Nacional de Bilingüismo* (PNB)—which advanced the goal of having Colombian public-school students reach a B1 pre-intermediate level of English, as described by the Common European Framework of Reference (CEFR). Cecilia María Vélez, Minister of Education from 2002 to 2010, said that the CEFR was chosen because "it was the clearest and the most widespread at the world level" (personal interview, 2012). The partnership between the MEN and the British Council in Colombia started in 1991 with the Colombian Framework for English (COFE) project. The PNB has developed and changed its name twice: between 2010 and 2014 it was known as the *Programa de Fortalecimiento al Desarrollo de Competencias en Lenguas Extranjeras* (PFDCLE), and since 2015 it has been known as *Programa Nacional de Inglés Colombia—Very Well*. In its latest version, the organization set new objectives for the year 2025, including a milestone of 50% of all high school graduates achieve the B1 level.

Responsible ELT

English Language Teaching has usually been seen as helping students progress economically. Speaking English is seen as an advantage for candidates in the job market. For instance, Vélez's letter introducing MEN's

Estándares básicos de competencias en lenguas extranjeras: inglés (hereafter referred to as *Estándares*), a document developed with assistance from the British Council in 2006, stated:

> Having a good level of English facilitates access to working and educational opportunities that help improve the quality of life. Being competent in another language is essential in the globalized world … Being bilingual increases the opportunities to be more competent and competitive. (MEN, 2006, p. 3)[2]

However, as Macedo et al. (2003) pointed out, the association of English with success is misleading. Even inside the United States, "the fact that approximately 30 million African-Americans speak English as their mother tongue did not prevent the vast majority of them from being relegated to ghetto existence, economic deprivation and, in some cases, to the status of sub-humans" (p. 16). Macedo (2006) himself observed how most English as a Second Language (ESL) teachers believe their mission is to *save* their students from their *non-English speaker status*. Unfortunately, seldom do ESL teachers think about consequences of supporting the hegemony of English, thus unknowingly becoming advocates of linguistic imperialism (Phillipson, 1992).

To understand how one may inadvertently maintain the myth that learning English will help students progress economically, let us take a look at concepts promoted by Skutnabb-Kangas (2000) and Tollefson (1991).

First, Skutnabb-Kangas (2000) referred to the spread of English worldwide in terms of

1. *the diffusion of English paradigm*, where perpetuating the hegemony of English—that is, the dominance of English as an international language—is due to its uncontested status among languages, leading to monolingualism, linguistic genocide, and cultural imperialism; and
2. *the ecology of languages paradigm*, where one becomes critically aware of linguistic hegemony and linguicism (cf. racism, sexism, classism) and advocates for multilingualism, linguistic diversity, and cultural pluralism.

Skutnabb-Kangas's two paradigms seemingly relate to two ideologies of language-policy research described by Tollefson (1991):

1. The *traditional approach*, which places all variables of language acquisition and learning on individual linguistic decisions—that is, language learning is determined by individual factors such as age, language aptitude, motivation, attitude toward the target language, and so on; and
2. The *historical-structural approach*, which has as its goal the "[examination of] the historical basis of policies and [making] explicit the mechanisms by which policy decisions serve or undermine particular and economic interests" (Tollefson, 1991: 32); in other words, this approach considers social, political, and economic factors that may condition or constrain language learning.

Figure 8.1 should assist in understanding the relationship between these two paradigms and ideologies.

To help teachers become more aware of the issues above, I developed a model called Responsible ELT. It contains three principal components: (a) awareness of the hegemony of English, (b) critical language-policy research, and (c) resistance.

Awareness of the Hegemony of English

Teachers aware of the hegemony of English understand that their role is not neutral. Indeed, teachers must realize that by reinforcing the myth that English will *save* their students from socioeconomic hardship, they may also be reinforcing linguistic and cultural imperialism, thereby contributing to the diffusion of English paradigm. Teachers must therefore ask themselves how they may contribute to an ecology of languages paradigm by advocating for linguistic diversity and cultural pluralism. To contribute to linguistic diversity, teachers could resolve to learn a language different from English—perhaps the language of where they are teaching English or the language of a neighboring region. Teachers would

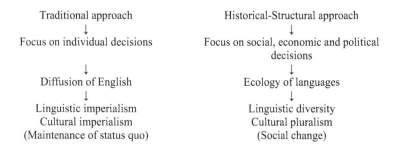

Fig. 8.1 Language-policy research and the spread of English

therefore help de-hegemonize English by celebrating the beauty and the status of other tongues.

Meanwhile, in contributing to cultural pluralism, teachers should foster dialog that examines not only English-speaking cultures but also those of the students. In other words, rather than aspire for students to imitate the culture of English, teachers could aim to have students learn about cultures of different languages and foster understanding among them.

Critical Language-Policy Research

The concept of critical language-policy research (Tollefson, 2006) poses questions regarding how language policies may create inequalities among learners, or how language policies may marginalize some students while granting privilege to others. It also examines the relationship between language policies and processes such as the global spread of English. This component within the Responsible ELT model asks teachers to become familiar with the impetuses of foreign language teaching policies.

Resistance

The third component of Responsible ELT, resistance, is an adaptation of the concept of resistance to linguistic imperialism described by Canagarajah (1999). Canagarajah sees the dominance of English as not only a *result* of political and economic inequalities, but also a *cause* of those. Then, the resistance model of English teaching (a) calls for micro-social perspectives in ELT, and (b) is carried out by periphery scholars (like the author of this chapter).[3] In other words, this component demands that teachers ask themselves how English can be learned as a means of resistance to (linguistic) imperialism. Teachers should consider how English can be "used to empower the local communities, or to further their own cultural, social, and educational interests" (Canagarajah, 1999, p. 42).

Methodology

Colombia's PNB set objectives for 2019, and the current *Programa Nacional de Inglés Colombia Very Well* has set objectives for 2025. Thus, it is worth viewing this study, carried out in 2013, as a means to explore the objectives for 2019, as well as assessing any current changes to foreign language teaching policy in the country.

Research Questions

Some questions arise regarding the PNB and its policies, such as: Were the objectives of the PNB reached? If so, did the CEFR help accomplish those objectives? Does ELT policy in the country consider any suggestions from people who work in the field?

Regarding *Escuela Nueva*: If this model has been so successful, has it contributed to ELT practices within the country? What recommendations could teachers in an *Escuela Nueva* give to ELT colleagues?

Setting

Following the call for micro-social perspectives in ELT carried out from the periphery (Canagarajah, 1999), I conducted a case study in an *Escuela Nueva* school in order to explore perspectives that students, teachers, and administrators at a community education school may have of EFL policy.

Thus, I contacted the school in Medellín where I performed my study: the Octavio Calderón. The idea of getting these people's perspectives was triggered, on the one hand, by the idea that English teachers and policy makers need to "create pedagogical responses that are more appropriate for the country and better address the real needs of learners at all levels" (Vélez-Rendón, 2003, p. 196), and, on the other hand, by the suggestion that exploring teachers' methodological practices through teacher interviews can provide a starting point to understanding and transforming the context of foreign language education in Colombia (Cadavid Múnera et al., 2004).

Octavio Calderón

The *Institución Educativa Octavio Calderón Mejía*, commonly known as the Octavio Calderón (OC), is a school in Medellín that started implementing the *Escuela Nueva* model in 2005. The OC is located in a middle-to-low socioeconomic class neighborhood known as Campo Amor, located in the city's industrial sector called Guayabal. One of the OC's main achievements was winning the 2008 city award for Best School in the Public Sector.

Indeed, the OC is considered a successful example of the *Escuela Nueva*, and the story is usually told of how this school was transformed from a school with a terrible reputation into a model school, thanks to the effort of Claudia Holguín, who became the school's principal in 1995, and who had previously been an *Escuela Nueva* teacher. By 2011, the school had gone (a) from having 76 students in 1995 to having 1280; (b) from not offering all grades to offering all grades from kindergarten to 11th grade, and (c) from not having specialization options to offering three different options: fashion design, graphic design, and software design. By 2011, there were 332 students enrolled in technical and technological programs of professional formation articulated with the *Servicio Nacional de Aprendizaje* (SENA) (*Fundación Escuela Nueva Volvamos a la Gente,* 2020).

Participants

I carried out interviews with 15 participants: six students, five teachers, and four school administrators. The students were chosen from Grades 9 to 11: two from Grade 9, two from Grade 10, and two from Grade 11.[4] Of the five teachers, three were high school English teachers, one was the main primary English teacher, and one was a chemistry teacher familiar with *Escuela Nueva*. Of the four school administrators, three were school employees (the school principal and two academic supervisors) and one was an expert in the development of self-instructional learning guides at the FEN.

Interviews and Coding

I spent from August 5 to August 21, 2013, at the OC campus. Two semi-structured interviews, each lasting approximately 30–40 minutes, were carried out with each participant. The second interview occurred one week after the first. In order to explore how the subjects perceived foreign language education policy, some of the questions asked included:

- What do you know about the PNB?
- What do you think about the PNB?
- What do you think are the main needs regarding foreign language education in Colombia?
- What kind of policies would you like to have regarding foreign language teaching and learning in Colombia?

Transcribed interviews were coded (Bogdan & Biklen, 2007) deductively, according to categories I had selected beforehand such as PNB, PNB objectives, *Estándares*, CEFR, advantages/disadvantages of *Escuela Nueva* for teaching foreign languages, and suggestions for foreign language education policy. Then, interviews were coded inductively for any topics emerging from the interviews that were unique and relevant to the research questions. A third and last stage of data analysis was performed to compare the two sets of coding to avoid excessive theme reiteration.

Findings

English as the "Universal Language"

Most participants saw English as the "universal language," reflecting the national attitude that English is indispensable in students' pursuit of higher education or better paying jobs. The Ministry of Education in Colombia has mandated that English be taught from first grade in all public schools, requiring general education teachers, without a degree in English or ELT, to teach it. If general education teachers are not proficient in English, they are offered courses of professional development. Unfortunately, teachers seldom reach an advanced level of proficiency in English. What, then, is the message that these teachers send to students? The principal of the Octavio Calderón could not have said it more eloquently: that teachers seem to be telling students: "You don't like English. Get bored with English!"

Misinterpretation of 1994 General Law of Education

Several teachers referred to the 1994 General Law of Education (MEN, 1994), which mandates the teaching of a foreign language at the elementary level; however, they noted that they thought the law mandates the teaching of English. The teachers' attitude, though, suggests that the promotion of "bilingualism" as dictated by the PNB does not include a wider view of bilingualism even though, in actuality, the word *English* does not appear within the law.

The teachers may be perpetuating a limitation of bilingualism as being exclusively Spanish and English, thereby reinforcing English hegemony and contributing to the diffusion of English paradigm. The comments omit consideration of indigenous students in Colombia who speak an indigenous language and then had to learn Spanish, as well as students in areas neighboring Brazil, who may have had contact with Portuguese and could actually become proficient and professionally active in that (foreign) language.

Unrealistic Expectations of English Proficiency Levels

Most participants found the PNB goals—having half of Colombia's public-school students bilingual in English and Spanish at the B1 level by 2025—unrealistic. As it turns out, according to the MEN, in 2020 not even 10% of students in public schools achieved this level. Such results may not be surprising given that, as described by the MEN (2013): "it is estimated that between 63% and 86% [of teachers] have a level lower than B2."[5] Meanwhile, higher education students are not only tested for their English knowledge as an admission requirement, but also are expected to reach a minimum level of B2 before graduation.

Policy Inhibiting English Learning

Teachers and administrators reported a lack of articulation between elementary and high school ELT policies that may be discouraging students in Colombian public schools from learning English. According to these professionals, in elementary school, there are few teachers with a B1 level of English; thus, demands on students do not support advancing proficiency in earlier grades. However, once students reach high school, they are suddenly taught in English by a teacher with greater proficiency. Some of the students in this study expressed their frustration at suddenly being asked to perform in proficient English. One student said they felt, "I will never be able to do this." Furthermore, several participants noted that "The students who reach the objectives of the PNB have been students who see that the amount of English that they learn at school is not enough."

Top-Down Policy

Most teachers and administrators indicated that they view PNB policies as top-down. English has been imposed in Colombian public schools as the foreign of language of choice and there is no way students can escape it. Respondents reported that it is important not only to set objectives for the future, but also to stop at some time in that "future," look back and see if objectives were met, and then analyze and recalibrate objectives based on these reflections.

It should be clear by now that, on the one hand, foreign language policy has possibly been misunderstood by ELT specialists, and, on the other hand, that policies set by bilingual programs in Colombia are not being effective in terms of English language learning. Equally noteworthy though are the efforts by the MEN in terms of "establishing English requirements for quality accreditation" as one of the "tools to improve the level of English in higher education institutions" (MEN, 2013) are efforts in the wrong direction. Such policy may be contributing to English becoming a gatekeeper for higher education and employment in Colombia. In other words, the "virtuous circle that motivates and supports English training" (MEN, 2013) has become, instead, a vicious circle that excludes and maintains inequality.

Role of *Escuela Nueva* in English Learning

A goal of this study was to find out what the community education model known as *Escuela Nueva* could contribute to ELT practices in Colombia—that is, to see if teachers at the OC could give any recommendations to Colombia's ELT community at large. In this sense, teachers at the OC mentioned the advantages of the *Escuela Nueva* model for the learning of English: (a) students being used to working in groups; (b) students having freedom in their learning process; (c) students learning at their own pace; and (d) a variety of lessons less adherent to textbooks.

Additionally, I wanted to uncover how students at this *Escuela Nueva* school could bring their experiences with English to their community. Unfortunately, most student responses referred to mostly superficial actions—for example, posting announcements in English regarding community outreach on information boards within the school. One student mentioned how teachers would choose outstanding students of English to take visitors who did not speak Spanish on a tour of the school in English. The OC, being one of the few schools implementing the *Escuela*

Nueva model in an urban setting, periodically receives delegations from Asian or African countries interested in observing how the model works.

Aside from that, instances of using English as a means of empowerment were still hypothetical. One administrator conjectured about the possibility of having a vocational course on tourism in English. Due to the school's proximity to a nearby airport and bus terminal, students could guide visitors in English on a city tour. However, there were no plans to actually do so. Instead, participants were more likely to lament the lack of in-depth English experiences, as indicated by this comment:

> Has the school studied the possibility of developing the theme of tourism in its articulation with the SENA?[6] There's a [bus] terminal and there's an airport. Why haven't they considered this? And if you talk about tourism, you need a foreign language. Why did the school choose fashion design? As far as I'm concerned, fashion is in Itagüí,[7] not around [the Octavio Calderón]. Having software design makes a lot of sense because that's what's hot today, the theme of technology, no need to discuss that. But, why fashion design? Couldn't the school have a fourth vocational course called, I don't know, a foreign language? Or a course to train tourism or tourist guide professionals? For a city like Medellín, having those two important focal points near the school, I would have common sense, you know what I mean?

Discussion

The logic goes like this: (Learning) English is crucial to pursuing a higher education or to get a better job. Students in public schools in Colombia have no choice in learning a foreign language different from English. However, the learning of English is mandated by a program prescribing standards that have little to do with students' experiences with English. In fact, English in elementary schools is more likely taught by teachers who are not ELT experts, and students end up barely communicating the simplest idea in English. Next comes secondary school shock: students enter high school and are taught English in English only by a teacher who expects students to understand everything and communicate with classmates in English.

The result is that students may end up *not* wanting to learn English even if they believe that it is good for them. Thus, enforcing the learning of English may be a way of sustaining inequality by having the language become a gatekeeper for higher education and employment (Tollefson, 1991). In this way, the diffusion of English paradigm is reinforced, and social inequality is maintained. Responsible EFL teachers in Colombia would ask themselves questions regarding whose interests are served by the language policies that they help implement. In fact, asking ourselves *why* we teach English is more important than asking ourselves *how* we can teach it effectively (Kincheloe & McLaren, 2003). Let us, then, look back and assess foreign language teaching policy as dictated by the PNB, and of the role (if any) of the *Escuela Nueva* model in foreign language teaching and learning.

Were the objectives of the PNB reached? Definitely not. Students in public schools in Colombia did not become bilingual in English and Spanish in 2019, and prospects for 50% of graduating students achieving the B1 level by 2025 seem slim.

Does ELT policy in Colombia consider suggestions from people who work in the field? The general feeling of teachers and administrators interviewed in this study was that ELT policies are top-down policies coming from capital city desks, which have little or no connection to what really happens in schools or with students' experiences with a foreign language, schedule scant self-reflection, and solicit little or no input from people who work in the field.

Finally, are foreign language teaching policies really helping students achieve a better social or economic status, as stated in the document *Estándares*? Seemingly, only those who can pay for English outside of school will achieve English proficiency. Thus, we see how policies may play a role in helping English become a gatekeeper for higher education and employment, a means for maintaining the status quo, and a tool for sustaining social *in*equality.

As for the *Escuela Nueva*, we could also look back and assess the model since 2013. The *Escuela Nueva* has continued its process of organic growth throughout the country and the Escuela Activa Urbana has been adapted successfully. However, the question that matters the most to this chapter is this: Has the *Escuela Nueva* model contributed to EFL or ELT practices in the country? The answer is *no*. Unfortunately, the connection between a successful community education model as the *Escuela Nueva* and foreign language teaching as a means of empowerment within the community has not been made. It seems the *Escuela Nueva* model—as it is mostly implemented in rural areas of the country—is still too busy working on first language learning and acquisition and has not given too much thought to foreign language teaching and learning.

Conclusion

This is perhaps the hope of this study revisited: that one day not only education in Colombia is informed by the benefits of a successful community education model as the *Escuela Nueva*, but also that one day there is a "quiet revolution in schooling" in terms of foreign language learning in the country because students' experiences and needs of a foreign language are actually addressed by foreign language teaching policy.

An additional aspiration is to bring students' voices to the forefront. Although students were asked about their perception of foreign language teaching and learning, I was already seen as an English teacher; thus, students may have politely expressed deference toward English. In future program self-reflection studies, we might recommend having students answer questions to non-ELT specialists, as then they might willingly share openness to other languages.

In the meantime, results of this inquiry buttress my concern that ELT specialists seldom realize their role in the design and implementation of foreign language teaching policies: they have implicitly and uncritically assumed as their "mission" to teach English as the foreign language required by Colombian law, so that they "save" their students from their "non-English speaker status." Therefore, this study leaves two main recommendations for future foreign language policy makers:

1. Foreign language teaching policy (and research) needs to become a more comprehensive field of education in which specialists from other

foreign languages participate: perhaps in this scenario the true role of English is understood and a step away from the diffusion of English paradigm is taken; and
2. Foreign language policy needs to consider the real needs of learners regarding foreign language learning, and in order to get to know these, teacher interviews are necessary.

Thus, another kind of "virtuous circle" could be added to the equation: one in which teachers' perceptions feed foreign language teaching policy and assess this policy periodically.

Notes

1. Meaning "New School."
2. All translations from the Colombian document *Estándares* are mine.
3. Canagarajah's term *periphery* is related to Phillipson's *periphery-English countries*, that is, countries where English is learned as a second or foreign language.
4. The Colombian school system ends in Grade 11.
5. My translation.
6. Acronym for National Service of Learning, a Colombian public institution focused on the development of programs of professional formation.
7. A town near Medellín.

References

Bogdan, R., & Biklen, S. K. (2007). *Qualitative research for education: An introduction to theories and methods*. Pearson.
Cadavid Múnera, I. C., McNulty, M., & Quinchía Ortiz, D. I. (2004). Elementary English language instruction: Colombian teachers' classroom practices. *PROFILE*, 5, 37–55. Retrieved from: http://www.revistas.unal.edu.co/index.php/profile/article/viewFile/11213/11877
Canagarajah, A. (1999). *Resisting linguistic imperialism in English language teaching*. Oxford University Press.

Colombia. Departamento Nacional de Planeación. (2006). *Visión Colombia II Centenario: 2019*. Retrieved from: http://repositorio.colciencias.gov.co/bitstream/handle/11146/132/1247-1Vision%20Colombia%20II%20 Centenario%202019.pdf?sequence=1&isAllowed=y

Colombia. Fundación Escuela Nueva Volvamos a la Gente (FEN 2020). Retrieved from: http://escuelanueva.org/portal1/es/

Colombia. Fundación LUKER. (2020). Retrieved from: https://fundacionluker. org.co/fundacion/historia/

Colombia. Ministerio de Educación Nacional [MEN]. (1994). *Ley General de Educación (Ley115 8 February 1994)*. Retrieved from: http://www.oei.es/quipu/colombia/Ley_115_1994.pdf

Colombia. Ministerio de Educación Nacional [MEN]. (2006). *Estándares básicos de competencias en lenguas extranjeras: inglés. Formar en lenguas extranjeras: ¡el reto!* [Basic standards of competences in foreign languages: English. Teaching in foreign languages: the challenge!] Retrieved from: http://www.colombiaaprende.edu.co/html/mediateca/1607/articles-115375_archivo.pdf

Colombia. Ministerio de Educación Nacional [MEN]. (2013). *Programa Nacional de Inglés Colombia Very Well*. Retrieved from: https://www.mineducacion.gov.co/1759/articles-343837_Programa_Nacional_Ingles.pdf

Farrell, J. P. (2008). Community education in developing countries: The quiet revolution in schooling. In F. M. Connelly, M. F. He, & J. A. Phillion (Eds.), *The Sage handbook of curriculum and instruction* (pp. 369–389). Sage.

Kincheloe, J. L., & McLaren, P. (2003). Rethinking critical theory and qualitative research. In N. K. Denzin & Y. S. Lincoln (Eds.), *The landscape of qualitative research: Theories and issues*. Sage.

Macedo, D. (2006). *Literacies of power: What Americans are not allowed to know*. Westview.

Macedo, D., Dendrinos, B., & Gounari, P. (2003). *The hegemony of English*. Paradigm.

Phillipson, R. (1992). *Linguistic imperialism*. Oxford University Press.

Skutnabb-Kangas, T. (2000). Linguistic human rights and teachers of English. In J. K. Hall & W. G. Eggington (Eds.), *The sociopolitics of English language teaching* (pp. 22–44). Multilingual Matters.

Tollefson, J. W. (1991). *Planning language, planning inequality: Language policy in the community*. Longman.

Tollefson, J. W. (2006). Critical theory in language policy. In T. Ricento (Ed.), *An introduction to language policy: Theory and method*. Blackwell.

Vélez-Rendón, G. (2003). English in Colombia: A sociolinguistic profile. *World Englishes, 22*, 185–198.

9

Broken Promises? The Florida Consent Decree, Multilingual Learners in Mainstream Classes, and Assimilationist Practice

Eric Dwyer and Carolyn O'Gorman-Fazzolari

K-12 schools encounter ESOL-related issues almost daily; thus, teaching [MLLs] is part of the mainstream in the educational system across the U.S. When it comes to the preparation of teachers, Florida leads the way, as its teacher education programs provide ESOL-integrated course work and field experiences… The Consent Decree addresses the civil rights of [MLLs], foremost among those their right to equal access to all educational programs. In addressing these rights, it provides a structure that ensures the delivery of comprehensible instruction and the expectations for all teachers and personnel. (Artecona-Pelaez, 2010: 7–8)

E. Dwyer (✉) • C. O'Gorman-Fazzolari
College of Arts, Sciences & Education, Florida International University, Miami, FL, USA
e-mail: dwyere@fiu.edu; cvill108@fiu.edu

Introduction

In 1990, the law office Multicultural Education Training and Advocacy (META) filed a class action complaint against the Department of Education (FDOE) within the U.S. state of Florida for not supporting multilingual learners (MLLs)—namely students whose English proficiency precludes easy comprehension of in-class material. In a settlement, the state agreed to the *Florida Consent Decree* (FDOE, 1990)—a set of rules requiring that teachers with MLLs be trained in *basic ESOL*—such that these students have "equal access to appropriate programming" (FDOE, 1990: 11). In this report, we examine the degree to which one school district, Miami-Dade County, has lived up to the promise of providing its approximately 77,000 MLLs (FDOE, 2017) "equal access" to subject area content.

With the Consent Decree came promises. Explicitly, the Consent Decree asserts that MLLs shall have "equal access to appropriate programming" (FDOE, 1990: 11) in terms of intensive English instruction and understandable subject matter. Implicitly though, under the scheme of *basic ESOL*, a term asserted 28 times in the Decree, the approach suggests an additive model (Lambert, 1975), where students learn content and English simultaneously while building upon the educative and linguistic experiences they bring to class—rather than an invisibilizing model (Ndhlovu & Makalela, 2017), where those experiences are mostly ignored.

As it turns out, a quarter century of Consent Decree implementation has yielded modest results. Florida's MLL graduation rate of 59% (Civic Enterprises, 2017) and Miami-Dade's of 62% (Lipsey & Innocent, 2017) rank Florida 37th among U.S.'s 50 states (Mitchell, 2016). Given that the Consent Decree was authored with the U.S.'s Federal Civil Rights Act of 1964 in mind, the resulting Decree is considered a civil rights victory for language minority students (Erben & Goussakova, 2020). With respect to how teachers engage with policy, this inquiry examines the degree to which mainstream teachers, in implementing the Consent Decree, foster understandable access to in-class materials for all language minority students.

Previous Inquiries and Research Questions

Our inquiry is situated in Hornberger's (2009) positioning multilingual education as a means for upcoming "generations to participate in constructing more just and democratic societies" (198). Certainly, the Consent Decree's established goal that MLLs receive schooling from teachers trained in *basic ESOL* implies, as Ndhlovu and Makalela (2017) suggest, that the melding of training amid this policy provides environments promoting multilingual education, social inclusion, and active citizen participation. Indeed, a key product of the Consent Decree has been an advance in positive teacher attitudes toward language minority students (Mitchell, 2017).

Still, graduation rates are of concern. In reaction to them, Mary Jane Tappen, the state's former executive vice chancellor for K-12 education, proclaimed:

> We need to take a really critical look at the quality of education that is going on in our ESOL classrooms" . . . She added that … it's important that students are "pushed to high expectations, as opposed to loved a lot. (Solochek, 2017)

Research supports Tappen's concerns. Platt, Harper, and Mendoza (2003) found many Florida teachers not appropriately trained to handle ESOL issues. Meanwhile, Harper and de Jong (2004) found that mainstream teachers believe that (a) needs of MLLs do not differ significantly from those of other diverse learners, and (b) ESOL teaching is "a menu of pedagogical adaptations appropriate for a variety of diverse learners" (152). A decade later, Coady, Harper, and de Jong (2015) found that their own graduates "rarely instituted specific [MLL] practices" (340).

We had heard from our own pre-service students that they were observing very little ESOL—anecdotes suggesting that the acculturation goals touted within the Consent Decree were leading instead to assimilationist practice (Ruiz, 1984). Our students' anecdotes, coupled with colleagues' previous studies, led us to worry, much as Tollesfson (1995) did, that teacher education programs may be emphasizing L2 acquisition, teaching methods, and linguistics without placing these into what Pennycook

(1994) calls "part of the cultural and political moments of the day" (34). We decided we had better visit a bunch of mainstream classes to see

1. to what extent mainstream teachers with ESOL credentials make use of *basic ESOL* strategies, and
2. to what degree they implement strategies designed to address MLLs in early stages of additional language development.

Methodology

In asking how teachers implement state-levied curricular requirements considering their required Consent Decree training, we wanted, following Canagarajah (2011), to develop an ethnographically derived "insider's view" on how mainstream teachers, most of whom are multilingual citizens in Miami, "negotiate, explain, and resolve [any] conflicting aspirations and claims" (95). More specifically, we desired a contextualized instrument where we initially collect and analyze qualitative data but then administer statistical analysis to derive generalizations we would not ordinarily expect in an ethnography. For these reasons, we constructed an exploratory sequential mixed-methods design (Creswell & Creswell, 2017) where we would accomplish the following (please see Fig. 9.1):

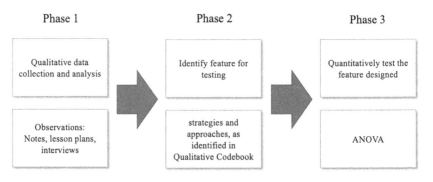

Fig. 9.1 Exploratory sequential design. (Based on Creswell & Creswell, 2017: 217)

Phase 1: conduct observations in a large number of mainstream classes where we take copious notes, acquire teacher lesson plans, and conduct impromptu post-class interviews

Phase 2: identifying parallel variables of both the qualitative and quantitative analysis, namely the strategies and approaches as identified in a qualitative codebook (Guest et al., 2012), and establish codes derived from the observations

Phase 3: code the data, count occurrences of specific phenomena, and then statistically analyze the occurrences to understand which strategies are implemented with specificity

Phase I: Observations

The school district granted us permission to visit 40 classes in 12 schools, ranging from kindergarten to 7th grade. No classes had more than 25 students. Observations lasted between 40 and 60 minutes. We typed notes onto laptops (Reid, 1992), paying attention to teacher lesson plans (when provided), as well as teachers' comments. We journaled our impressions immediately after school visits (Taylor & Bogdan, 1984).

Phase 2: Qualitative Codebook—ESOL Strategies and Approaches

We devised a lens—a qualitative codebook (Guest et al., 2012), if you will—which establishes predetermined codes through which we might observe and assess classes. We began by asserting that simply providing content does not guarantee language acquisition. Indeed, de Oliveira (2016) insists that teachers ponder language elements first when planning. Thus, we may contemplate reciprocity in lesson planning: rigorous lessons implementing language specific to content, as well as content specifically supporting language development. Supporting methodology has included Language-Based Approach to Content Instruction (LACI) (de Oliveira, 2015), Sheltered Instruction Observation Protocol (SIOP) (Echevarria et al., 2010), Cognitive Academic Language Learning

Approach (CALLA) (Chamot & O'Malley, 1994), Structured English Immersion (SEI) (Clark, 2009), Specially Designed Academic Instruction in English (SDAIE) (Peregoy & Boyle, 2008), and "Teach the text backwards" (Jameson, 1999). In addition, a Florida-specific text (Govoni, 2015) was compiled to address MLL language needs.

To help us gauge the extent mainstream teachers scaffold focus on language into focus on content, we applied these methodologies. Inquiry began with the Florida Teacher Standards for ESOL Endorsement (FDOE, 2010) and our school district's ESOL Strategies Matrix (Miami-Dade County Public Schools, 2017). With these provisos, we selected well-known approaches—themes, if you will—taught in our teacher education program and throughout the state, creating a means of notating ESOL approaches mainstream teachers implement:

Proficiency

The World-class Instructional Design and Assessment (WIDA, 2012) focuses on language development showcases how proficiency crescendos so long as it is paired with contextualized academic content.

Lesson Preparation

A key aspect of lesson preparation has been teachers' assembly of activities promoting linguistic development and understanding of new concepts. Language objectives can, in accordance with students' proficiency levels, be differentiated such that teachers scale guiding questions and other linguistic challenges (de Oliveira, 2015). Meanwhile, content standards identify what students are expected to learn or be able to do (Echevarria et al., 2010).

Code Breaking

De Oliveira (2015) describes code breaking as mortar connecting content with underlying language, suggesting teachers "focus on language from three angles: *presenting ideas, enacting a relationship with the reader or listener*, and *constructing a cohesive message*" (220). Specifically, linguistic elements present opportunities for students to interact with and contextualize language through content (WIDA, 2012).

Connection: Building Background

MLLs bring unique language and content resources to classrooms. Therefore, teachers' accessing those funds of knowledge (Moll, 2007) can advance developing these resources by promoting home languages (de Jong, 2011), appropriate translanguaging (O'Gorman-Fazzolari, 2017), and language brokering (Orellana et al., 2014).

Culture

Of key importance will be professionals' understanding of multiculturalism, particularly with respect to concepts of assimilation and acculturation. Rosa (2019) refers to *assimilation* as either "a disavowal of [one's] Latinidad[1] or [maintenance of one's] cultural authenticity while accepting a subordinate racial and socioeconomic status" (11). Meanwhile, Esposito, Sirkin, and Bauer (2018) report that *acculturation* is additive, a position "associated with benefits to academic performance, social development, and possibly cognitive benefits for both minority- and majority-language speakers" (243). To that end, following Gilmore (1983), we ask if teachers have been recontextualizing mainstream activities by seeking out and applying overt acculturative reference to MLLs' backgrounds and histories, household and family life, functional skills in other languages, or their sources of knowledge and potential.

Comprehensible Input

After decades of implementing $i + 1$ (Krashen, 1977), we look to where comprehensible input is fostered. Several colleagues have posed means of promoting $i + 1$, including:

- adjusting speech by simplifying vocabulary (Abedi et al., 1997);
- using visual aids, graphic organizers, and vocabulary previews (Jameson, 1999);
- incorporating adapted texts (Echevarria et al., 2010);
- using sentence starters (Shin, 2016), language frames, or highlighted text (Robertson, n.d.);
- using multimodal techniques including maps, charts, timelines, outlines (Choi & Yi, 2015);
- promoting higher-order thinking skills (Anderson & Krathwohl, 2001);
- providing supportive review and assessment techniques based on students' proficiency levels (Govoni, 2015); and
- supporting native language, including use of technology-based resources (Cummins & Swain, 1986).

ESOL Strategies

School districts have been stalwart in offering online ESOL materials. Miami-Dade County Public Schools (2017) offers a chart known as "the ESOL Strategies Matrix." Teachers report using these strategies by number code in lesson plans submitted to administrators.

Classroom Interactions, Community, and Collaboration

Wright (2015) details means of grouping students for language and content development, implementing aspects of cooperative learning and peer tutoring. To this end, de Oliveira (2016), via *interactional scaffolding*, shifts the responsibility of scaffolding from instructors to students, suggesting that functional language skills—such as negotiating meaning, confirming information, describing, comparing, and persuading—be taught overtly but developed through in-class teamwork.

Challenges

De Oliveira (2016) reminds us of goals, including standardized test results; however, she directs us to students' prior knowledge and their comfortable development upon it. Doing so entails challenging MLLs toward creating portfolios, including pictorial, hands-on, performance-based assessments; group tasks; oral reports; and written assignments.

Among these 9 themes, 72 in-class activities were identified (Table 9.1). The activities were further classified with respect to whether they applied to (a) new MLLs of lower proficiency or (b) all students in class, regardless of their English proficiency. We then coded our notes (Mackey & Gass, 2005) with respect to the 72 ESOL strategies.

Table 9.1 In-class strategies, identified by theme and by student base

Approach/Theme	MLL-based strategies	All-students-based strategies
Proficiency	Understanding Ss' language proficiency	
Lesson preparation	Language challenges (attending to linguistics)	Language objectives
	Analysis of instructions/directions	Content objectives
	Guiding/overarching questions	Content concepts
	Adaptation of text content	Meaningful activities
	Operational ESOL-specific technology	
Code breaking	Language skills and functions (speech acts)	Learning strategies
	Language structure (word order, syntax, etc.)	Promoting higher-order thinking
	Vocabulary preview	
	Content vocabulary (subject-specific/technical terms)	
	General academic vocabulary	
	Word parts and affixes	
	Contextualizing key vocabulary	
	Pronunciation issues	
Connection: building background	Ss' home language literacy proficiency	Connections with S experiences
	Proficiency in each of the 4 skills	
	Reference to home language or bilingualism	
	Appropriate translanguaging	
	Attention to word frequency	

(continued)

Table 9.1 (continued)

Approach/Theme	MLL-based strategies	All-students-based strategies
Culture	Respectful of Ss' home culture Inclusion of MLLs' home culture in culturally relevant materials Efforts in treating MLLs equitably Additive/transformational approaches exhibited (not deficit model) Advocacy for MLLs	
Comprehensible input	Adjusting speech Simplifying text Keying in on what Ss learn from text Concrete items → abstract items BICS → CALP Reducing nonessential details Native language support Sentence starters or language frames Highlighted text	Scaffolding Modeling academic tasks Multimodal techniques (maps, timelines, outlines, etc.) Visual aids Graphic organizers
ESOL strategies	Multicultural resources: cultural sharing, guest speakers, worldwide holidays Accommodations: heritage dictionary, extended time, flexible setting, flexible scheduling	Listening: LEA, TPR, illustrations Speaking: brainstorming, group projects, meaningful practice, repetition, role play, think aloud Reading: prior knowledge, picture walk, KWL, QAR, task cards, read-aloud, jump-in, chunking, word walls, cognates Writing: dialogue journals, letter writing, process writing, spelling, rubrics, summarizing, writing prompts Audiovisuals: audio books, videos, music, listening centers, tech software, realia, charts, pictures, graphs

(*continued*)

Table 9.1 (continued)

Approach/Theme	MLL-based strategies	All-students-based strategies
Classroom interactions: differentiating for multilevel classes	Modifications, accounting for interrupted education or language issues	Cooperative learning
	Identifying how language is used in different situations	Promotes student engagement
	Grouping students for language and content development	Peer tutoring
	Forwarding activities to practice and extend language, content learning	Fluency building activities
	Enacting a relationship with the reader or listener	Close reading
		Pre-, during, and post-reading activities
Challenge	Procedural knowledge	Declarative knowledge
	Functional language skills (e.g., negotiating meaning, confirming information, describing, comparing, persuading)	Portfolios
	Modified assessments	Performance-based assessments
		Oral reports
		Attention to standardized tests
		Test-prep, implementing accommodations

Phase 3: Data analysis

On an Excel spreadsheet, we listed strategy codes vertically and each visited class horizontally. Each time a strategy occurred, we entered a tick under the class corresponding to its occurrence. We then calculated the number of ticks per strategy. If any strategy was implemented in a single approach, that approach was also given its own tick so that we could calculate the number of times an approach was applied in a class. From this Excel file, we could then find the following:

1. the proportion of classes with an observed MLL-based strategy,
2. the proportion of classes with an observed all-students-based strategy,
3. the overall proportion of classes with respect to a qualitative codebook approach,
4. the mean number and standard deviation of classes per strategy,
5. an ANOVA-calculated p-value distinguishing MLL-based and all-students-based strategies per approach, should there be two or more strategies named in an approach, establishing significance at the 0.05 level, and
6. an overall ANOVA-calculated p-value distinguishing MLL-based and all-students-based strategies for the entire data set, again with significance set at the 0.05 level.

Results

Which ESOL Strategies Are Currently Implemented in Mainstream Classrooms?

We tallied the results with respect to each strategy and the school in which it occurred. Tallies are presented in Table 9.2. Proportions of classes per strategy, as distinguished by each lens approach, are presented in Table 9.3.

To What Extent Are Mainstream Teachers with ESOL Credentials Making Use of ESOL Strategies in Their Classrooms?

We witnessed ESOL strategies implemented in all 40 classes. On average, each of the 72 strategies appeared in an average of 8.83 (SD = 7.02) classes. Furthermore, each class showcased average of 15.95 (SD = 10.43) strategies per class.

Of the nine approaches in the qualitative codebook, six were showcased in more than half the classes. Four of these—lesson preparation

Table 9.2 Times each ESOL approach was observed among 40 classes

Approach	MLL-based strategy	Number of classes with observed strategy	Proportion of classes with MLL-based strategies by %	All-students-based strategy	Number of classes with observed strategy	Proportion of classes with All-students-based strategies by %
Proficiency	Understanding Ss' language proficiency	6	15			
Lesson preparation	Language challenges (attending to linguistics)	4	10	Language objectives	16	40
	Analysis of instructions/directions	4	10	Content objectives	30	75
	Guiding/overarching questions	19	47.5	Content concepts	24	60
	Adaptation of text content	2	5	Meaningful activities	25	62.5
	Operational ESOL-specific technology	4	10			
Code breaking	Language skills and functions (speech acts)	4	10	Learning strategies	0	0
	Language structure (word order, syntax, etc.)	4	10	Promoting higher-order thinking	21	52.5
	Vocabulary preview	10	25			
	Content vocabulary (subject-specific/technical terms)	12	30			
	General academic vocabulary	12	30			
	Word parts and affixes	4	10			
	Contextualizing key vocabulary	11	28			
	Pronunciation issues	4	10			

(*continued*)

Table 9.2 (continued)

Approach	MLL-based strategy	Number of classes with observed strategy	Proportion of classes with MLL-based strategies by %	All-students-based strategy	Number of classes with observed strategy	Proportion of classes with All-students-based strategies by %
Connection: building background	Ss' home language literacy proficiency	2	5	Connections with S experiences	8	20
	Proficiency in each of the 4 skills	1	2.5			
	Reference to home language or bilingualism	5	12.5			
	Appropriate translanguaging	8	20			
	Attention to word frequency	1	2.5			
Culture	Respectful of Ss' home culture	3	7.5			
	Inclusion of MLLs' home culture in culturally relevant materials	1	2.5			
	Efforts in treating MLLs equitably	5	12.5			
	Additive/transformational approaches exhibited (not deficit model)	5	12.5			
	Advocacy for MLLs	1	2.5			

Category	Item			Item		
Comprehensible input	Adjusting speech	11	27.5	Scaffolding	8	20
	Simplifying text	9	22.5	Modeling academic tasks	12	30
	Keying in on what Ss learn from text	7	17.5	Multimodal techniques (maps, timelines, outlines, etc.)	19	47.5
	Concrete items → abstract items	0	0	Visual aids	22	55
	BICS → CALP	2	5	Graphic organizers	11	27.5
	Reducing nonessential details	6	15			
	Native language support	11	27.5			
	Sentence starters or language frames	14	35			
	Highlighted text	2	5			
ESOL strategies	Multicultural resources: cultural sharing, guest speakers, worldwide holidays	3	7.5	Listening: LEA, TPR, illustrations	15	37.5
	Accommodations: heritage dictionary, extended time, flexible setting, flexible scheduling	6	15	Speaking: brainstorming, group projects, meaningful practice, repetition, role play, think aloud	18	45
				Reading: prior knowledge, picture walk, KWL, QAR, task cards, read-aloud, jump-in, chunking, word walls, cognates	10	25
				Writing: dialogue journals, letter writing, process writing, spelling, rubrics, summarizing, writing prompts	20	50
				Audiovisuals: audio books, videos, music, listening centers, tech software, realia, charts, pictures, graphs	14	35

(continued)

Table 9.2 (continued)

Approach	MLL-based strategy	Number of classes with observed strategy	Proportion of classes with MLL-based strategies by %	All-students-based strategy	Number of classes with observed strategy	Proportion of classes with All-students-based strategies by %
Classroom interactions: differentiating for multilevel classes	Modifications, accounting for interrupted education or language issues	6	15	Cooperative learning	23	57.5
	Identifying how language is used in different situations	4	10	Promotes S engagement	21	55
	Grouping students for language and content development	9	22.5	Peer tutoring	7	17.5
	Forwarding activities to practice and extend language, content learning	10	25	Fluency building activities	7	17.5
	Enacting a relationship with the reader or listener	9	22.5	Close reading	4	10
				Pre-, during, and post-reading activities	4	10
Challenge	Procedural knowledge	6	15	Declarative knowledge	11	27.5
	Functional language skills (e.g., negotiating meaning, confirming information, describing, comparing, persuading)	10	25	Portfolios	3	7.5
	Modified assessments	1	3	Performance-based assessments	15	37.5
				Oral reports	0	0
				Attention to standardized tests	9	22.5
				Test-prep, implementing accommodations	6	15

Table 9.3 Proportion of classes per strategy

Approach	Focus of strategy (# of individual strategies)	# of classes exhibiting strategies	% of classes exhibiting strategies	mean # of classes per strategy	Standard deviation	p
Proficiency	MLL (1)	6	15	6	0	*
	All Ss (0)	n/a	n/a	n/a	n/a	
	Total 1	6	15	6	undefined	
Lesson preparation	MLL (5)	24	60	6.60	6.99	0.005
	All Ss (4)	35	87.5	23.75	5.80	*
	Total 9	36	90	14.22	10.89	
Code breaking	MLL (8)	19	47.5	7.63	3.93	0.293
	All Ss (2)	21	52.5	10.5	14.85	ns
	Total 10	26	65	8.20	6.16	
Connection: building background	MLL (5)	10	25	3.40	3.05	*
	All Ss (1)	8	20	8	undefined	
	Total 6	13	32.5	4.17	3.31	
Culture	MLL (5)	6	15	2.00	2.00	*
	All Ss (0)	n/a	n/a	n/a	n/a	
	Total 5	6	15	2.00	2.00	
Comprehensible input	MLL (9)	27	67.5	6.89	4.81	0.01
	All Ss (5)	27	67.5	14.40	5.86	*
	Total 14	35	87.5	10.31	5.81	
ESOL strategies	MLL (2)	8	20	4.50	2.12	0.007
	All Ss (5)	35	87.5	15.40	3.85	*
	Total 7	35	87.5	12.29	6.24	

(continued)

Table 9.3 (continued)

Approach	Focus of strategy (# of individual strategies)	# of classes exhibiting strategies	% of classes exhibiting strategies	mean # of classes per strategy	Standard deviation	p
Classroom interactions	MLL (5)	19	47.5	7.60	2.51	0.86
	All Ss (6)	31	77.5	11.00	8.65	ns
	Total 11	31	77.5	9.45	6.56	
Challenge	MLL (3)	15	37.5	5.67	4.51	0.332
	All Ss (6)	22	55	7.33	5.47	ns
	Total 9	27	67.5	6.67	4.94	
All approaches	MLL (43)	38	95	5.88	4.29	0.00001
	All Ss (29)	40	100	13.21	8.01	*
	Total	40	100	8.83	7.02	

(90%), comprehensible input (87.5%), ESOL Strategies (87.5), and classroom interactions (75%)—appeared in at least three-fourth of the classes. Three, however—proficiency (15%), culture (15%), and connection (32.5%)—were observed in less than half of all classes.

Data showed that the following strategies occurred in at least half of all visited classes: content objectives, content concept maps, meaningful activities, higher-order thinking questions, visual aids, dialogue journals, cooperative learning, and student engagement. These elements may not necessarily pertain directly to MLLs; however, they do accelerate access to course content. Other data showed moderate ESOL strategy implementation, occurring between 35% and 50% of classes: language objectives, guiding questions, multimodal techniques, sentence starters, brainstorming, group projects, performance-based assessments, and listening strategies that include Language Experience Approach techniques, illustrations, and Total Physical Response. Notably, a good number of these techniques apply more directly to MLLs.

Seven classes (17.5%) displayed between 20 and 34 strategies, and three (7.5%) featured 35 or more strategies, with one class offering 55 examples. In other words, only a quarter of all observed classes put forth more than a quarter of the strategies, and only 7.5% offered MLLs full access to content while simultaneously channeling multicultural experiences to NESs. Contrastingly, 30% of the classes implemented no more than an eighth of the esteemed ESOL approaches.

How those strategies were used is worth noting.

Proficiency

In only 15% of the classes did we witness instructors offering references to MLLs' proficiency level. Here we observed translanguaging and references to cognates. One teacher actually grouped Spanish-speaking kindergartners together for a quick Spanish-based explanation of the activity, while another differentiated reading tables based on students' proficiency levels.

Lesson Preparation

Impressively, 90% of all classes showed elements of lesson preparedness. Of the four strategies identified for all students, three appeared in between 40% and 75% of the classes. However, all-students-based strategies were implemented significantly more than MLL-focused strategies. In fact, the only MLL-based lesson preparation strategy used fairly often, in 47.5% of the classes, was that of offering guiding or overarching questions. Otherwise, MLL-based strategies were evident in only 10% of the classes, thereby suggesting that students of emerging or developing proficiency would struggle when negotiating in-class activities.

A quarter of the teachers shared lesson plans. An example is shown in Fig. 9.2. This prototypical lesson plan shows some ESOL elements: an essential question, a reading section, a writing section, an exercise in listening comprehension, and vocabulary. There are higher-order thinking questions, engaging activities and corresponding assessments.

Distinctions between language and content objectives were rarely made. Furthermore, there was little addressing students of emerging proficiency, thereby raising questions about equity and inclusion for MLLs. ESOL strategies, however, were named with corresponding ESOL codes—for example, A2, B6—as seen in Fig. 9.3.

Lack of corroboration between ESOL codes and actual ESOL implementation leads us to questioning lesson plans. In one extreme case, a teacher listed the same ESOL codes for three consecutive weekdays—Wednesday, Thursday, and Friday—as well as for Monday, a national holiday, and Tuesday, a teacher planning day.

Teachers tended to choose content objectives (75% of classes) over language objectives (40% of classes). In fact, language objectives often appeared only in language arts classes, as if language arts concepts *are* content objectives. In only 15% of the lessons did teachers address both.

Code Breaking

Code breaking appeared in 65% of the classes. The strategy most implemented, in 52.5% of the classes, was a promotion of higher-order

9 Broken Promises? The Florida Consent Decree, Multilingual…

Essential Question: What can people do to bring about a positive change?			Whole Group Instruction			
			Reading Component (40-55 Minutes) *Priority Skill & Planning Card* LAFS.5.RI.3.8, LAFS.5. RI.1.2	Gradual Release	Writing Component-(30 Minutes) *Priority Skill & Planning Card*	Eval: & HL
Day:	Objective:	DLT:	Instructional Resources & Activities			
Day 1 Source: *Multi-Media: Weekly Opener #1: Listening comprehension #2: RWW	SWBAT: Build background knowledge on taking action to bring about a positive change and listen for purpose, identify characteristics of a biography (LAFS.5.RI.3.7, LAFS.5.SL.1.2) (READING) Understand features of an informative essay, understand the prompt (LAFS.5.W.1.2) (WRITING)	I can identify characteristics of a biography	10 minutes Introduce the Concept/Build Background T10/Weekly Opener clip 10 minutes Listening Comprehension T141 10 minutes Vocabulary 264-265 10 minutes -DEA Routine 25-40 minutes Shared Read/Comprehension 25-40 minutes Frederick Douglass: Freedom's Voice Pgs. 266-269 -Introduce the Sample Response Mechanism Item (s) to set purpose to read/reread the RWW utilizing Close Reading of Complex text strategy (SPADE) to support comprehension skill(s) -Standard based mini lesson: Genre Lesson: Biography pg. 272 -Standard based mini lesson: Comprehension Strategy (Summarize) pg. 270 (Q1)RI.3.7 Multimedia Based on the information in the video clip, what are some things people can do to bring positive change? (Q2) RI.3.7 Multimedia Based on the text heard, what did Susan B. Anthony fight for and how did she go about making a positive change?	I DO: WE DO: THEY DO: YOU DO:	COLD WRITE: (90 MINUTES) –DAY 1 PLAN, WRITE, & REVISE **Topic:** Railroads in America **Prompt:** *The sources talked about railroads spanning the country. Write an informative essay in which you explain the purpose of the Transcontinental railroad, and the challenges the workers face. Use information from the sources in your essay.*	EVAL:E1, E2, E4, E5

Fig. 9.2 Screenshot of prototypical 5th-grade mainstream lesson plan

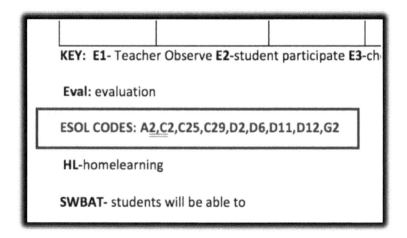

Fig. 9.3 Screenshot of mainstream lesson plan with highlighted ESOL codes

thinking, a tactic implemented for all students. MLL-based code breaking strategies were seen in 47.5% of the classes, with three different vocabulary strategies—content vocabulary (30%), general academic vocabulary (30%), and contextualization of vocabulary (27.5%)—appearing from time to time. On the other hand, language functions (10%), grammar (10%), word subdivisions (10%), and pronunciation issues (10%) seemed mostly overlooked.

Teachers focused on key vocabulary in context and posing higher-order thinking questions—strategies directed toward NESs and MLLs of higher proficiency. Few teachers, however, addressed the complexity of instructions or modified materials for students of emerging proficiency. Occasionally, students of emerging proficiency working slowly through tedious exercises while NESs finished early and progressed to compelling projects.

Connection: Building Background

Connection strategies appeared in only 32.5% of observations. MLL-based (25%) and all-students-focused strategies (20%) appeared in comparable proportions. No single strategy achieved presence in any more than 20% of the classes.

Drawing connections between target texts and MLLs' cultural contributions was seldom evident. Teachers rarely lent attention to students' heritage, opting instead to focus exclusively on text. In only 7.5% of the observations did we witness teachers pointing to a multilingual learner's background. Additionally, state sanctioned accommodations (e.g., heritage dictionary use or flexible timing) were evident in only 15% of the classes.

More surprising, though, was the lack of promoting home language. In a county where two thirds of the population speaks Spanish, we saw only 7 occasions (17.5% of the classes) when teachers used Spanish. Outside these puffs of Spanish, most classes exhibited English immersion where the culture of the textbooks determined lesson focus. The study revealed no evidence where teachers knew students' home language literacy level.

Culture

Reference to MLLs' home culture was largely non-existent. In only 12.5% of the classes did we witness teachers making extra effort to assert equitable access of materials to MLLs. In fact, in only one class did we see an MLL's home culture become part of the classroom design—a lesson on Japanese games where students implemented Venn diagramming to compare one Japanese game to that of a Mexican game described by a Mexican MLL. Only 7.5% of classes displayed any mention of any MLL's home culture.

Comprehensible Input

Teacher training regarding comprehensible input was abundant as 87.5% of all classes showed examples of such. And while an equal proportion of classes (67.5%) showed either MLL-based or all-students-based comprehensible input strategies, significantly more ($p = 0.01$) classes displayed all-students-based strategies (mean = 14.40, SD = 5.86) than MLL-based strategies (mean = 6.89, SD = 4.81).

Regarding teachers' speech, strategies such as slowing down, paraphrasing, or repeating occurred in no more than a quarter of the classes. Otherwise, teachers spoke at rates suitable for NESs, or faster! Strikingly, many teachers, at a rate of over a quarter of the classes, sent students of developing proficiencies to computers to work via ESL software, effectively abdicating their responsibility to tweak language while presenting.

Teachers, however, regularly implemented multimodal support such as maps, timelines, graphs, or charts. They also used extensive use of video and sentence frames upon which both NESs and MLLs might build academic language.

ESOL Strategies

In terms of district-recommended ESOL strategies, most purportedly benefit all students. Only those pertaining to multicultural resources (cultural sharing, guest speakers, worldwide holidays) and testing accommodations (heritage dictionary, extended time, flexible setting, flexible scheduling) refer to experiences unique to MLLs. Unsurprisingly, all-students-oriented strategies were implemented in 87.5% of the observed classes. However, elements referring to individual MLLs' cultures were observed in 7.5% of classes.

Most teachers required journaling (shown in 50% of all classes). Students were also given rubrics when performing writing tasks. With respect to speaking (demonstrated in 45% of classes), teachers made strong use of brainstorming and group projects. When promoting listening (observable in 37.5% of all classes), teachers often tried illustrations. With respect to reading (seen in 25% of classes), the most observable strategies related to word walls, read-aloud, jump-in reading, and an occasional prior knowledge question. Audiovisuals were a regularly implemented ESOL strategy (35% of classes), with computer software and videos implemented most.

Classroom Interactions, Community, and Collaboration

With respect to classroom interactions, distinctions between MLL-related and all-students-based strategies were not significantly different. Many classes (57.5% of the sample) involved cooperative learning, with students bunched in groups of 3 to 6 with students showing high degrees of engagement. Teachers openly touted grouping MLLs with NESs; however, this strategy occurred in only 22.5% of classes.

Challenge

A narrative we hear is that teachers are teaching to the annual state exams. However, test-prep reference was far more tempered than expected, appearing in only 15% of all classes. Instead, we saw far more examples of students working through performance-based assessment pieces with data revealing no significant differences in implementation of ESOL-based and native-speaker-based assessment activities.

MLL-Focused Versus All-Students-Focused Strategies

When teasing out activities oriented as MLL- or all-students-focused, we found two classes (5% of the sample) didn't implement MLL-based activities at all. Indeed, the degree to which all-students-based strategies were implemented was significantly more (p = 0.00001), occurring at a clip of 13.21 classes per strategy (SD = 8.01), while those for MLL-based strategies occurred at only 5.88 classes per strategy (SD = 4.29).

Conclusion

We found mainstream teachers are engaging with ESOL techniques emerging from their training. Every observed teacher demonstrated some use of ESOL techniques, particularly with respect to lesson preparation, linguistic puzzle pieces, comprehensible input, and ESOL strategies touted by their school district. However, the most important result may be that all-students-focused techniques were implemented at more than double the rate that MLL-specific strategies were. In other words, Tollefson's (1995) concerns are still pertinent: Teachers still address language acquisition, teaching methods, and linguistics but exclude cultural agency on behalf of multilingual learners.

Observations revealed clear teacher respect for MLLs, and the graduation rate of multilingual learners in Florida exceeds that of states where no ESOL is expected (Mitchell, 2016). However, the rate is still one of the lowest in the U.S. and reminiscent of research seen decades ago (Collier & Thomas, 2002), where MLLs often take 5 to 7 years to reach academic proficiency. In other words, Tappen's question regarding why Florida's ESOLers need 6 years to achieve bridging level is predictable: Florida's 300,000 MLLs are by-and-large working in assimilation settings (Ruiz, 1984) the Consent Decree authors were clearly trying to avoid.

We observed a non-localized curriculum that replaces any potential for Miami teachers to connect with their students' (or even their own) cultural and linguistic funds of knowledge (Moll, 2007). Instead, ESOL strategies implemented in classes seem geared almost exclusively toward MLLs learning majority views rather than incorporating those from their communities. Remarkably, in Miami, doing so entails multilingual teachers with multilingual students excluding the cultures they all bring into classes, exclusively projecting the hegemonic interests of the state, which are then policed by more multilingual officials.

In other words, despite the additive spirit espoused within the Consent Decree, we instead observed a clear example of Makoni and Pennycook's (2007) admonition of how additive bilingualism ends up as monolingualism. More alarmingly, the results indicate a strong degree of invisibilizing (Ndhlovu & Makalela, 2017) both teachers' and students' home lives. In other words, the structures in place across the state and acted upon within Miami's school district purposefully and successfully delegitimize the backgrounds of practically everyone in any classroom. Instead, what is legitimized is monocultural deficit-model practice (Valencia, 2020), via locally touted state test scores and graduation rates. It does not appear that efforts in Miami's MLL context are those with reference to emergent multilingualism but to emerging monolingualism. Rosa's (2019) concept of young students growing into young Latinx professionals on the terms of their community does not resonate in these data; instead, oddly, we may be witnessing a community acquiescing to assimilative practice.

These results bring ESOL credentials for Florida's mainstream teachers into question. A system restricting the use of students' background knowledge suggests that education is fundamentally more difficult for its students than need be, a result that challenges the Consent Decree as a full-fledged promoter of civil rights. We therefore propose that colleagues attend to how the Consent Decree addresses linguistic and cultural capital as part of its messaging, professional development, and documentation. Most specifically, we suggest, as a point of departure within professional development programs, a "knowing your students" element laced deeply in acculturative contexts of MLLs.

In the meantime, the results of this study point to monolingual practice for multilingual learners. Such is likely a key contributor to why today's students are progressing at the rates of the last century. The promise of equal access to all MLLs has not been kept.

Note

1. This of course can refer to anyone's personal identity. Rosa here refers to his own.

References

Abedi, J., Lord, C., & Plummer, J. R. (1997). *Final report of language background as a variable in NAEP mathematics performance* (CSE Report No. 429). National Center for Research on Evaluation, Standards, and Student Testing.

Anderson, L. W., & Krathwohl, D. R. (Eds.). (2001). *Taxonomy for learning, teaching, and assessing. A revision of Bloom's Taxonomy of Educational Objectives*. Longman.

Artecona-Pelaez, G. M. (2010). Understanding the implications of the Florida consent decree. In J. Govoni (Ed.), *Preparing the way: Teaching ELLs in the K-12 classroom*. Kendall Hunt Publishing.

Canagarajah, A. S. (2011). Diaspora communities, language maintenance, and policy dilemmas. In T. McCarty (Ed.), *Ethnography and language policy*. Routledge.

Chamot, A. U., & O'Malley, J. M. (1994). *The CALLA handbook: Implementing the cognitive academic language learning approach*. Addison-Wesley Publishing Company.

Choi, J., & Yi, Y. (2015). Teachers' integration of multimodality into classroom practices for English language learners. *TESOL Journal, 7*(2), 304–327.

Civic Enterprises. (2017). *Building a grad nation: Progress and challenge in raising high school graduation rates*. Civic Enterprises; Everyone Graduates Center at the School of Education at Johns Hopkins University.

Clark, K. (2009). The case for structured English immersion. *Educational Leadership., 66*(7), 42–46.

Coady, M. R., Harper, C., & de Jong, E. J. (2015). Aiming for equity: Preparing mainstream teachers for inclusion or inclusive classrooms? *TESOL Quarterly, 50*, 340–368. https://doi.org/10.1002/tesq.223

Collier, V. P., & Thomas, W. P. (2002). Reforming education policies for English learners means better schools for all. *The State Education Standard, 3*(1), 30–36. Alexandria, VA: National Association of State Boards of Education.

Creswell, J. W., & Creswell, J. D. (2017). *Research design*. SAGE.

Cummins, J., & Swain, M. (1986). *Bilingualism in education: Aspects of theory, research, and practice*. Longman.

de Jong, E. J. (2011). *Foundations for multilingualism in education: From principles to practice*. Caslon Publishing.

de Oliveira, L. (2015). A language-based approach to content instruction (LACI) for English language learners. *Journal of Language and Literacy Education*. Found May 27, 2017 at http://jolle.coe.uga.edu/wp-content/uploads/2014/01/SSOODecember_FINAL.pdf

de Oliveira, L. (2016). A language-based approach to content instruction (LACI) for English language learners: Examples from two elementary teachers. *International Multilingual Research Journal*, 217–231.

Echevarria, J., Vogt, M. E., & Short, D. (2010). *Making content comprehensible for elementary English learners: The SIOP® model*. Allyn & Bacon.

Erben, T., & Goussakova, K. (2020). SSTESOL presidents and the educational context of ESOL in Florida 1975–2020. In T. Erben (Ed.), *45 years SSTESOL: A chronicle of ESOL advocacy, research and practice in Florida*. Sunshine TESOL Press.

Esposito, A. G., Sirkin, R. E., & Bauer, P. J. (2018). Bilingual education. In M. H. Bornstein (Ed.), *The SAGE encyclopedia of lifespan human development*. SAGE.

Florida Department of Education. (1990). CASE NO. 90-1913. Found April 10, 2017 at http://www.fldoe.org/core/fileparse.php/7582/urlt/Consent-Decree.pdf

Florida Department of Education (2010). Florida Teacher Standards for ESOL Endorsement 2010. Found October 22, 2022 at https://www.fldoe.org/core/fileparse.php/7502/urlt/0071748-approvedteacherstandards.pdf

Florida Department of Education. (2017). Enrollment. Found April 9, 2017 at https://edstats.fldoe.org/SASWebReportStudio/gotoReportSection.do?sectionNumber=1

Gilmore, P. (1983). Spelling "Mississippi": Recontextualizing a literacy-related speech event. *Anthropology and Education Quarterly, 14*(4), 235–255.

Govoni, J. (Ed.) (2015). *Preparing the way: Teaching ELs in the PreK-12 classroom* (2nd ed.) [Bookshelf Online]. Retrieved from https://online.vitalsource.com/#/books/9781465279712/

Guest, G., MacQueen, K. M., & Namey, E. E. (2012). *Applied thematic analysis*. SAGE.

Harper, C., & de Jong, E. (2004). Misconceptions about teaching English-language learners. *Journal of Adult & Adolescent Literacy, 48*(2), 152–162.

Hornberger, N. H. (2009). Multilingual education policy and practice: Ten certainties (grounded in indigenous experience). *Language Teaching, 42*(2), 197–211.

Jameson, J. H. (1999). *Enriching content classes for secondary ESOL students* (pp. 206–233). Center for Applied Linguistics and Delta Systems Co., Inc., Passim.

Krashen, S. (1977). Some issues relating to the monitor model. In H. In Brown, C. Yorio, & R. Crymes (Eds.), *Teaching and learning English as a Second language: Trends in research and practice: On TESOL '77: Selected Papers from the Eleventh Annual Convention of Teachers of English to Speakers of Other Languages* (pp. 144–158). Teachers of English to Speakers of Other Languages.

Lambert, W. E. (1975). Culture and language as factors in learning and education. In A. Wolfgang (Ed.), *Education of immigrant students*. OISE.

Lipsey, R. F., & Innocent, D. (2017). *Creation and implementation of policies affecting English learners*. Miami-Dade TESOL Symposium. November 4.

Mackey, A., & Gass, S. M. (2005). *Second language research – Methodology and design*. Lawrence Erlbaum.

Makoni, S., & Pennycook, A. (Eds.). (2007). *Disinventing and reconstituting languages*. Multilingual Matters.

Miami-Dade County Public Schools. (2017). *ESOL strategies matrix. Division of World Languages and Bilingual Education.* Found April 12, 2017 at http://bilingual.dadeschools.net/BEWL/pdfs/ESOL_Strategies_Matrix.pdf

Mitchell, C. (2016). English language learner graduation rates are all over the map. *Learning the Language. Blog. Education Week.* January 4. Retrieved May 29, 2017 from http://blogs.edweek.org/edweek/learning-the-language/2016/01/english-language_learner_gradu.html

Mitchell, C. (2017). What can educators do to increase graduation rates for English-learners? *Learning the Language. Blog. Education Week.* May 11. Retrieved August 19, 2017 from http://blogs.edweek.org/edweek/learning-the-language/2017/05/to_boost_graduation_rates_for_.html

Moll, L. C. (2007). Bilingual classroom studies and community analysis: Some recent trends. In O. García & C. Baker (Eds.), *Bilingual education: An introductory reader* (pp. 272–280). Multilingual Matters.

Ndhlovu, F., & Makalela, L. (2017). *Decolonising multilingualism in Africa: Recentering silenced voices from the global south.* Multilingual Matters.

O'Gorman-Fazzolari, C. (2017). *Becoming bilingual: Examining teachers' perceptions and practices for achieving bilingualism and biliteracy in English and Spanish in a two-way dual language bilingual education program.* PhD dissertation, Florida International University.

Orellana, M. F., Martínez, D. C., & Martínez, R. A. (2014). Language brokering and translanguaging: Lessons on leveraging students' linguistic competencies. *Language Arts, 91*(5).

Pennycook, A. (1994). *The cultural politics of English as an international language.* Longman.

Peregoy, S. F., & Boyle, O. F. (2008). *Reading, writing, and learning in ESL: A resource book for teaching K-12 English learners* (5th ed.). Pearson Education Inc.

Platt, E., Harper, C., & Mendoza, M. B. (2003). Dueling philosophies: Inclusion or separation for Florida's English language learners? *TESOL Quarterly, 37*(1), 105–133.

Reid, A. O., Jr. (1992). Computer management strategies for text data. In B. F. Crabtree & W. L. Miller (Eds.), *Doing qualitative research* (Vol. 3). Sage.

Robertson, K. (n.d.). Increasing academic language knowledge for English language learner success. *¡Colorín Colorado!* Retrieved May 27, 2017 from http://www.colorincolorado.org/article/increasing-academic-language-knowledge-english-language-learner-success

Rosa, J. (2019). *Looking like a language, sounding like a race.* Oxford University Press.

Ruiz, R. (1984). Orientations in language planning. *NABE Journal, 7*(2), 15–34.

Shin, D. (2016). Disciplinary language development in writing: Science reports and common core state standards. In L. C. de Oliveira & T. Silva (Eds.), *Second language writing in elementary classrooms: Instructional issues, content-area writing and teacher education*. Palgrave Macmillan.

Solochek, J. (2017). Florida Board of Education raises concerns over services for English-language Learners. *Tampa Bay Times*. March 22. Found April 10, 2017 at http://www.tampabay.com/blogs/gradebook/florida-board-of-education-raises-concerns-over-services-for/2317519

Taylor, S. J., & Bogdan, R. (1984). *Introduction to qualitative research methods* (2nd ed.). Wiley.

Tollesfson, J. W. (1995). *Power and inequality in language education*. Cambridge University Press.

Valencia, R. R. (2020). *International deficit thinking: Educational thought and practice*. Routledge.

WIDA. (2012). *Amplification of the English language development Standards*. Retrieved from https://www.wida.us/standards/eld.aspx

Wright, V. (2015). Applying literacy strategies for ELs in the classroom. In J. Govoni (Ed.), *Preparing the way: Teaching ELs in the Pre-K-12 classroom* (2nd ed.). Kendall Hunt.

Part III

Teachers' Position in Policy Innovation

10

Policy on Global Issues in Sub-Saharan Africa: A Possible Role for ELT from Examples in Guinea Bissau, Senegal and DRC

Linda Ruas and Ali Djau

Introduction

We believe English teachers have a broader role than simply teaching English language as a code. We consider it important to expand the teaching of grammar, vocabulary and the four skills towards educating, developing critical thinking and engaging learners in global issues. We also contend we have a duty and social conscience, as educators, to integrate social, local and global issues into English classes. The tendency in different countries has been to get content rated relevant for learners into the school curricular through top-down policy reforms in education ignoring teachers who are the major stakeholders in the implementation process (Holmarsdottir, 2005; Harris & Richard, 2019; Enever, 2020).

L. Ruas (✉)
London South East Colleges, Bromley, UK

A. Djau
Action Guinea Bissau, London, UK

However relevant global issues are felt in different educational contexts, teachers, unfortunately, do not have the liberty to get them into the classroom, unless required by laid down policy guidelines. It seems unusual that, for more than two decades, research has demonstrated how unproductive this top-down approach to policy implementation has been and has strongly recommended the foregrounding of teachers at the initial phase of any policy that requires teachers' agency in implementation (see Steans, 2012; Schweisfurth, 2013 for example). In spite of the well-stated need to involve teachers in the initial phase of policy crafting, very little exists on how this should be done. The attempt in this chapter is to analyse an experience in which teachers were involved in drafting an English language curriculum in three sub-Saharan African countries primarily with the intention of solving a practical need and not meeting any research agenda. The interest was to develop an English language curriculum that prioritises global issues and to find out the responsiveness in the contexts in view of supporting the teachers in the implementation process. This explains why the approach in this chapter is ontological and intended to knowledge the overall experience in the project. We will first provide an overview of global issues in ELT, the local contexts in the three selected countries and why global issues are so relevant, and the relevant educational policies. We will then discuss teachers' and students' perceptions and awareness of these policies, how they already bring social issues into class, if they do, and what further support they might need.

Why Global Issues in ELT?

We know we are not alone in our beliefs in that we are part of a worldwide movement, slowly gaining ground, of teachers who decide, and act, to make a change in the world through teaching. Cates (1997) focused on five areas where global education influenced ELT during the 1990s:

> (1) new thinking about the aims and mission of the English teaching profession; (2) new ideas about the content of English language teaching (ELT); (3) out-reach efforts by ELT associations to global issue speakers and organizations; (4) the growing emphasis in ELT conferences on global

issue themes; and (5) the formation of global issue interest groups within the English teaching profession.

Educators began to think and write about why we were teaching English, as many learners seemed to be learning English for no particular purpose at all. This general *TENOR* (Teaching English for No Obvious Reason) was reflected in large-scale production and sales of general coursebooks around the world. Publishers could not afford to risk offending anyone, and therefore stuck to invented, unreal contexts. Together with learning English, as we need meaning and context for all language we use, could we actually address pressing world issues such as ecological disasters, racism, human rights and war, *and* make a difference? Could we incorporate a moral dimension into English teaching and get learners to think, critically evaluate and change their worlds?

Many published materials have always included what can be called *softer* global issues, those which are less contentious. However, this is often restricted to 'shallow environmentalism' (Stibbe, 2004: 243) and superficially nods to gender issues and recycling. Big publishers understandably usually avoid all the PARSNIP topics—Politics, Alcohol, Religion, Sex, Narcotics, -Isms and Pork—as they aim to sell in as many different contexts as possible—a practice that often conditions teachers to believe that they should not bring these topics into class. This limitation also makes it more difficult for teachers to include them, as there are fewer ready materials to use.

It was in the 1990s that several Global Issues Special Interest Groups started up, as part of larger teaching associations in Japan, the UK, Korea and the US, to address these points and support teachers with materials, training and sharing experience. These Special Interest Groups mobilised international and national conferences to address global issues more publicly, link teachers with shared interests, put on events which specifically addressed various global issues, and produced relevant publications. One such recent publication is *Global Issues in an Uncertain World* (Sowton, 2018), which includes excerpts from many IATEFL Global Issues Special Interest Group (GISIG) newsletter articles over the past 20 years. The Special Interest Groups also encourage, support and disseminate the increasing research accomplished in the area of global issues in ELT.

Brown (2018), in researching global issues-related topics and exploring power relations within the teaching of English, concluded that our goal should be the full emancipation of learners, going beyond the oft-hyped *empowering*. We can disempower learners by keeping the world, contentious issues, politics and authentic social problems out of the English class, but we can emancipate them by providing opportunities to critically evaluate social structures and contexts. As an example, we highly recommend exploring the Participatory Tools exhibited in from Reflection Actions (2022)[1] webpage regarding Tools and Methods.

On Policy Reforms

Despite recurrent calls on and argument for the involvement of teachers in the initial phase of policy conception, very few studies have provided evidence of this happening. To find out factors that influence history teachers' voluntary engagement in curriculum reforms in England, Harris and Richard (2019) noted a general sense of laxity in teachers' agency in the process. They equally noted that push factors to agency in curriculum reforms were subject identity and accountability. The absence of adequate evidence on teacher's involvement in policy conception reveals power relations inherent in conceiving policies. This partly explains why the whole process of conception is described as top-down. However, some stories of successes of stakeholders' involvement in policy reforms are reported in Wales, with factors such as effective follow up communication strategies being the major push factor (OECD, 2018; 2020). On the outcome of teachers' involvement in policy reforms, Steans (2012) shares the following:

> E4E teachers in Los Angeles spent several months researching the most effective way to improve the feedback and support teachers receive to improve their performance in the classroom. They published a report this summer advocating for the creation of a flexible evaluation system that would base 50 percent of a teacher's annual review on multiple classroom observations by administrators and peers and 40 percent on multiple measures of student growth. One of E4E teachers put it best, saying, 'We have taken on the complexity and controversy of this issue and produced a new

way forward for teacher evaluation, one that unites ideas from our union and our district and considers input from our peers, community members and, most important, our students. Our goal is to start a conversation about solutions that create pathways for collaboration and consensus.' (p. 1)

Major immediate benefits of involving teachers in policy conception include the mitigation of resistance (OECD, 2020) and a sense of ownership (Schweisfurth, 2013). The easily translate into commitment in implementation. The few instances of successes in involving teachers in policy reforms are generally from countries in the global North. In the global South, in African countries, for example, where power structures intensely permeate educational culture, the tendency for tension between teachers and administrators abound. This, more or less, reduces the possibilities of engaging teachers in curriculum reforms. To add value to calls for teachers' involvement in policy reforms, there is the urgent need to provide data-driven evidence of how teachers' involvement leads to better policy implementation, improved teacher quality and increased students' achievement.

The ELT Context in Guinea Bissau, Senegal and DRC

Guinea Bissau, Senegal and DRC have several commonalities. Among these are that they all are under-resourced educational contexts in Sub-Saharan Africa and learners learn English as a foreign language in secondary school in large classes.

Guinea Bissau differs from the other two. Being an ex-Portuguese colony, the official language of education is Portuguese. Portuguese, however, is hardly used outside education and formal occasions, as Kriol and other local languages take precedence. Senegal and DRC have French as the official language and language of education, although several other local languages are also spoken. Senegal and DRC, for various political and economic reasons have more government support within education than Guinea Bissau, with government-endorsed national curriculum and tests.

Senegal has its own national coursebooks, *Keep in Touch* (Hodder Education Group, 2010), produced in conjunction with the government. These texts include some local and national and African topics, such as mention of the Kenyan environmentalist Wangari Maathai; role models such as Ellen Sirleaf Johnson, President of Liberia; an article about the education of women in Senegal and how this is now more equal to that of men; and a page about how the sea-level rise is affecting the area of Saly. The inclusion of the topics of gender equality and the environment could lead to valuable discussions.

Guinea Bissau, due to the more fragile government, has no national curriculum at the time of this writing, even though the English Language Teaching Association—ELTA-GB—has been pushing for this for some time. In Guinea Bissau, the education system is not at the same levels as other ECOWAS countries because there is no regional educational system.

The government seems to take no interest in education at all. As there is no national curriculum, each school develops its own syllabus and exams, and teachers are left alone to prepare. There is no supervision of teachers or in-service training. As government officials send their children abroad or to private schools for study, they have no direct incentive to improve state schools. When state school teachers strike because they are not paid, the ones to suffer are the students.

One particular situation in Guinea Bissau is that of girls in school. Parents prioritise the education of boys over that of girls. Nevertheless, there have been various strategies to encourage more girls to attend school in the last 20 years, but the majority still do not complete secondary school due to issues such as early marriage, pregnancy, or lack of ability for families to pay school fees.

Both DRC and Guinea Bissau have experienced comparatively recent civil wars since independence. While the wars caused of millions of deaths, not only directly as a result of violence but also because of associated disease and starvation. Both countries still have fragile governments and have experienced several coups.

Senegal, meanwhile, has had a relatively peaceful transition to democracy and is now seen as one of the few stable democracies in West Africa. While Senegal is mainly Muslim, Guinea Bissau has a non-confrontational mixture of Islam and Christianity, and DRC is mostly Christian. The issue of peace-building is therefore extremely relevant. Thus, education promoting understanding and respect for other religions and a growing awareness of the many environmental problems have recently become key emphases for schools in these regions. As examples, student awareness regarding rising sea levels and increases in pollution from discarded plastic water bottles and bags have become deeper emphases for these countries.

In all three countries, poverty is an issue, especially in rural areas. The health and education systems are all severely lacking. There is exploitation of natural resources, slavery and a horrific amount of corruption. FGM, HIV and Koranic school street-begging are common in Guinea Bissau and Senegal. And the conflict, mass rape and humanitarian state of emergency continues in DRC.

There have been, however, some glimmers of hope and positivity, apart from the general resilience of the majority of the populations. Once such high point was the inspirational revolutionary leader, Amilcar Cabral in Guinea Bissau. In leading the resistance to the Portuguese colonialists, he created a strong system of equality for women, and education for all in simple bush schools. He brought in Brazilian educator Paulo Freire to advise on education and literacy, empowering people to spread literacy and critically question political leadership.

With regard to conflict in DRC, Kaleba Walingene and Tombola Barabara (2017) describe how peace initiatives, one being English Clubs, raise awareness of and give expression to peace-building via English:

> The learning of a language can allow us to see issues from another perspective, put ourselves in someone else's shoes and challenge some of the embedded prejudices that may go unchallenged in our communities. This may be particularly important in the context of the DRC where people come from a wide range of ethnic and linguistic backgrounds. Moreover, given the global spread of English, engaging with the language can allow us to consider our views in relation to the wider world and outside our local context. English can allow access to information from outside our communities and also allow us to contribute to global discussions in English. (132)

There is also a move to create a new 'African pedagogy', in opposition to the culturally imposed, often contextually irrelevant coursebooks that were exported as part of colonialism. In fact, Whitehead (2011) argued that English can combine with local indigenous languages so that colonial French and historically imposed Lingala may be somewhat neutralised with respect to the power structures imposed by those languages in many communities. To do so, teachers then rely on communicative methodologies that are often more relevant to small, well-resourced classrooms in Europe than the English classes in Senegal, Guinea Bissau and DRC, which often have 60 or 70 learners in one class and no materials but a blackboard and chalk.

'Global Issues' in the Educational Policies

We decided to conduct an initial investigation into how far these beliefs are supported by policy and practice in the teaching contexts of three Sub-Saharan African countries. More specifically, we wanted to discuss interpretations of education policy with both teachers and students to see whether they share our convictions and understand what type of support they need. Our selection of three countries—Guinea Bissau, Senegal and DRC—was based on personal connections and familiarity, ease of access and communication and relevance of global issues. All three countries are now linked to the IATEFL Global Issues Special Interest Group.

It was interesting to look through educational policies of the three countries to see how they were similar and how they differed with respect to global issues. Guinea Bissau has no formal educational policy, but the official recommendation for educational policy from the two teachers' unions SINAPROF and SINDEPROF have been used instead.

As can be seen in the policy excerpts in Table 10.1, all three countries include the topic of peace-building. Both DRC and Senegal include the topic of human rights. Each country also has an individual focus: Guinea Bissau on gender equity and the environment, DRC on moral education and improvement of living conditions and Senegal on discrimination and violence against women.

Table 10.1 Relevant policy excerpts

Guinea Bissau: 1.Promover a equidade entre géneros; Promover e melhorar a saúde escolar e desenvolver os comportamentos cívicos relativos à paz 3.3 Adaptação e reforço dos programas relativos a melhoria da saúde escolar, a protecção do ambiente e educação para a paz; Adaptação de módulos de formação dos alunos e professores em saúde escolar, conservação do ambiente e educação para a paz
Senegal: Article premier … à promouvoir les valeurs dans lesquelles la nation se reconnaît : elle est éducation pour la liberté, la démocratie pluraliste et le respect des droits de l'homme, développant le sens moral et civique de ceux qu'elle forme, elle vise à en faire des hommes et des femmes dévoués au bien commun respectueux des lois et des règles de la vie sociale et œuvrant à les améliorer dans le sens de la justice, de l'équité et du respect mutuel Article 6 … en même temps qu'elle est ouverte sur les valeurs de civilisation universelle et qu'elle inscrit dans les grands courants du monde contemporain, par là, elle développe l'esprit de coopération et de paix entre les hommes Article 11 … de contribuer, avec la famille notamment, à assurer l'éducation sociale, morale et civique de l'enfant Article 12 … de contribuer à compléter l'éducation sociale, morale et civique de l'élève Article 17 … l'éducation et la formation nécessaire à l'amélioration des conditions d'existence (santé, alimentation, habitat)
DRC: Article 14: Les pouvoirs publics veillent à l'élimination de toute forme de discrimination à l'égard de la femme et assurent la protection et la promotion de ses droits. Ils prennent, dans tous les domaines, notamment dans les domaines civil, politique, économique, social et culturel, toutes les mesures appropriées pour assurer le total épanouissement et la pleine participation de la femme au développement de la nation. Ils prennent des mesures pour lutter contre toute forme de violences faites à la femme dans la vie publique et dans la vie privée Article 15: Les pouvoirs publics veillent à l'élimination des violences sexuelles. Sans préjudice des traités et accords internationaux, toute violence sexuelle faite sur toute personne, dans l'intention de déstabiliser, de disloquer une famille et de faire disparaître tout un peuple est érigée en crime contre l'humanité puni par la loi

(*continued*)

Table 10.1 (continued)

Article 45: Les pouvoirs publics ont le devoir de promouvoir et d'assurer, par l'enseignement, l'éducation et la diffusion, le respect des droits de l'homme, des libertés fondamentales et des devoirs du citoyen énoncés dans la présente Constitution. Les pouvoirs publics ont le devoir d'assurer la diffusion et l'enseignement de la Constitution, de la Déclaration universelle des droits de l'homme, de la Charte africaine des droits de l'homme et des peuples, ainsi que de toutes les conventions régionales et internationales relatives aux droits de l'homme et au droit international humanitaire dûment ratifiées
Article 51: L'Etat a le devoir d'assurer et de promouvoir la coexistence pacifique et harmonieuse de tous les groupes ethniques du pays. Il assure également la protection et la promotion des groupes vulnérables et de toutes les minorités

Given the contexts and these accompanying policies, we decided it would be useful and interesting to investigate how both teachers and learners of English see these topics as relevant to their English classes, and how coverage of the topics might be expanded and improved.

The Voices of Teachers and Learners

We started with a simple list of questions:

1. Did you know the following ideas are included in the educational policy for your country? (Brief summary of these areas)
2. Do you think it is a good idea to include these ideas in English classes?
3. Do you/Does your English teacher ever cover any of these topics in class? If so, how?
4. How else can teachers cover these topics?

We had three teacher respondents from each of the three countries, as well as two or three student respondents from each. We are, of course, aware that this is a small number and that no real conclusions can be drawn from such a small study. However, as an initial inquiry, we hope their responses may serve as a springboard for further work.

We also organised discussions on the IATEFL/Africa WhatsApp groups in each of the three countries. Discussions were structured around topics of politics, gender, the environment and social issues to see how they felt about bringing these issues into their English classes. We also left room for teachers to offer anything else they wanted to say.

All the teachers except one said that they agreed that social topics should be included. One participant explained:

> Definitely! Yes, I do agree that it is important to cover these topics when teaching English because we are not only teachers of English but we are also educators. We need to widen our learners' knowledge; to teach them the life skills in order to prepare them for a bright future. This is important again in the sense that as the leaders of tomorrow, our learners need to be such citizens who know their rights and duties.

Half the teachers said they include global issues in class through discussion and student presentations. The other half do not, mainly due to lack of time. In fact, one teacher defended their choice: 'No, I don't cover it since we need to follow the state curriculum with specific materials.' To cover global issues more effectively, all teachers said they need more time and materials. Among the requests for additional materials were documents pertaining to international conventions of human rights, textbooks, pictures, videos, audios, newspapers, videos, CDs and sample syllabi dealing with these topics. No-one mentioned the need for any training or support in creating materials.

Within the spirited discussions in the WhatsApp groups, some teachers chatted about one-off lessons they had taught on gender equality, the environment or peace. Others conversed about how they worked on raising the confidence of girls by encouraging them to speak or take on class management roles in class, thereby helping to question, challenge and change traditional ideas. A particularly boisterous conversation surrounded the topic of girls being housewives where teachers advocated for

- making boys share or take over the supportive role of cleaning the board,
- providing a girls-only after school English club to give extra encouragement and support,

- ensuring there are more women English teachers to act as role models to girls, and
- reading about inspirational women figures.

One teacher spoke about projects he had conducted in class on local environmental issues like rubbish and recycling. Another teacher organised a Saturday excursion for students and teachers to plant trees and Saturday seminars focusing on Koranic street-begging and family discussions regarding girls' education. As predicted, most teachers knew that these particular issues were in their educational policy. Students, on the other hand, students did not. The students interviewed from DRC gave different answers to those from Senegal and Guinea Bissau, most likely due to differing school syllabi.

The Senegalese and Bissau Guinean students thought it was a good idea to include social and global issues in English classes because, as one student relayed, the topics 'are so interesting and important in general'. Students said their English teachers don't often include these topics, though they occasionally get them to write dialogues about one of the issues. They do however sometimes have opportunities to talk to them about such topics after class or during breaks. Students did agree that it would be valuable to have reading texts about global issues that include, as one student mentioned, 'moral education and politics so we will be able to debate the situation of the country'.

The students from DRC, however, did not think these topics should be included in English classes, suggesting there is clearly no need. One student expounded by noting that 'we have them in Civics and Moral Education classes'.

Suggested Materials and Resources

Publishers have been accused of putting forth materials that propagate, consciously or unwittingly, a 'wholesale, unthinking export of consumerist neoliberalist materials' from the UK and the US to the rest of the world, through the type of contexts and texts they include and, more importantly, by what they omit. Maybe a better solution is to work with local materials and local contexts. This has worked to a certain degree in Senegal, where local materials have been produced. But these materials do not go far enough. If we are to develop critical pedagogy and encourage learners to question systems and create change, we may need to develop ways of training teachers to integrate more crucial issues.

We have several suggestions. The United Nations (2022) Sustainable Development Goals could be one structure to base classes on, taking each goal in turn and basing English lessons on them, making example sentences and practice exercises reflect the goal, and getting learners to think about water, gender, life under the ocean, energy and other considerations. We cannot teach a language with no content, so it makes far more sense to have meaningful content than use vague, random, decontextualised examples, as we have seen in the past. For example, which of the following comments, which help students practise the present continuous, would make students think more, when practising the present continuous:

1. He is opening the door. She is walking to the shop.
2. Brazilians are voting for a new President. We are destroying the ocean.

Another idea is for teachers to direct specific projects around global issues through English in English clubs. The Grand Yoff secondary school in Dakar actually did this by preparing for and putting on an English programme highlighting the local environment and its problems. Small groups of students prepared and acted out short dialogues about street rubbish blocking drains when it rains, sang songs about our duty to look after nature and gave short speeches about recycling and re-using plastic.

Kaleba Walingene and Tombola Barabara (2017) reported that, in DRC, schools have gone much further and used English clubs as a way to use English as a neutral language to allow students to become to change agents with respect to their communities' peace and reconciliation processes:

> Such activities promote critical thinking and use English to discuss issues such as democracy, elections, corruption, interpersonal conflicts, and community problems'. (132)

In fact, some clubs have presented shocking skits about crime, theft, violence and rape.

A further idea is to tap into and use the work of the many international organisations that work towards peace, gender equity and environmental issues. We can link up classes in remote areas of Sub-Saharan Africa with world movements towards cleaning up the oceans, protesting against commercial logging for palm oil plantations and encouraging improved techniques, environmental destruction from oil extraction or mining, or shaking up traditional gender roles. There is plenty of material and opportunity to join movements online, and teachers need to find ways of involving learners and having them use and practise their English while also making international connections.

Perhaps the easiest starting point for bringing important local and global issues into class is for teachers to get together and produce some of the materials that they feel they need. In Guinea Bissau, the ELTA-GB has identified topics such as supporting and encouraging girls to continue their schooling and protecting the local environment for their new National Curriculum. They will each find or write short texts about these topics, create simple lessons around them and then share the materials with other teachers across the country.

Communities of practice are important for discussing issues we want or need to bring into class, as well as sharing ideas for how to do this. By making use of various social media channels—WhatsApp, Facebook, Telegram and others—we can, as IATEFL GISIG and other groups have shown recently, easily link up teachers who may feel isolated and share teaching ideas and materials. It is our experience that when published materials and training opportunities about global issues are lacking, enthusiasm and passion abound when motivated individuals connect.

One objection for working on global issues together with English is that there are other priorities in Sub-Saharan African education—for example, literacy, motivation of learners, retention of learners, low teacher pay, and lack of materials and resources. However, all these issues can be improved by bringing greater motivation of a world-changing cause to teaching. By working on issues such as peace-building, empowering women and protecting the environment and the planet, we can build positivity and hope, link learners with cohorts working towards the same ideals. Students and teachers from disparate locales maybe even help one another with their local issues.

Maybe the inclusion of some global issues in the national education policy does not go far enough and should be extended to include many more pressing topics. We have a wonderful opportunity with language to teach and express meaningful, change-creating ideas. While we lament that internet access is not, unfortunately, available and affordable to all in Sub-Saharan Africa, we do have, in the twenty-first century, access to more information and high-quality materials. Furthermore, more than ever before, we have instant opportunities to link up with others across the world every day.

Conclusion

Although the focus of this has been to demonstrate how teachers placed global issues at the centre of their own English language curriculum similar to the Indonesian experience (see Widodo, 2016), the outcome of the exercise in the project is consistent with calls for teacher agency in policy design in English Language Teaching (ELT). It was noticed that the teachers involved in the project felt a sense ownership of the curriculum, which re-invented their identities during the process. They felt positioned in countries whose policy structures undermine teachers. Three major policy issues implicational in this approach include (1) teacher communities of practice, (2) learning content and (3) material design. While the overall goal was to create a context-responsive curriculum, teachers' agency was critically cultivated with immediate feedback from their learners on the relevance of the content. This was crucial in enhancing both student and teacher communities of practice, which became a major booster to the project outcomes. The choice of content to be included in the curriculum reduced the abstraction that generally characterises ELT content in the global South. There has been a long standing tradition of the North outsourcing the South with learning content, which has built a myth around the English language. Getting teachers involved in developing their own materials was a catalyst in reconstructing their ideologies about English language learning by raising their cultural awareness in

ELT. Many context-specific evidence of how power relations in ELT can be deconstructed through global issues and/or curriculum innovation are necessary to bring ELT closer to the learners in the global South.

Note

1. Formerly known as Networked Toolbox.

References

Brown, S. (2018). Exploring ELT as emancipatory practice. *IATEFL Online 2018*. [Video]. Teaching English. https://www.teachingenglish.org.uk/article/exploring-elt-emancipatory-practice

Cates, K. A. (1997). New trends in global issues and English teaching. *The Language Teacher* Issue 21.5; May. Found at https://jalt-publications.org/tlt/articles/2139-new-trends-global-issues-and-english-teaching

Enever, J. (2020). Global language policies: Moving English up the educational escalator. *Language Teaching for Young Learners, 2*(2), 162–191.

Harris, R., & Richard, S. (2019). Engaging with curriculum reform: Insights from English history teachers' willingness to support curriculum change. *Journal of Curriculum Studies, 51*(1), 43–61.

Hodder Education Group. (2010). *Keep in touch* (Textbook series). Édicef.

Holmarsdottir, H. (2005). *From policy to practice: A study of the implementation of the Language-in-Education Policy (LiEP) in three South African Primary schools*. PhD dissertation submitted to the Faculty of Education, Universitetet i Oslo.

Kaleba Walingene, J., & Tombola Barabara, J. (2017). English as a language of community problem solving and conflict resolution: The case of English Clubs in the Democratic Republic of the Congo. In E. Erling (Ed.), *English across the fracture lines*. British Council. Found at https://www.teachingenglish.org.uk/article/english-across-fracture-lines

OECD. (2018). Education policy in Japan: Building bridges towards 2030. *Reviews of National Policies for Education*. https://doi.org/10.1787/9789264302402-en

OECD. (2020). *Curriculum reform: A literature review to support effective implementation* (Working Paper No. 239). OECD.

Reflection Actions (2022). *Tools and methods.* Found at https://www.reflection-action.org/tools_and_methods/

Schweisfurth, M. (2013). Learner-Centred education in international perspective. *Journal of International and Comparative Education, 2*(1), 1–8.

Sowton, C. (Ed.). (2018). *Global issues in an uncertain world.* IATEFL Global Issues Special Interest Group. Found at https://gisig.iatefl.org/wp-content/GIUW/GIUWp.pdf

Steans, R. (2012). Engaging teachers in Ed Reform. *PIE.* (Available at www.pie%2D%2D-network.org)

Stibbe, A. (2004). Environmental education across cultures: Beyond the discourse of shallow environmentalism. *Language and Intercultural Communication, 4*(4), 242–260. https://doi.org/10.1080/14708470408668875

United Nations Department on Economic and Social Affairs. (2022). *Sustainable development: The 17 goals.* Found at https://sdgs.un.org/goals

Whitehead, D. (2011). English language teaching in fragile states: Justifying action, promoting success and combating hegemony. In H. Coleman (Ed.), *Dreams and realities: Developing countries and the English language.* British Council. Found at https://www.teachingenglish.org.uk/sites/teacheng/files/Z413%20EDB%20Section16.pdf

Widodo, H. P. (2016). Language policy in practice: Reframing the English language curriculum in the Indonesian secondary education sector. In R. Kirkpatrick (Ed.), *English language education policy in Asia. Language policy* (Vol. 11). Springer. https://doi.org/10.1007/978-3-319-22464-0_6

11

English Language Proficiency for All University Graduates Stipulated by Law: A Realistic or Idealistic Goal? An Appraisal of a Tertiary ELT Policy from Montenegro

Vesna Bratić and Milica Vuković-Stamatović

Introduction

Global social and political factors have given rise to English being seen as a necessity across the world. In this light, governments worldwide have been introducing various English language teaching (ELT) policies mainly for the primary and secondary levels of education. However, little attention has been devoted to the design of language policies at the university level (Ramos García & Pavón Vázquez, 2018). In consideration of this shortcoming, Jenkins (2014) surveyed 166 teachers from 24 countries regarding their ELT policies at university level. Most respondents answered that they "did not have an official or stated policy," often

---

V. Bratić (✉) · M. Vuković-Stamatović
University of Montenegro, Podgorica, Montenegro
e-mail: vmilica@ucg.ac.me

adding that they followed "some kind of informal understanding or 'unwritten rule'" (129) and that such policies were indeed necessary.

Still, some countries have actually attempted regulating tertiary ELT policies. Montenegro is among them. Specifically, the Montenegrin government recently mandated EFL courses in higher education, stipulating that all students achieve advanced English proficiency for their graduation. However, this ambitious policy is seen by many as unrealistic and "divorced from practice." By discussing the nature and effects of this tertiary ELT policy, we hope we to contribute to sparse literature on university language policies (Lauridsen, 2013; Ramos García & Pavón Vázquez, 2018).

ELT Policies

ELT Policies at Tertiary Level Around the World

Tertiary-level ELT policies vary greatly, not only by region or country, but by universities themselves, especially where governments have not adopted binding EFL policies. In this short review of the tertiary ELT policies around the world, we will focus on the EFL contexts, as the ELT policy which is the subject of this chapter is implemented in such a context. The European tertiary ELT policies, as policies which are the most relevant for this chapter, will be covered separately, in the ensuing section of the chapter.

Tertiary ELT policies for EFL contexts have best been described for Asia. Some countries—for instance, China (Li, 2018; Zhao, 2012; Rao & Lei, 2014), Taiwan (Timina & Butler, 2011; Kelsen & Liang, 2012), and Vietnam (Nguyen et al., 2015)—have chosen to make English mandatory for all their university students, where it is both an entry and a graduation requirement (Fryer et al., 2014). Still, tertiary-level education policies in Asia vary (Park, 2017).

Most universities in Asia require a certain entrance level of English, typically checked via standardised tests. Upon entering a university, students are required to attend mandatory English courses so that all students achieve a desired level. This scenario is showcased in China, where English is a mandatory course in most universities, with the College English Test Band as an assessment method (Li, 2017). In 2007, the country issued the College English Curriculum Requirements (Han & Yin, 2016) that recommends that universities tailor syllabi to local contexts.

The Japanese Ministry of Education has been promoting English instruction at their universities for almost a decade, recognising the mastery of English as necessary for job-seeking young people in the era of globalisation (Terauchi, 2017). In South Korea, a certification of English proficiency is a graduation requirement (Lee, 2017). The significance of English proficiency for Thai students has resulted in international programmes and bilingual courses at a number of colleges in Thailand (Sanpatchayapong, 2017). Vietnam has even launched the National Foreign Language Project 2020, whose overall aim is the enhancement of standard English proficiency among Vietnamese millennials. To this aim, abundant funds have been allocated to the professional advancement of English language teachers through the mandated standardisation of both instructors' and students' English proficiency (Le, 2017).

In the Middle East and North Africa (MENA) region, English is synonymous with academic success (Kirkpatrick & Barnawi, 2017). Thanks to the oil industry, the Gulf Cooperation Council States place a particular importance to the English language education through their policies (Abou-El-Kheir & MacLeod, 2017). However, despite this, in general, Arabic language users have a low proficiency in English across all four skills (Aloreibi & Carey, 2017). Many of the region's tertiary ELT policies have centred on developing locally produced English language teaching materials and textbooks which are culturally and socially appropriate for their context (cf. Aghagolzadeh & Davari, 2017; Bianchi & Abdel Razeq, 2017), but many of these focus on grammar and reading, which is seen as one of the reasons why the region's students generally score low on English tests, in addition to the teacher-centred style of teaching which is still dominant in the region (Aloreibi & Carey, 2017; Barnawi & Al-Hawsawi, 2017).

In the MENA region, university programmes in fields such as science, engineering, and dentistry are often offered in English (Rugh, 2002; Abou-El-Kheir & MacLeod, 2017) and so entry into university is often conditioned on the knowledge of English. Social sciences and humanities courses are not typically delivered in English, however. This method of using both English and Arabic (as well as other regional languages) has been one of the ways through which the regional policymakers have sought to strike a balance between the necessity of English and the cultural duty of fostering national languages (Abou-El-Kheir & MacLeod, 2017).

Most Latin American countries also represent EFL contexts. In many of these, universities receive students who have poor knowledge of English, many of them at the level of near-beginners, despite having learned this language for years prior to applying for university (Harmer, 2017). Bearing this in mind, at many universities, students are offered EFL courses at the elementary level before attending the English language courses offered by the university's language centres (cf. Vazquez et al., 2013; Pérez, 2017). Typically, English features strongly across university curricula for undergraduates (cf. Vazquez et al., 2013) but it is not always compulsory (Cronquist & Fiszbein, 2017).

Many Latin American governments are investing significant efforts into remedying the deficiencies in the typically low attainment of English by their students, but the gaps remain (Cronquist & Fiszbein, 2017). Still, some results are already visible and the university entrants have been demonstrating somewhat better mastery in Chile, Colombia and Uruguay, Cronquist and Fiszbein (2017) show. However, these government efforts are mostly centred on K-12 education and most universities in Latin America remain autonomous in setting their own tertiary ELT policies as well as entry requirements in terms of foreign language knowledge. There are exceptions, however. For instance, Peru's 2016 university law prescribes a foreign language requirement for entry into undergraduate programmes and mentions a preference for English, while the Colombian national strategy prescribes that English should be mandatorily taught at all university study programmes (Cronquist & Fiszbein, 2017), similar to the Montenegrin tertiary policy that we are investigating in this chapter. In addition, Colombia and Ecuador have university exit exams which include testing English. In Ecuador, the prescribed exit level for public universities is lower intermediate (National English Curriculum Guidelines—Ecuador, 2013), much lower than the Montenegrin.

Generally, in many countries around the world, regardless of whether they have given English some type of an official status or not, English is encouraged as a medium of instruction in higher education, where all or some courses are offered in English and students are just expected to come to university with their knowledge of English at a functional level. In her survey covering 55 countries worldwide, Dearden (2014) determined that English as a medium of instruction (EMI) was in place in 22 countries (40%)—a significant share. This especially seems to be the case in the private sector and at high-ranking universities with competitive admissions.

EMI programmes generally do not provide English language instruction and support (Arnbjörnsdóttir & Prinz, 2017). It seems that universities offering these programmes generally believe EFL lessons will become extinct and language teachers will be substituted by the EMI lecturers teaching academic content in English, whereby their students will somehow learn English automatically (Dearden, 2018), solely through Content and Language Integrated Learning (CLIL). A number of studies (e.g. Byun et al., 2011; Hu & Lei, 2014) have reported that such practices are often problematic as students and even professors do not have the necessary English level and that resources needed to implement such programmes are lacking (Dearden, 2014). Thus, Dearden (2018) stressed that English language teachers are needed more than ever to be part of EMI programmes, offering support to both professors and students. This promotion of EMI and English, especially when justified as a *lingua franca* of higher education, can be double-edged, as Coleman (2006) warned, since such a spread of English may suppress or threaten minority languages.

ELT Policies at Tertiary Level in Europe

In Europe, policies and practices vary, but generally EMI is on the rise, not only in higher education, but in secondary and even in primary schools. Even though internationalisation cherishes multilingualism, in the EU, it "pervades the policy discourse of higher education," whereby instruction in English has contributed to the attractiveness of many EU universities and English has become the "academic *lingua franca*" (Doiz et al., 2011). European tertiary-level policies have been influenced by (a) the 1998 Sorbonne Joint Declaration envisaging "the creation of the European area of higher education as a key way to promote citizens' mobility and employability and the Continent's overall development" (1–2), and (b) the Bologna Agreement (1999), signed by 31 European Ministers of Education. At the heart of these agreements was the belief that language competence would increase "employability across national borders" and the learning of at least two foreign languages, other than English, would be strongly advocated (Räisänen & Fortanet-Gómez, 2008: 11).

Paradoxically, European legislative actions towards restructuring of national tertiary education systems have endangered EFL teaching and learning across the wider European area. As observed by Räisänen and Fortanet-Gomez (2008), "the prevalence of English in the global and European markets […], and the Bologna requisite of learning at least two other foreign languages apart from English […] result[ed] in more and more European universities shifting to English as the medium of instruction [but also] […] in reductions in the number of hours of English teaching offered to the students" (12). Facing the pressure to respond to different reform requirements and meet many criteria, higher-education policymakers in Europe have either reduced EFL teaching in favour of content subjects and teaching of other languages or warned stakeholders that funding will be reduced. In addition, presupposing that their students already have a reasonable command of general English, most European universities teach EFL as English for Specific Purposes (ESP), a decision that has fostered a reduction in teaching general English.

A number of European universities have resorted to integrating content and language teaching, and some optimistic results have been reported (Räisänen, 2004; Jacobs, 2006). However, this practice has been found fruitful in those countries—for example, Sweden or the Netherlands—in which general knowledge of English is exceptionally high across all strata of population, where English is more of a second than a foreign language. European universities deal with this issue in different ways, but scholars are mostly unanimous about the collaboration between content and language teaching as being vital to the future of language teaching and learning.

Still, we note that, despite efforts to find a one-size-fits-all solution, as proposed by the Bologna Agreement and similar ELT policy tendencies, the knowledge of English varies greatly across Europe, which is best reflected in the versatility of the university entry-level requirements, which range between as low as elementary to as high as advanced English. Hellekjaer (2006) warned that many European students are not proficient enough to study content subjects in English. Certainly, the varying entry levels make it considerably difficult to apply comparable ELT policies at tertiary level for those countries where English is still taught as a foreign language; furthermore, where the entry proficiency level of students, in practice, is intermediate at best, the reduction in general English teaching with a fast transition to ESP, and particularly to EMI, seems ill-advocated.

ELT Policy at Tertiary Level in Montenegro

According to census data, English is the most spoken foreign language by Montenegrins– 26% of those older than 15 years of age speak some level of English as a foreign language (*Strategy of the Education of Adults in Montenegro for the period 2015–2025*, 2014). This is far below the EU level, where, according to a Eurobarometer 386 Special, 2012 survey over a half of all Europeans (54%) can have a conversation in at least one foreign language, a quarter (25%) can speak two foreign languages and 10% can converse in three non-mother tongue languages. In addition, tests carried out among secondary school students in 14 EU countries showed that the "independent user levels B1 and B2 in any skill are achieved in English by about 50% of tested pupils" (European Commission, 2012a: 9). Montenegro has aspired to join the EU for two decades. Therefore, for reasons of internationalisation, fostering mobility and competitiveness in the international labour market, Montenegro has recently adopted many foreign language policies at various levels, which all prescribe EFL courses as mandatory in all grades of primary and secondary education, as well in higher education, and the introduction of EMI in all levels.

In 2014, Montenegro passed its new Higher Education Act, whose Article 80 reads as follows: "A higher education institution shall, within the curricula it organises, provide conditions for its students to learn a minimum of one foreign language at the upper advanced level." In addition, the *Strategy of Higher Education in Montenegro for the period 2016–2020*, also passed in 2014, prescribes that English—and not other foreign languages—shall be compulsory at universities, due to the "global presence of English" and the "availability of literature written in English." Moreover, this Strategy recommends introducing "as many EFL lessons as possible" into the university curricula, so that the students may speak at a C1 (advanced) or C2 (proficiency) level when they graduate. The Strategy was adopted by the then Ministry of Education of Montenegro. This authority has not commented on the said policy since its introduction.

For the purposes of accreditation renewal for 2017–2022, the University of Montenegro, where approximately 80% of the Montenegrin student population studies, in September 2017 introduced many new EFL courses whose syllabi were set at an advanced exit level. However, soon after introduction, new management allowed individual departments to reduce the number of English teaching hours as they see fit (as of September 2018). As a result, the number of English teaching hours varies per department; some have English for two semesters (typically 1.5 hours per week, totalling 45 hours), whereas some teach English for four semesters (90 to 120 hours in total).

Prior to implementation of this policy, the level of English was not prescribed by any documents: Teachers were, in practice, free to change the EFL syllabi at their discretion, adapting them unrestrictedly to the needs of their students, who were typically tested for level upon entry. Teachers were also free to choose whether to teach general English or ESP, which was typically reserved for more advanced groups.

Research Aims and Methodology

The aim of this chapter is to analyse how the tertiary ELT policy of setting the advanced English proficiency level as a graduation requirement (presented in the previous section of the chapter) has been received by some of the main stakeholders of this policy in Montenegro: tertiary content teachers, tertiary English language teachers, and tertiary students. In addition, we intend to analyse the results which have been achieved under this policy so far, as well as the problems with which its implementation has met.

In order to fulfil the stated aims of the study, in autumn 2018 we performed our study at the University of Montenegro, which is by far the largest university in Montenegro, as said earlier. This was one full year after the introduction of the said policy at this university. The study involved conducting semi-structured interviews and administering written questionnaires. In the interviews, the content teachers were asked several questions: what they thought about Article 80 of the Higher Education Act (i.e. the new policy), the number of EFL courses offered at the University so as to implement this provision, and whether they thought their students needed such good mastery of English. The questionnaires were administered to the university's EFL teachers and the students; they were similar in content and included the following open- and close-ended questions: what the stakeholders thought of Article 80 of the Higher Education Act, how they felt about this policy, whether they thought that fulfilling this legal provision was realistic, whether they were ready for implementing this policy, whether they thought that such good mastery of English was needed for the students, what they thought about the number of classes offered in connection with implementing the said policy, and whether they thought that the policy would be successfully implemented. The written questionnaires were disseminated electronically.

After presenting the main results of the data collected through the methods described above, we qualitatively analyse the problems in the implementation of the policy based on these results and on some previous findings from the literature.

The final subsection of the analysis is devoted to the results achieved by the first generation of students who graduated from their bachelor studies under the Montenegrin tertiary ELT policy which we are here examining. For this purpose, we tested their English levels in June 2020. A total of 130 students from four departments of the University of Montenegro was tested. The aim was to investigate how many students achieved the advanced level of English stipulated by the Montenegrin Law. The results were also compared to the English language entry-level results for this university, which were already available in the literature, in order to assess the progress attained under this tertiary ELT policy.

Results and Analysis

This part of the chapter presents the main findings of the semi-structured interviews and questionnaires conducted with the three stakeholders, as explained in the previous section. Additionally, we present the problems in implementing the said Montenegrin tertiary ELT policy in the period 2017–2020, as well as the results achieved after three years of its implementation (2020).

First Survey: The Opinion of Content Teachers

We first conducted semi-structured interviews with members of the non-philological teaching staff working at the university. A total of 30 professors teaching content courses participated.

The content teachers all thought that Article 80 of the Higher Education Act should be deleted from the Act and that tertiary institutions should be autonomous in setting their own ELT policies (100%). Regarding the introduction of the additional EFL lessons into the curricula, needed to implement the policy, the professors interviewed were largely dissatisfied (83.3%), most of them citing the consequent reduction of content subjects as the main reason. Some of them even expressed fear that their study programmes would begin to resemble philological studies, as there were, in their opinion, too many EFL courses. They all agreed (100%) their students needed an advanced knowledge of English, and most (86.6%) believed their students needed more EFL lessons; however, they also reported that these should be organised outside the curricula, as non-credit courses, or even outside the university (at private language centres).

Second Survey: The Opinion of EFL Teachers

We surveyed 26 EFL teachers out of a total of 39 teaching at the university. We used a written questionnaire, as explained earlier.

The 2014 Higher Education Act generated mixed feelings among tertiary EFL teachers, with all of them welcoming the fact that English was prescribed as mandatory in all types of studies and departments (100%). At the same time, all teachers voiced concerns regarding the level of English prescribed for all students. Few teachers (only 23.1%) were satisfied that their students' level of English was proficient enough to reach the advanced level before graduation and thought that they were ready for the implementation of the policy. In fact, two thirds of them (66.67%) felt pressured to assist students towards perceptibly an unrealistic prescribed level. The remainder, however, felt responsibility rests squarely with the policymakers. All of them doubted that the policy would be fully successful (100%).

Third Survey: The Opinion of Students

We surveyed 88 students from three non-philological departments of the University of Montenegro regarding their opinions of the policy setting an advanced exit level for all students.

The majority of the students (82.4%) thought that they should be proficient in English at graduation and that the policy could work. Most students (88.6% of the sample) also thought that at least three or four semesters of the EFL lessons were needed to reach this level, and even more (90.9%) felt that EFL courses should be part of their curriculum. Strikingly, regarding the degree they believed they would actually be proficient in English by the end of their bachelor studies, just over half (54.5%) said they would, approximately a third (38.6%) said they might, and the remaining 17.6% were sure they would not be. As the content and the EFL teachers, they all thought that such good knowledge of English was necessary for them (100%).

Problems in Implementing the Policy

According to the results of the semi-structured interviews, the policy was met with resistance from some stakeholders—mainly non-philological staff teaching content, who perceived the initial increase in EFL courses as unnecessary intrusion on their curricula. Simultaneously, the questionnaires with the EFL teachers showed that they felt increasingly pressured by sudden unrealistic demands. Certainly, a key problem is students' low university entry level of English, as some of them pointed out. Officially, Montenegrin secondary school leavers are believed to have an upper-intermediate proficiency level, and vocational secondary school leavers an intermediate knowledge of English, as attested by high-school leaving examinations (Examination Centre of Montenegro, n.d.). In practice, though, this is often not the case. As in many European countries, Montenegro's universities cannot perform additional entry testing and must rely on the school-leaving examinations (Wilkinson, 2008: 69).

With these phenomena in mind, Božović & Piletić (2020) tested the CEFR entry levels of 853 students entering three Montenegrin universities. Their results are presented in Fig. 11.1:

According to an assessment made by the Association of Language Testers of Europe (ALTE) (European Commission, 2012a, b), the number of teaching hours needed to reach each one of CEFR levels is as follows (the figures refer to the number of hours of formal, classroom teaching, and the additional learning hours are not included in the estimate):

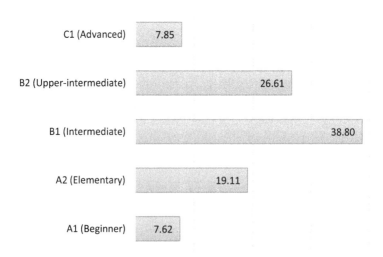

Fig. 11.1 Entry level of Montenegrin students (in %) (Božović & Piletić, 2020)

A1	90–100 hours
A2	180–200 hours
B1	350–400 hours
B2	500–600 hours
C1	700–800 hours

As can be seen, the ALTE found that some 200 teaching hours are generally necessary to progress from one level to another. However, various departments of the University of Montenegro teach English from 45 to 120 hours in total, which is what is needed to master a quarter to approximately half of one single level only. Based on Božović and Piletić's (2020) results and taking into account the number of teaching hours available, we can conclude that, apart from students having achieved the advanced level (7.85%), the C1 exit level is likely only attained by students who enter with a B2 level. In other words, for 65.5% of the students entering university, it is unrealistic that the C1 level can be reached.

As previously noted, to meet the newly levied legal requirements, the management opted initially to enlarge the number of the EFL lessons. In 2016, language experts were consulted (among them one of the authors of this chapter), who suggested that, based on the actual entry level of the students, English would have to be taught in every semester, as intensively as possible, at least four hours per week (360 hours) (Lakić et al., 2016). This, however, proved impossible to implement as doing so would require a substantial reduction in the number of content courses. The management, therefore, decided to take into account not the actual knowledge of English, but rather the level students are supposed to have upon completing secondary education—their rationale being that universities are not supposed to remedy the faults of other education system sectors. Thus, the number of lessons from the initial recommendation was reduced significantly, ultimately to between 45 and 120 hours, depending on the department (Bogojević et al., 2016).

Results Achieved So Far Under This Policy

The first generation of students studying under the reformed ELT system and the new legal framework graduated in June 2020. Student experiences operating under this framework were assessed. We tested 130 second- and third-year students from the departments of Biology, Mathematics, Physics, and Electrical Engineering, who completed all the English courses foreseen by their curricula. We used the same test as Božović and Piletić (2020) so we could compare our results with theirs. Results are revealed in Fig. 11.2. (A more comprehensive study—i.e. one including more departments—was not possible at the time, June 2020, due to COVID-19 circumstances.)

Results showed that 84.6% of the students from the four departments had an upper-intermediate or an advanced level; however, even after completing all the courses, 6.15% of the students still tested at the elementary level, whereas 9.23% were at the intermediate level. The results show a significant improvement in students' overall levels of English, likely as a consequence of the increase in number of EFL lessons in three of the four departments, as well as tougher assessment criteria, applied under the new Act.

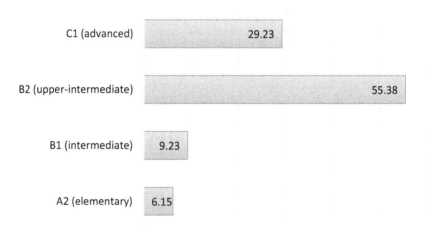

Fig. 11.2 Exit level of students from four departments of the University of Montenegro (in %)

In addition to proficiency-level statistics, we offer the following observations:

Prior to the ELT reform, English teachers were free to choose the levels and draft their own syllabi. Teaching was often adjusted to the weakest students. English courses varied in the levels (from elementary to advanced) across departments and even across generations within the same departments (Vuković-Stamatović et al., 2020). Highly proficient students were discouraged from attending EFL classes since they could pass all tests without much preparation and focus on content courses instead. Such a set up contributed to the perceived inferior status of EFL courses.

Under the new framework, EFL courses have become more uniform and standardised. Furthermore, the demand that *all* students reach proficiency has had serious side-effects. Both students and teachers report additional stress as the weakest students now struggle to keep up with the level of teaching. Both faculty are clearly disheartened that the target level set by the law will not be reached by a great number of students.

Discussion

A major issue with the European harmonisation directives is their imposition from the highest levels of authority (Räisänen & Fortanet-Gómez, 2008). This means that the main stakeholders—university staff and students—are typically excluded from the policymaking even though they are expected to implement policy (Johnston, 2003; Vazquez et al., 2013). Montenegro is no exception. Aspiring to reach the level of English equal to that in most advanced European economies, Montenegrin lawmakers have uncritically copied ELT policies from these countries, which assume the highest level of English but disregard both (a) the actual entry knowledge of its students and (b) their lack of resources. Moreover, Montenegro went one step further by legally prescribing the advanced exit knowledge of its graduates, which, to our knowledge, is *not* the case in any European country.

The EFL teachers we surveyed were satisfied that foreign language courses had become mandatory, but they were all sceptical about the level to be achieved by their students: they called it "unrealistic," "too demanding," "wishful thinking," "too ambitious" and "unfeasible," *inter alia*. Upon passing the Act, university EFL teachers were then asked to provide advice on the number of teaching hours needed to attain the required level. Ultimately, their guidelines were not followed, as the management found it unfeasible to have mandatory English courses every semester, particularly since the content teachers also opposed this idea.

Effectively, tertiary ELT teachers have neither participated in designing policy nor in devising its implementation. Based on our findings, we strongly recommendation that policymakers involve the practitioners who implement ELT policies in decision-making processes. As Ricento and Hornberger (1996) argue, educational change often begins with the grass roots and, even if not consulted, ELT practitioners should play a role in reaffirming or opposing a language policy.

On the basis of this study, useful guidelines for amending the Montenegrin ELT policy can also be recommended. First, all stakeholders agreed that all graduates should possess a good knowledge of English and that the EFL courses should be mandatory. Regarding the prescription of the exit level of English, all stakeholders were dubious. The Act assumes that all students should have the upper-advanced knowledge of English, which is, in practice, impossible. Indeed, the Act seems to have been drawn with limited consideration for classroom realities. Still, without prescribing a level, the danger is that many teachers, under pressure to both lower the criteria and indulge the students devoted to content courses, will teach towards lower proficiency levels. We therefore suggest prescribing the upper-intermediate and the advanced level as the levels at which English must be taught, without precisely defining the mandatory exit level for all students. In this way, students would be motivated to learn English intensively and the teachers would raise the bar, but without the pressure of graduating all students at an unrealistic milestone.

Conclusion

Although the evidence described here comes from one country—Montenegro—we believe its results and implications may be of interest to professionals in other countries. Prescribing mandatory foreign language courses and regulating the ELT tertiary policy at the level of a law may prove beneficial, judging by Montenegrin results: the knowledge of the students has increased, and tertiary ELT has gained more recognition. On the other hand, prescribing an extremely high exit level may not work in even a well-resourced country. Nevertheless, just as Jenkins' (2014) respondents indicated, we recommend that governments and ministries formalise and pass ELT tertiary policies; however, to reap the best results, we also recommend that tertiary ELT teachers be consulted when both passing and devising an implementation plan for such policies.

References

Abou-El-Kheir, A., & Macleod, P. (2017). English education policy in Bahrain–a review of K-12 and higher education language policy in Bahrain. In R. Kirkpatrick (Ed.), *English language education policy in the Middle East and North Africa* (pp. 9–32). Springer.

Aghagolzadeh, F., & Davari, H. (2017). English education in Iran: From ambivalent policies to paradoxical practices. In R. Kirkpatrick (Ed.), *English language education policy in the Middle East and North Africa* (pp. 47–62). Springer.

Aloreibi, A., & Carey, M. D. (2017). English language teaching in Libya after Gaddafi. In R. Kirkpatrick (Ed.), *English language education policy in the Middle East and North Africa* (pp. 93–114). Springer.

Arnbjörnsdóttir, B., & Prinz, P. (2017). From EFL to EMI: Developing writing skills for the humanities. *ESP Today-Journal of English for Specific Purposes at Tertiary Level, 5*(2), 172–195.

Barnawi, O. Z., & Al-Hawsawi, S. (2017). English education policy in Saudi Arabia: English language education policy in the Kingdom of Saudi Arabia: Current trends, issues and challenges. In R. Kirkpatrick (Ed.), *English language education policy in the Middle East and North Africa* (pp. 199–222). Springer.

Bianchi, R., & Razeq, A. H.-A. (2017). The English language teaching situation in Palestine. In R. Kirkpatrick (Ed.), *English language education policy in the Middle East and North Africa* (pp. 147–169). Springer.

Bogojević, D., Kostić, N., & Vuković-Stamatović, M. (2016). *Recommendations of the Representatives of the Faculty of Philology regarding Foreign-Language Teaching at Non-Philological Departments of the University of Montenegro.*

Bologna Declaration. (1999). Retrieved September 10, 2018: https://www.eurashe.eu/library/bologna_1999_bologna-declaration-pdf/

Božović, P., & Piletić, D. (2020). *Reforming Foreign languages in Academia in Montenegro: Status Quo analysis report.* Project Reflame.

Byun, K., et al. (2011). English-medium teaching in Korean higher education: Policy debates and reality. *Higher Education, 62*(4), 431–449.

Coleman, J. A. (2006). English-medium teaching in European higher education. *Language Teaching, 39*(1), 1–14.

Cronquist, K., & Fiszbein, A. (2017). *English language learning in Latin America.* The Dialogue.

Dearden, J. (2014). *English as a medium of instruction-a growing global phenomenon.* British Council.

Dearden, J. (2018). The changing roles of EMI academics and English language specialists. In Y. Kırkgöz & K. Dikilitaş (Eds.), *Key issues in English for specific purposes in higher education* (pp. 323–338). Springer.

Doiz, A., Lasagabaster, D., & Sierra, J. M. (2011). Internationalisation, multilingualism and English-medium instruction. *World Englishes, 30*(3), 345–359.

Eurobarometer 386 Special. (2012). *Europeans and their languages.* June. https://ec.europa.eu/commfrontoffice/publicopinion/archives/ebs/ebs_386_en.pdf

European Commission. (2012a). *First European survey on languages competences. Executive summary.* http://ec.europa.eu/languages/eslc/docs/executive-summary-eslc_en.pdf

European Commission. (2012b). *First European survey on languages competences. Final report.* http://ec.europa.eu/languages/eslc/docs/en/final-report-escl_en.pdf

Examination Centre of Montenegro. (n.d.). *Website of the Examination Centre of Montenegro.* Retrieved July 2022: https://iccg.co.me/

Fryer, L. K., et al. (2014). Instrumental reasons for studying in compulsory English courses: I didn't come to university to study English, so why should I? *Innovation in Language Learning and Teaching, 8*(3), 239–256.

Han, J., & Yin, H. (2016). College English curriculum reform in Mainland China: Contexts, contents and changes. *Asian Education Studies, 1*(1), 1–10.

Harmer, J. (2017). ELT realities in Latin America, and… um…: A modest proposal. In P. Davies (Ed.), *English language teaching in Latin America* (pp. 8–16). TESL-EJ Publications.

Hellekjaer, G. (2006). Screening criteria for English-medium programmes: A case study. In R. Wilkinson, V. Zegers, & C. van Leeuwen (Eds.), *Bridging the assessment gap in English-medium higher education* (pp. 43–60). AKS-Verlag.

Hu, G., & Lei, J. (2014). English-medium instruction in Chinese higher education: A case study. *Higher Education, 67*(5), 551–567.

Jacobs, C. (2006). Integrated assessment practices–when language and content lecturers collaborate. In *Bridging the assessment gap in English-medium higher education* (pp. 141–160). AKS Verlag.

Jenkins, J. (2014). *English as a Lingua Franca in the International University: The politics of academic English language policy*. Routledge/Taylor and Francis Group.

Johnston, B. (2003). *Values in English language teaching*. Lawrence Erlbaum Associates.

Kelsen, B. A., & Liang, L. H.-y. (2012). Indicators of achievement in EFL classes at a Taiwanese University. *Education Research International, 2012*, 1–8.

Kirkpatrick, R., & Barnawi, O. (2017). Introduction: English language education policy in MENA. In R. Kirkpatrick (Ed.), *English language education policy in the Middle East and North Africa* (pp. 1–8). Springer.

Lakić, I., Kostić, N., Vuković-Stamatović, M., Andrić, N., & Špadijer, S. (2016). *Report of the Working Group on Foreign language teaching at Non-Philological Departments of the University of Montenegro*.

Lauridsen, K. M. (2013). Higher education language policy. Working Group under the European language council. *European Journal of Language Policy, 51*(1), 128–138.

Le van Canh. (2017). English language education in Vietnamese universities: National benchmarking in practice. In E. S. Park & B. Spolsky (Eds.), *English education at the tertiary level in Asia: From policy to practice* (pp. 183–202). Taylor & Francis.

Lee Hee-Kyung. (2017). Heading toward the global standardization of English education in Korean universities: A case study of an English program in a Korean University. In *English education at the tertiary level in Asia* (pp. 84–108). Routledge.

Li, X. (2017). ELT at tertiary institutions in China: A developmental perspective. In *English education at the tertiary level in Asia* (pp. 6–45). Routledge.

Li, J. (2018). *An evaluation of pragmatic elements in university EFL textbooks in China*. Master thesis, University of Liverpool.
National English Curriculum Guidelines. (2013). *Ecuador: Ministerio de Educacion*. Retrieved on June 6, 2022: https://educacion.gob.ec/wp-content/uploads/downloads/2013/04/Curriculum_Guidelines-EFL-1.pdf
Nguyen, H. T., Fehring, H., & Warren, W. (2015). EFL teaching and learning at a Vietnamese University: What do teachers say? *English Language Teaching, 8*(1), 31–43.
Park, E. S. (2017). Introduction English education at the tertiary level in Asia. In E. S. Park & B. Spolsky (Eds.), *English education at the tertiary level in Asia: From policy to practice* (pp. 1–5). Taylor & Francis.
Pérez, C. (2017). ELT in a Mexican university's language centres. In P. Davies (Ed.), *English language teaching in Latin America* (pp. 74–78). TESL-EJ-Publications.
Raisanen, C. (2004). Multiple literacies for the "new" engineer: Learning to learn. In *Integrating content and language: Meeting the challenges of a multilingual higher education* (pp. 264–274).
Räisänen, C., & Fortanet-Gómez, I. (2008). The state of ESP teaching and learning in Western European higher education after Bologna. In *ESP in European higher education: Integrating language and content* (Vol. 4, pp. 11–51).
Ramos García, A. M., & Pavón Vázquez, V. (2018). The linguistic internationalization of higher education: A study on the presence of language policies and bilingual studies in Spanish universities. *Porta Linguarum, Monográfico, III*, 31–46.
Rao, Z., & Lei, C. (2014). Teaching English as a foreign language in Chinese universities: The present and future: An appropriate way to teach English in China is to balance teaching activities for elaborating linguistic details and developing students' communicative competence. *English Today, 30*(4), 40–45.
Ricento, T. K., & Hornberger, N. H. (1996). Unpeeling the onion: Language planning and policy and the ELT professional. *TESOL Quarterly, 30*(3), 401–427.
Rugh, W. A. (2002). Arab education: Tradition, growth, and reform. *The Middle East Journal, 56*(3), 396–414.
Sanpatchayapong, U. (2017). Development of tertiary English education in Thailand. In *English education at the tertiary level in Asia* (pp. 168–182). Routledge.

Sorbonne Joint Declaration. (1998). Retrieved January 17, 2020 from http://ehea.info/media.ehea.info/file/1998_Sorbonne/61/2/1998_Sorbonne_Declaration_English_552612.pdf

Strategy of Higher Education in Montenegro for the period 2016–2020. (2014). Government of Montenegro. Retrieved on September 10, 2018: http://www.mps.gov.me/ResourceManager/FileDownload.aspx?rid=244534&rType=2&file=Strategija%20razvoja%20visokog%20obrazovanja%20u%20Crnoj%20Gori%202016-2020.doc

Strategy of the Education of Adults in Montenegro for the period 2015–2025. (2014). Government of Montenegro. Retrieved on September 10, 2018: http://www.mps.gov.me/ResourceManager/FileDownload.aspx?rId=177228&rType=2

Terauchi, H. (2017). English education at universities in Japan: An overview and some current trends. In *English education at the tertiary level in Asia* (pp. 65–83). Routledge.

Timina, S. A., & Butler, N. L. (2011). *Uncomfortable topics and their appropriateness in Asian EFL classes*. Retrieved from ERIC Database (ED515120).

Vazquez, A. M., Guzmán, N. P. T., & Roux, R. (2013). Can ELT in higher education be successful? The current status of ELT in Mexico. *TESL-EJ, 17*(1), 1–26.

Vuković-Stamatović, M., Živković, B., Piletić, D., Bratić, V., & Božović, P. (2020). *Foreign language syllabi assessment*. Reflame Project. Retrieved in July, 2022: https://www.reflame.ucg.ac.me/dokumenta/FL_syllabi_assessment.pdf

Wilkinson, R. (2008). Locating the ESP space in problem-based learning. In *ESP in European higher education* (pp. 55–74).

Zhao, Z. (2012). EFL teaching and reform in China's tertiary education. *Journal of Language Teaching & Research, 3*(6), 1105–1113.

12

Assessing Teachers' Perceptions of Relevant ELT Policies in Cameroon

Eric Enongene Ekembe

Introduction

The effective teaching of foreign languages is a sine qua non for breeding a culture in the increasingly diverse global village. Linguistic and cultural diversity is representative of the difficulties practitioners and policy makers have to deal with (Power, 2005). Many countries conceive of English Language policies as a way of keeping pace with the global economy, given the dominant global influence of English. In English as a medium of instruction (EMI) and specifically in English as a foreign language (EFL) contexts, cultural distinctiveness imposes various kinds of policy challenges to effective teaching of English given the relationship between English Language proficiency, access to knowledge, and economic empowerment (Milligan & Tikly, 2016). Throughout the world, there are few instances of successes and more instances of failures in the implementation of EFL policies in middle and lower income contexts

E. E. Ekembe (✉)
Higher Teacher Training College (ENS), Université de Yaoundé I, Yaounde, Cameroon

(Schweisfurth, 2013), with the failures mostly associated with lack of robust teaching procedures, analogue/traditional classroom settings, inattention to exams in policy formation, mismatch between policy requirements and the reality of various contexts. Studies examining the policy-practice link generally blame this on the neglect of teachers in policy design and posit the centrality of teacher agency from the conceptual to the implementation phases of any ELT policy reforms (Murray & Christison, 2012). They equally hold that sensitivity to contextual factors is central to the success of any innovations (Schweisfurth, 2011, 2013; Hayes, 2012; Gil, 2016). There has been a constant demand for contextually rooted methodologies and policies (Tomlinson, 2005; Shamin et al., 2007, Smith, 2011), and the argument has been to have practising teachers at the centre of any innovation process. It is, however, yet to be fully demonstrated how teachers' centrality in ELT policy innovation process can result in context-specific and implementable policies. Accordingly, this chapter seeks to investigate what Cameroonian teachers would consider appropriate ELT policy, drawing on their understanding of their work contexts. It also hopes to assess the relevance of policy recommendations in the light of commonly stated work constraints in Cameroon as in other low-resourced contexts. It begins by reviewing major concerns regarding ELT policies and moves on to describe the methods of the study and consequent findings.

Key Issues in English Language Education Policy Innovation

This section examines topical issues in policy design and implementation across different contexts. The idea is to assess the arguments advanced for ELT policy successes and failures in both high-and low-resource contexts and equally examine issues that complicate the adoption and implementation of new policies in local teaching contexts and how any such complications correlate with teachers' understandings of what they consider to be relevant policies.

Transportation

The tendency has been for ELT policies to be drawn up by people who have limited understanding of current classroom realities, and for the major agents of change—teachers—to be frequently left to implement the policies, whether or not they are appropriate. Given the inattention paid to teachers in the decision-making process (Bolitho, 2012), implementation tends to be fraught with resistance, either on grounds of inadaptability of the policies to local constraints or as a result of misunderstanding of how the policies work. Any assessment of inadaptable policies and misunderstandings of their requirements and scope, can be directly obtained from the feedback provided by grassroots implementers- teachers. In most cases in developing countries, policy innovations unfortunately do not emanate from baseline research. They are most often borrowed from other contexts where they have worked well. This, in particular, has led to a naïve belief among many policy makers and practitioners that policies and practices designed in one context can be unproblematically transported elsewhere (Hayes, 2012). One challenge is to implement policy and create a match between teachers' aspirations and the context in which they live and work, even if this means that the policy may have to change the context in some way (Kennedy, 2011). In some cases, resistance to the policies can be understood in two ways: (1) teachers resist policies that they know will not work, most often on the grounds that they (teachers) have a better understanding of what works well in their own contexts; (2) their common sense resistance to unworkable policies is interpreted as simple conservatism. So policy makers persist, assuming that greater force will eventually bring about the positive changes they seek.

Beliefs

Teachers' understanding and beliefs about teaching and learning can affect their abilities to adopt innovative approaches to instruction (Murray & Christison, 2012). Gil (2016) discusses resistance to

Computer Assisted Learning (CAL) in China by teachers who think it requires time and effort to develop courses. He equally cites lack of training and/or confidence in using computer technology to teach English and 'commonly held student and teacher beliefs which favour more traditional methods of teaching'. A stronger correlation between attitudes to perceived behavioural control (PBC) (Ajzen, 2006) and teachers' intentions to use technology in education was identified by Teo et al. (2016) from a sample of 592 primary and secondary schools teachers. The study measured their interest in the use of technology in teaching and learning in Singapore and found a negative impact of subjective norm, suggesting that regardless of the reasons for which teachers might have been asked to use technology, they would not find it useful. This is not very different from Lee et al.'s (2010) survey of secondary school teachers in Korea in which attitudes and beliefs were noted to have a stronger correlation with teachers' intentions to adopt computer technology in designing and delivering lessons than the other variables. Identifying pathways to successful implementation of innovations, Carless (2013) advocates the frontlining of teachers at an early stage and the perceived need to give them more than a token sense of belonging and ownership. He notes: 'these teachers may act as brokers, "champions" or opinion leaders' (p. 3).

With the aim of institutionalising preventive measures towards the risk of developing psychosis in 16+ educational institutions in 12 counties in Cambridgeshire, Path Analysis from a sample of 75 teachers showed that perceived behavioural control was noted to be the most significant predictor of intentions in teachers' beliefs and motivation for them to be engaged in detecting high risk of developing psychosis in school (Russo et al., 2015; see also Godin et al., 1992).

Training and Continuing Professional Development (CPD)

Generally, categories such as continuous support in the process of reforms power and leadership in managing innovation, constraints of local contexts, attention to examinations, and grassroots stakeholders' involvements in decision-making are integral to the process of ELT policy reforms (Bolitho, 2012). Researchers in this domain commonly argue for the consideration of these factors in policy innovation (Schweisfurth, 2011, 2013; Hayes, 2012; and Gil, 2016, for example). In fact, the best policies and practices will only be effective if teachers are the agents of implementation (Murray & Christison, 2012). The successful implementation of any policy reforms is linked significantly to practitioners' ability to translate it into concrete action in the classroom and this has a very high correlation with the type of support, motivation, and training they receive in the process. This translates directly into their assessments and appreciation of what is considered relevant. The MEXT Action Plan in Japan is reported to have failed due to a severe lack of pre-and in-service teacher training. Teachers depended more on their previous school learning experiences as a basis for their practice, contrary to the expectations of the Course of Study Guidelines innovation (Kikuchi & Browne, 2009). Canh (2015) reports the case of Vietnam where, in spite of a funded CPD initiative run by government officials, there was little evidence of improved practice and proficiency of teachers. Policy reformers generally believe that one or two instances of professional development activities in the policy reform in question will facilitate understanding and implementation. Certain behaviours are reported to pose difficulties with regard to execution (Siragussa & Dixon, 2009). A measure of PBC can serve as a proxy for actual control and as such contribute to the prediction of the behaviour in question. Many studies have demonstrated a higher predictive power of PBC over intentions (Siragussa, 2011; Armitage et al, 2004 cited in Knabe, 2012).

Willingness to Adopt/Change Policy

Whereas the greater majority of studies identify PBC as the highest predictor of intention, a good number of studies have also identified subjective norms to be a key determinant of intentions. A meta-analysis of 27 primary studies by Schulze and Wittmann (2003) demonstrated a non-significant value of PBC in predicting intention. Subjective norms predicted intentions more than PBC in faculty's interest in teaching public relations online (Knabe, 2012), a finding supported by Yan and Sin (2014), although the latter also found a high predictive value for PBC in teachers' intentions to practise inclusive education, but not as much as subjective norms. While the majority of studies limit agency in the innovation process to teachers, an account of how the whole context of teaching/learning can determine the appropriateness of policies is provided by Vavrus (2009). She reports teachers' resistance to learner-centred education policy that also met with resistance from the learners in Tanzania and advocates educational policy reform that can include an experiential component for those responsible for its formulation, implementation, and evaluation.

Teachers' Opinions in Policy Innovation

A good policy is one that takes into account the opinion of teachers and is based on a sustainable notion of change (Bolitho, 2012), and given inattention to this, patterns of classroom interaction and students' achievement have experienced no change as a result of innovations in policy (Hayes, 2012). Hayes (p. 59) warns that no matter how sound an innovation might be theoretically, if it does not secure the wholehearted support of the people who have to implement it, the chances of successful implementation tend to be very limited. Teachers' understanding of the values and conceptual framework of any reforms are intensely related to their engagement in implementing the reform. In such a situation, explicit theoretical and empirical explanation of the reform, which is too often neglected, (Russo et al., 2015) serves as a prerequisite for teacher commitment in the implementation process. There is very little research to demonstrate how teachers' teaching methodologies change as a result of their engagement in policy reform, and to claim a straight-forward correlation may seem too hasty a conclusion. This is termed 'hasty' because it has been suggested that teachers' previous school culture has a strong influence on their methodology (Vavrus, 2009).

Context of the Study

This study was carried out in the Cameroonian EFL context. It is important to review how English became part of the Cameroonian educational system. The British-French colonisation of Cameroon led to the adoption of English and French as the country's official languages in 1972 (Simo Bobda, 1992, 1994; Mbangwana, 1989; Kouega, 1991, 2002). Since its introduction in Cameroon in 1972, the development of English, in terms of use collocates with historical trends (see Mbassi Manga, 1976), and it became popular as a language of communication during the French/British colonial administration. Between 1961 and 1972 English became the official language of Cameroon alongside French, with its use restricted to the former West Cameroon (Simo Bobda 1992, p. 46). With the proclamation of the unitary state in 1972, English in Cameroon was given a new impetus both in terms of status and function. It could be used everywhere in Cameroon depending on circumstances and the competence of its users.

As a long-standing tradition, English is learned as a foreign language (EFL) in eight of the ten regions of Cameroon. While it is learned as a second language (ESL) in the two anglophone regions, it is equally learned as a second language in some of the regions, which traditionally were believed to be fundamentally French-speaking. French serves as a lingua franca in the francophone zone whereas English is used mostly in specific domains such as education, administration, diplomacy, and politics. It is an obligatory school requirement with a weekly teaching contact time of three hours and assessed in all certification examinations. Due to the economic crisis that hit the country in the mid-1980s and increased awareness of its significance in global education, business, and politics, English has attracted a lot of attention from the overwhelmingly francophone population (Simo Bobda, 2001), leading to an extremely high demand for the language. This makes it difficult to identify a clear dichotomy between the terms 'anglophone' and 'francophone' in the country or between 'ESL' and 'EFL', an issue well handled by Anchimbe (2006).

English Language learning in Cameroon is steered by the government's efforts to promote and consolidate the French-Engish bi-cultural status of the country. This is enshrined in section 1.1.3 of the 1996 version of the Cameroon Constitution, which recognises English and French as the official languages of Cameroon, 'both having the same status'. The Constitution asserts that 'the state shall guarantee the promotion of bilingualism throughout the country'. This is implemented through mainstream schools and pilot language centres traditionally created through presidential decrees to upgrade the language competences of state employees. In spite of the seemingly strong political will of the government, Wolf (2001) remains critical of its design, since the policy was historically and politically motivated. He cites Chumbow's (1980, p. 288) critique of a language policy that was not the result of careful planning based on detailed study of a wide range of socio-economic and political variables relevant to the state's development needs. To advance government's policy to increase the use of English, the Ministries of Secondary and Basic Education (MoE) have made significant curricula reforms over the last two decades. Unfortunately, Kuchah (2016) observes that unfortunately, the policies are driven by a political agenda with no sensitivity to local realities. Consequently, implementation tends to be met with either resistance or misapplication.

What have we learnt from the literature?

Meaning made from the literature on policy innovation can be summarised into five key statements:

1. Transported/imported policies are likely to meet resistance because of local constraints and teachers are the most appropriate people to appreciate the relationship between new policies and local realities, as they are in direct contact with the local pedagogical context and are the ones to implement the policies.
2. Teachers' attitudes and beliefs towards policies are influenced by their perceived behavioural control over the policies, and this is reciprocally linked with their involvement in the policy at the conceptual phase of the policies.
3. Policy implementation significantly correlates with teachers' professional abilities to translate the policies into practice, and this is based on the quality of training and support they receive during practice.

4. In translating policy into concrete action, there is an interface between subjective norms and perceived behavioural control over the policies in question and both are culturally constructed in the broader pedagogical context.
5. Teachers' opinions are cardinal in policy innovation and successful implementation of policies depends on the wholehearted support of teachers.

Methods

Given the need to probe understandings and beliefs about the functionality of ELT policies vis-à-vis local realities, this chapter was designed to be primarily qualitative. Teachers' perception of a policy is deeply rooted in their interaction between the curriculum and teaching/learning environments. Deriving from the diverse nature of their experiences and perspectives in their local educational contexts, the approach in this study was to seek interpretations on what characterises their understandings of relevant policies. This is consistent with previous approaches that posit the need to investigate people's conception of their experiences (Stolz, 2020; Tantawy, 2020). In keeping with this, 113 practising English language teachers with between 3 and 30 years' teaching experience, randomly sampled from four secondary schools in Cameroon, were required to freely share their opinions on policy reforms they would make in order to teach effectively if they were in decision-making positions. This was intended as a non-formal interaction to avoid self-conscious responses designed to make an impression on a public audience. Some were members of the Cameroon English Language Teachers' Association (CAMELTA) while others did not belong to any formal groups. Their opinions were obtained through WhatsApp and face-to-face interaction over a period of two weeks and their responses were coded following recurrently stated themes and assigned the code TR to signify 'teacher's response'. 'Recurrent' themes were those that were stated at least three times in either a participant's opinion or in many responses from different participants. These were derived through a categorisation of their descriptions, an approach that aligns with phenomenographic research

(Marton, 1986; Stolz, 2020). The themes proposed were not directly linked to the number of participants, as each participant's response could be lengthy enough to contain many ideas that could be associated with multiple themes. They were edited for typos, classified under different categories, and given a quantitative appraisal to be able to appreciate high-frequency suggestions from the teachers. From the coding, the issues raised by the teachers ranged from raising learners' awareness of the importance of English to teachers' responsibilities; from curriculum reforms and human capital, to professional development.

Raising the Value of English to Learners

It has been suggested that the perceived value learners associate with a language influences their attitudes towards that language. However, it has not yet been clearly proven that learners' engagement in the classroom is the result of the perceived value they associate with the language or teachers' pedagogic ability to manipulate their interest in the language. As reported in Kuchah and Smith (2011, p. 127) Kuchah's students' change of attitude towards English as well as their more constant interaction in English around the school…' were more associated with practice and not the least with the credit weight given to English. As the government attempts to create awareness of the importance of English in Cameroon, greater credit weight is given to the subject. Comparatively, English is one of the subjects with the highest credit weight in Arts subjects in high school, and this has not yet been reported to have changed students' attitudes towards a language described by learners as 'God-given' language, meaning it can only be learned through God's intervention. Yet, teachers sampled in the study made the following suggestions:

[TR 1] *I think if I were the Minister of secondary education, I will lay more emphasis on English language teaching in the francophone subsystem of education*
[TR 2] *By giving more value to the language in terms of advantages and opportunities they can have through the mastering of the language*
[TR3] *I will increase the time and period allocated for English language*

[TR4] *If I were the minister of secondary education, I would emphasise on sensitising learners on the importance and advantages of learning English and the advantages both at the academic, professional, and job level*

[TR5] *I'd adopt policies like making English obligatory in all classes especially at the francophone section; more so, I'd give English the highest coefficient for both sciences and art classes and finally I'd set an elimination mark (5/20) in this subject with the hope of boosting especially francophones to learn English*

[TR6] *Increase the coefficient of English language to ensure seriousness of students*

The opinions above fall into two categories: vague and specific responses. Opinions such as 'laying emphasis' [TR1], 'giving more value to language in terms of advantages and opportunities' [TR2], and 'emphasise and sensitise learners on the importance of English' [TR4] lack pragmatic focus and may not properly typify the context in question. However, they raise issues that affect learners' motivation. Whether raising learners' motivation is the direct job of the policy maker or teacher is a different question. The rest of the responses have direct resonance with practice. For example, increasing the number of hours allocated for English and adding the credit weight demonstrate teachers' understandings of inadequacies in existing policies, probably weighed against practical classroom experience. It was surprising to find suggestions regarding 'making it an obligatory subject' in school curriculum, given that exiting policies require it to be learnt as an obligatory school subject. While this is generally essential in raising the motivational scales of learners, it still remains hypothetical claiming their incidence on improved classroom practice and learners' attitudes towards English in Cameroon. In a recent study, Ekembe (2021) noticed high negative student attitudes towards English, contradicting the general claim about the high quest for English in Cameroon. Learners in urban areas with increased access to new technologies are likely to have a better understanding of the value of English than those in rural communities. Even with this, their attitudes towards English are more likely to be associated with their personal life goals than with the credit weight or policy provisions.

Teacher Responsibility

The responses coded as 'teachers' responsibilities' are related to what any teacher would do in the classroom. This constitutes responses associated with policy requirements by the teachers sampled, which we judged to be the teachers' responsibilities in the language classroom. They include raising students' awareness of the value/importance of English, classroom management, learning activities, in-class assessment, models of teaching and so on. These were found to be high-frequency concerns that featured far more than any other. Characteristic features of their suggestions included the following:

[TR 6] *Making them feel it important and part of them and not only a subject to be validated*
[TR 7] *I will implement the cooperative learning Method which encourages group work*
[TR 8] *I will increase peer work*
[TR 9] *Encourage translanguaging in the teaching of foreign learners*
[TR 10] *The method of assessment, and the different stages of a lesson*
[TR 11] *Include lessons that involve real-life situations. more practice than lectures related to their students' daily activities*
[TR 12] *The teaching outcome or objective should be what the students can do with knowledge acquired*
[TR 13] *If it's a first, I would strongly recommend the use of a bilingual game in classes to reinforce learning, promote a communicative approach of learning which entails linguistic aspects and pragmatic aspects with competency, promote e-learning and enhance a more efficient network system*
[TR 14] *Focus on language as a means of communication and the status of a subject in school it seems to have*
[TR 15] *Role playing, simulation, brainstorming, interview, storytelling, debate can do*
[TR 16] *I would want to ensure that speaking is done intensely just like the other sections reading, listening, and writing.*

[TR 17] *I will include language workshops in the school program. This will enable students to give out practically what they have been learning theoretically in a classroom context*

[TR18] *First of all I think the programmes and the syllabi are to be designed in such a way that students learn English instead of studying it.*

[TR19] *Liberalise methodology*

[TR20] *My method prescription will be: do what works for you systematically; teachers are so creative and are better placed to know what works for them.*

'Liberalising teaching methodology', as suggested by one participant, is eclecticism in the classroom, of which every trained teacher is aware. Many other concerns raised demonstrate teachers' meta-knowledge of basic learner-centred classroom activities and procedures such as using language workshops, role play, simulation, cooperative learning, peer work, which they claim should have been policy provision. Their association of classroom activities with policy constraints can be associated with their inability to use the activities in the classroom. This interrogates the issues of teacher quality and professional development ranked the least in participant's suggestions. Teachers are most likely not to see themselves as part of failures in the classroom and they are usually tempted to associated failures with either administrative or policy constraints. There are two possible explanations for the prominence of this reaction: teachers either do not understand the extent of their responsibilities in the classroom or lack basic understanding of practical classroom procedures. Such lack of procedural awareness can partly be blamed for the kind of top-down control from administrative school management observed by Kuchah and Smith (2011, p. 127). They noted that Kuchah taught in the Cameroonian context 'where administrative decisions override pedagogic reality to depart from what is believed to be the traditional way of doing things'. On the other hand, inability to practically handle local constraints in the classroom was unusually associated with policy constraints by the respondents in this study.

Curriculum Reforms

Varied opinions were provided by teachers regarding areas of innovations in the ELT curriculum. These included materials development, teaching approach, learners' proficiencies, managing work progress, and the introduction of ICT.

[TR21] *Design a syllabus that reflects local realities*
[TR22] *The course books in remote areas especially in francophone schools should be different given that their contact with English is difficult*
[TR23] *Replace competency-based approach with the traditional approach in ESL contexts*
[TR24] *Harmonise textbooks, syllabuses, and schemes in relation to levels and specialisations and make sure the right institutions remain faithful to respective programmes*
[TR25] *I will improve on the syllabus (scheme of work)*
[TR26] *I will include a speaking test at exams*
[TR27] *Focusing on performance rather than syllabus coverage*
[TR28] *I will encourage online learning for now and try to make it accessible to all*
[TR29] *One class per week for drills in a language laboratory*
[TR30] *I will love us to make our own curricular by using books written about us, environment, and our wellbeing to be used in nursery and primary schools*
[TR31] *I will love French and English to be used in teaching all subjects in nursery and primary schools*
[TR32] *I will create schools where bilingual teachers that are to teach these students are trained*
[TR33] *I will create schools for specialty learning, that means as of form three I child should focus only what he is interested in making them self-independent than focusing on many things without having a focus*
[TR34] *Introduction of oral evaluation in official exams. This would make learners more serious in speaking activities*
[TR35] *Expansion of the Special Bilingual Education Programme (SBEP) to all students in secondary schools, not only a few selected ones*

Although a few of the issues raised by the teachers were not very specific, there is sufficient evidence attesting that teachers feel a great need to be involved in designing their syllabuses, and textbooks, and to take part in important decisions regarding teaching approaches. Their interest in learners' output ranges from raising students' attention to English in class work, assessing speaking in the official exam, to expanding the English immersion scheme. The need to be involved in curriculum and materials development suggest to learners' needs that existing materials and programmes may seem irrelevant or non-responsive Curiously, teachers' desire to shift from the competency-based approach to structuralism does not correlate with current thinking in language learning in the Expanding Circle. As studies in perceived behavioural control have suggested, teachers are likely to be committed to policy implementation when they have been involved in policy design. It is, however, not yet proven whether such commitment can be translated into change of practice (Le, 2015). However engaged a teacher is in the process of policy innovation, learners' output is more affected by direct classroom practice than with the adoption of policy, regardless of whether or not the procedures are relevant.

Human Capital Resources and CPD

If teachers are to comfortably manage their learners and learning, they must be trained in keeping with current ELT methodologies. This lies at the heart of classroom practices and it was a very crucial aspect as reflected in the quantity of suggestions on training. Respondents thought as follows about training and CPD.

[TR36] *The constant evaluation of ELT teachers*
[TR37] *Teachers of ELT be constantly trained*
[TR38] *Constant recycling of English teachers through numerous in-service trainings*
[TR39] *Regular training of English teachers on the effective use of ICTs in teaching*

[TR40] *Make it a policy to provide human, material, and other resources in ELT*
[TR41] *Start with getting more teachers*
[TR42] *I think I will ensure that only trained English teachers teach the subject because it seems people are mistaking origin with professionalism*

The majority of the teachers sampled were members of CAMELTA who were actively involved in professional development activities. The suggestions made were specific at the level of using ICTs and the other suggestions were mostly generalisations about training. No other specifications were made on training that could be associated with the realities of their work contexts. Constant evaluation, recycling, and training of teachers is general government policy that transcends all professions and is not restricted to ELT. It is not clear whether teachers sampled were unaware of the challenges of their contexts described in the literature as 'difficult' or they had mastered what it takes to teach in such circumstances. Unfortunately, this did not receive as much attention from the teachers as might be supposed from the challenges of their contexts. Quality training and availability of resources have generally been documented to be in disproportion with the reality of ELT learning across contexts (Kuchah & Smith, 2011). This partly explains why classes in the global South are described as large, containing low proficiency teachers/learners, and the context referred to as low-resource. Availability of learning resources provides opportunities for teachers to diversify practice and create more interesting learning activities in the language classroom. Mindful of this, whatever is conceived to be (low) resource is concomitantly related to the teacher's perception and appreciation of relevant resources for classroom activities. For example, a significant proportion of Cameroonian teachers would require well-equipped classrooms for effective teaching when they are unable to access available local infrastructure in the classroom as practical resources for teaching aspects of the language. The limited number of suggestions in this area does not reflect the extent to which the paucity of resources in the context is globally stated in discourse about ELT.

The Relevance of Teachers' Opinions in Policy Innovation

The majority of the suggestions made by teachers emphasised curriculum reforms, with a lot more recommending matching the syllabus with the reality of the context. It is difficult, thus far, to concretely determine whether or not the teachers sampled have an in-depth understanding of the workings of their contexts and how/when these affect classroom procedures. Of the commonly stated local classroom challenges expressed by Cameroonian teachers (see Ekembe, 2016, Ekembe & Fonjong, 2018), only learner motivation was stated as an area requiring policy reforms in this study. Even so, the suggestions made were rather associated with teachers' classroom responsibilities that had very little to do with policy requirements. Raising learners' awareness of the importance of English is implicitly contained in the credit weight given to English and there is no evidence that poor attitudes towards English are the result of government inattention to its value. The issues of large classes, limited material resources, low proficiencies, lack of textbooks that have commonly been cited as characteristic features of 'difficult' circumstances were not any of the concerns expressed by teachers in the study. It could either be that West's (1960) (supported by Kuchah, 2008; Maley, 2001; and Smith, 2011) definition of the 'difficulty' of the circumstances in the South does not resonate with teachers' understandings of their working environment or that what is conceived of as 'difficult' is mainly their inability to adapt their Northern ELT experience to the workings of the teaching ecologies in the South. A major issue noticed in teachers' opinions was the high number of suggestions on policy reforms related to teachers' responsibilities in the classroom. Their numerical strength vis-à-vis other suggestions begs one major question: How competent would teachers be in making concrete policy recommendations? Where they associate basic classroom procedures with policy limitations suggests their inability to define the scope of their work within their work environment.

The second highest number of suggestions made were associated with curriculum reforms to ensure equity in learning. The rural-urban divide is seen as a major constraint in the implementation of policy. This raises issues of inequality. The teachers' suggestions for the provision of professional development opportunities was the least in terms of frequency of ideas and, curiously, all the teachers (at the time of this study) had just experienced the challenges imposed by Covid19, irrespective of the fact that no policy recommendation was made in the light of this. Putting together the inattention to the supposed difficulty of their work environment with the critical Covid19 situation, it is important to further investigate at what point teachers would demonstrate mastery of their work environment and how to address the constraints in policy reforms where they have the opportunity. Curriculum innovation recorded the second highest area of concern. There is no evidence in the data collected to give a clue to teachers' potentials to address their work constraints with curriculum provisions, given that they failed to demonstrate consciousness of the very issues that impose constraints on them in the classroom. The extent to which teachers can be resourceful in policy innovation processes where they are given the chance remains critically problematic.

The Link Between the Suggestions

Having made sense from the types of suggestions, it was deemed necessary to examine the relation between the suggestions. One approach was to examine the types the suggestions to find out dominant types. To realise this, different types of suggestions related to the various themes were extracted from the responses and counted and the percentage for each theme worked out from the total number of suggestions retained. A total of 457 suggestions occurred more than three times, ranked below from the highest to the lowest (Table 12.1).

Table 12.1 Frequency of suggestions according to themes

Theme	Number of occurrence	%
Curriculum reforms	162	35.45
Raising the value of English	114	24.95
Teacher responsibility	103	22.54
Human capital resources and PD	78	17.07
Total number of suggestions	457	100

This major relationship between the themes in found in the frequency of occurrence of responses related to the various themes. It is difficult to ascertain whether the frequency of the types of suggestion is consistent with perceived local needs. However, the frequency here highlights common issues with language education concerns prevalent in various contexts as is found in all the chapters in this volume. Policy reforms is a matter of general concern in most of the countries that have adopted the English language education trend. The illogical transportation of curriculum reforms is common across the globe. Whether or not the participants in this study think better curriculum reforms will make them better teachers who can raise student achievement is assessed here to be critically hypothetical. Another pointer to a global phenomenon in the literature is teachers' attitudes towards CPD. Stories of lack of interest in CPD are common across the globe. This probably explains why the participants in this study were least concerned with innovations regarding CPD. In any case, it is necessary to knowledge the responses proposed by the participants.

Conclusion

Research on ELT policy innovation and implementation has demonstrated a serious disconnect between the two and the tendency has been to blame this disconnection on the neglect of teachers during policy conception. This is supported by findings from studies in the theory of planned behaviour, which have mostly posited participants' commitment in implementing new policies when they are part of the policy. In an attempt to shed light on this, studies (Vavrus, 2009, for example) have reported that teachers' previous learning and training experiences tend to determine classroom practices and this plays a fundamental role in classroom decision-making. Appropriate policies and context-specific classroom practices correlate significantly with mastery against the constraints of work contexts. This study did not investigate classroom practices in the light of policies but checked with real-time practitioners what would count as relevant EFL policies, with the understanding that they were competent enough to do this. While the results demonstrate various areas of policy concern, what have been the *de facto* constraints of the teachers' teaching context was not part of their concern in their policy recommendations. Given that appropriate policies must capture local constraints, this chapter holds that teachers' mastery of their work contexts has a high influence on their ability to propose relevant policy innovations. High-frequency policy recommendations in this study were rather related to basic classroom practices identified as teachers' circumstantial responsibilities. Teachers' ability to make relevant recommendations that can address specific context issues in policy conception remains highly questionable. While their agency in the policy innovation process is not contested, their role in the process requires serious attention to be able to provide a more appropriate account of reasoned action.

References

Ajzen, J. (2006). *Constructing a TpB questionnaire: Conceptual and methodological considerations.* Available at http://www.people.mass.edu/aizen/tpb.html. Accessed 11 Nov 2016.
Anchimbe, E. (2006). *Cameroon English: Authenticity, ecology and evolution.* Peter Lang.
Armitage, C. J., Sheeran, P., Conner, M., & Arden, M. A. (2004). Stages of change or changes of stage? Predicting transitions in transtheoretical model stages in relation to healthy food choice. *Journal of Consulting & Clinical Psychology, 72*(3), 491–499.
Bolitho, R. (2012). Projects and programmes: Contemporary experience in ELT change management. In C. Tribble (Ed.), *Managing change in English language teaching: Lessons from experience* (pp. 33–46). British Council.
Canh, L. (2015). Uncovering teachers' beliefs about intercultural language teaching: An example from Vietnam. *The European Journal of Applied Linguistics and TEFL, 4*(1), 83–103.
Carless, D. (2013). Innovation in language teaching and learning. In C. A. Chapelle (Ed.), *The encyclopedia of applied linguistics.* Blackwell Publishing. https://doi.org/10.1002/9781405198431
Chumbow, B. S. (1980). Language and language policy in Cameroon. In N. Kale (Ed.), *An African experiment in nation building: The Bilingual Republic of Cameroon since reunification* (pp. 281–311). Westview Press.

Ekembe, E. (2016). Do 'Resourceful' methodologies really work in 'Under-resourced' contexts? In A. Murphy (Ed.), *New developments in Foreign language learning*. NOVA Science Publishers.

Ekembe, E. (2021). Revisiting attitudes towards English in Cameroon and the rush for EMI: Positioning education for all vision. *Journal of English Learner, 12*(1).

Ekembe & Fonjong. (2018). Teacher Association Research for Professional Development in Cameroon. *ReSIG ELT Research, 33/1.*

Gil, J. (2016). English language education policies in the People's Republic of China. In R. Kirkpatrick (Ed.), *English language education Policy in Asia* (pp. 49–90). Springer.

Godin, G., Valois, P., Lepage, L., and Desharnais, R. (1992). Predictors of smoking behaviour-an application of Ajzen's theory of planned behaviour. *British Journal of Addiction 87*(9), 1335–1343.

Hayes, D. (2012). Mismatched perspectives: In-service teacher education policy and practice in Korea. In C. Tribble (Ed.), *Managing change in English language teaching: Lessons from experience* (pp. 99–104). British Council.

Kennedy, C. (2011). Challenges for language policy, language and development. In H. Coleman (Ed.), *Dreams and realities: Developing countries and the English language* (pp. 24–38). British Council.

Kikuchi, K., & Browne, C. (2009). English educational policy for high schools in Japan. *RELC, 40*(2), 172–191. https://doi.org/10.1177/0033688 209105865

Knabe A. (2012). *Applying Ajzen's theory of planned behavior to a study of online course adoption in public relations education.* Dissertation, Marquette University. Available at http://epublication.Marquette.edu/dissertations_mu/186

Kouega, J. P. (1991). *Some speech characteristics of Cameroon media news in English, An exploratory study of radio and television news.* Unpublished 3rd cycle doctorate thesis, University of Yaounde.

Kouega, J. P. (2002). Uses of English in Southern British Cameroons. *English World-Wide, 23*(1), 93–113.

Kuchah, H. 2008. Developing as a professional in Cameroon: challenges and visions. In Garton, S and Richards, K (eds.). Professional Encounters in TESOL (pp. 203 – 217). Palgrave

Kuchah, K. (2016). English-medium instruction in an English–French bilingual setting: Issues of quality and equity in Cameroon. *Comparative Education, 52*(3), 311–327.

Kuchah K., & Smith, R. (2011). Pedagogy of autonomy for difficult circumstances: From practice to principles. In *Innovation in language learning and teaching* (Vol. 5/2, pp. 119–140). http://www.tandfonline.com. https://doi.org/10.1080/17501229.2011.577529. Accessed April 2013.

Le, V. C. (2015). English language education innovation for the Vietnamese secondary school: The Project 2020. In B. Spolsky & K. Sung (Eds.), *Secondary school English education in Asia: From policy to practice* (pp. 182–200). New York, NY: Routledge.

Lee, J., Cerreto, F. A., & Lee, J. (2010). Theory of planned behaviour and teachers' decisions regarding use of educational technology. *Educational Technology and Society, 13*(1), 152–164.

Maley, A. (2001). The teaching of English in difficult circumstances: Who needs a health farm when they're starving? *Humanising Language Teaching 3/6.* http://www.hltmag.co.uk/nov01/martnov014.rtf. Accessed April 2013.

Marton, F. (1986). Phenomenography – a research approach to investigating different understandings of reality. *Journal of Thought, 21*(3), 28–49.

Mbangwana, P. (1989). Flexibility in lexical usage in Cameroon English. In O. Garcia & R. Otheguy (Eds.), *English across cultures, cultures across English* (pp. 319–333). Mouton de Gruyter.

Mbassi Manga, F. (1976). *The state of contemporary English. Cameroon Studies in English and French (CASEF).* Pressbook.

Milligan, D., & Tikly, L. (2016). English as a medium of instruction in postcolonial contexts: Moving the debate forward. *Comparative Education, 52*(2), 227–280. https://doi.org/10.1080/03050068.2016.1185251

Murray, D. E & Christison, M. (2012). Understanding innovation in English Language education: Contexts and issues. In Tribble, C (ed.). *Managing Change in English Language Teaching: Lessons from Experience.* (pp. 48–61). British Council.

Power, C. (2005). Beyond Babel: Language policies for the 21st century. In D. Cunningham & A. Hatoss (Eds.), *An international perspective on language policies, practices and proficiencies* (pp. 37–50). FIPLV.

Russo, A., Stochl, J., Painter, M., Shelley, F., Jones, B., & Perez, J. (2015). Use of the theory of planned behaviour to assess factors influencing the identification of students at clinical high-risk for psychosis in 16+ Education. *BMC Health Services Research, 44*(6), 839–847. https://doi.org/10.1186/s12913-015-1074-y

Schulze, R., & Wittmann, W. W. (2003). On the moderating effect of the principle of compatibility and multidimensionality of beliefs: A meta-analysis of the theory of reasoned action and the theory of planned behavior. In R. Schulze, H. Holling, & D. Böhning (Eds.), *Meta-analysis: New developments and applications in medical and social sciences* (pp. 219–250). Hogrefe & Huber.

Schweisfurth, M. (2011). Learner-centred education in developing country contexts: From solution to problem? *International Journal of Educational Development, 31*(5), 425–432.

Schweisfurth, M. (2013). Learner-Centred education in international perspective. *Journal of International and Comparative Education, 2*(1), 1–8.

Shamin, F., Negash, N., Chuku, C., & Demewoz, N. (2007). *Maximizing learning in large classes*. British Council.

Simo Bobda, A. (1992). *Lexical integration in Cameroon Standard English*. Unpublished Doctorat de 3eme Cycle thesis, University of Yaounde 1.

Simo Bobda, A. (1994). Lexical innovation process in Cameroon English. *World Englishes, 13*(2), 245–260.

Simo Bobda, A. (2001). Various statuses and perceptions of English in Cameroon: A diachronic and synchronic analysis. *TRANS, Internet-Zeitschrift fur Kulturwissenschaften*, No 11. http://www.inst.at/trans/11Nr. Accessed 22 Feb 2010.

Siragussa, L., & Dixon, K. C. (2009). Theory of planned behaviour: Higher education students' attitudes towards ICT-based learning interactions. *Same places, different spaces. Proceedings Ascilite* Auckland 2009. Available at http://www.ascilite.org.au/conference/auckland09/procs/Siragussa.pdf

Siragussa, L. (2011). Theory of planned behaviour: Higher education students' Attitudes towards ICT-based learning interactions. Paper presented at Ascilite 2011. (Available at http://www.ascilite.org.au).

Smith, R. (2011). *Teaching English in difficult circumstances: A new research agenda*. Available at: http://www.warwick.ac.uk/go/telc

Stolz, S. A. (2020). Phenomenology and phenomenography in educational research: A critique. *Educational Philosophy and Theory, 52*(10), 1077–1096. https://doi.org/10.1080/00131857.2020.172408

Tantawy, N. (2020). Investigating teachers' perceptions of the influence of professional development on teachers' performance and career progression. *Arab World English Journal, 11*(1), 181–194. https://doi.org/10.24093/awej/vol11no1.15

Teo, T., Zhou, M., & Noyes, J. (2016). Teachers and development: Development of an extended theory of planned behaviour. *Educational Technology Research and Development, 64*(3), 1–20. https://doi.org/10.1007/s11423-016-9446-5

Tomlinson, B. (2005). English as a foreign language: Matching procedures to the context of learning. In Henkle (Ed.), *Handbook of research in second language teaching and learning* (pp. 137–154). Lawrence Erlbaum Associations Pub.

Vavrus, F. (2009). The cultural politics of constructivist pedagogies: Teacher education reform in the United Republic of Tanzania. *International Journal of Educational Development, 29*(3), 303–311. https://doi.org/10.1016/j.ijedudev.2008.05.002

Wolf, H. (2001). *English in Cameroon*. Mouton de Gruyter.

Yan, Z., & Sin, K. F. (2014). Inclusive education: Teachers' intentions and behaviours analysed from the viewpoint of the theory of planned behaviour. *International Journal of Inclusive Education, 18*(1), 72–81. https://doi.org/10.1080/13603116.2012.757811

Part IV

Interface

13

So … What's the Interface? The Specter of Smush and Poof

Eric Dwyer

Introduction

The impetus for this book was our perception that there has been little consideration regarding how ELT policies subject practitioners to conflicting institutional requirements. Hornberger and Johnson (2011) warned of "mounting pressures toward a shift to English as far-flung" (282) as the Quichua highlands and the Tamil diaspora. In this volume, we see those pressures manifest in 11 countries, appearing in numerous postures of English as a medium of instruction (EMI). The thrust of EMI seems undergirded with ideologies based in socioeconomic benefits (Hu, 2005; Nomlomo & Vuzo, 2014; Erling et al., 2017) and instrumentalism (Miligan & Tikly, 2016). Thus, a goal of this volume has been to analyze

---

E. Dwyer (✉)
College of Arts, Sciences & Education, Florida International University, Miami, FL, USA
e-mail: eric.dwyer@fiu.edu

the impact of *de facto* language policy on colleagues' everyday experiences. To accomplish such, we asked colleagues around the world to look into how much ELTs *interface* with folks establishing policies.

Starting from Rather than Looking to the Global South

In asserting our investigation, we follow Ndhlovu and Makalela's (2021) lead in search of "broadening … the horizon of our conceptualization of language policies by integrating Southern and decolonial perspectives that draw attention to the *real* language practices of *real* people in *real* life" (76). In their call, they suggest researchers "take into account the voices of currently marginalized and ignored … communities of practice" (5). Our desire was to go further and actually front those voices—namely those of teachers. Thus, while we rhetorically write with our applied linguist research friends in mind—after all, they laid out a precursory research scape—this volume primarily captures the daily lives of key players responding daily to policy: the teachers themselves. We aspire to follow Fillerup's (2008) model "where each [teacher's and] child's language and culture are regarded not as a problem to be solved but as an indispensable resource" (1). Ultimately, we hope we can "unite research with effective change" by involving "the teachers as participants" in our ethnographic work (Hymes, 1980: 72).

Brown and Ganguly (2003) showed that language policies can determine who gains access to schools, economic development, government services, and even fair treatment, and Kuchah Kuchah (2016) found these policies usually etched in leaders' political agendas, which rarely take into account local conditions. Unsurprisingly, Ndhlovu and Makalela (2021) find that

> Language policies sometimes wrongly consign … cultural identities into bifurcated categories of "superior" and "inferior", "useful" and "less useful" and "important" and "unimportant". This breeds all sorts of injustices, inequities, and exclusions. (81)

Under these conditions Tuhiwai Smith (2012) suggested a Global South orientation for developing counter-practices and disrupting hegemonic rules, articulating research practice rooted in people's cultural experiences, weaving seemingly disparate research stories into broader encapsulations, and discovering new ways to know and discover. For us, in accepting these objectives, we anticipated observing gestures of exclusion, as posed by Connell (2007), where Global North perspectives yield discourses labeling Southern perspectives as irrelevant, pre-modern, or unsophisticated. In other words, by starting with the South, we might stumble upon and give extra attention to stories that yield new locally based policy and practice advancing contributions of individual communities, maintaining language and culture, and providing nuanced ideas worldwide. In fact, we might, as Ndhlovu and Makalela (2021) suggest, accommodate, and recognize those language practices that are generally ignored, and instead foster appropriate "forms of praxis and pedagogy against the colonial matrix of power" (Mignolo & Walsh, 2018: 17).

At the heart of our inquiry, we followed Hornberger and Johnson's (2011) simple recommendation to see just "what is going on in the classroom" (87). In our contemplation, we wondered if we would observe language practices that are generally ignored (Ndhlovu, 2015), or examples of *colonial schooling* and *epistemic violence* (see McCarty et al., 2011). We also hoped we might uncover any blind spots, issues colleagues may not have yet registered with which we might raise some awareness.

As a lens, we accept Ramírez Lamus's (2015) notion of *Responsible ELT*, where we maintain that a top-down generalist, likely colonialist, approach would be *irresponsible*, since it pays little attention to teachers and students, who must live with administrations' decisions, and omits innumerable contributions from myriad locales. Additionally, we share Macedo's (2006) concern that ELT training programs emphasize instrumental acquisition of English, where many ELTs and policymakers fall prey to hubristic zeal to save students from *non-English-speaker status*. And honestly, we worry that colleagues seldom realize their unintentional roles in expansion of imperialist policies.

Methodology Perspective

Approaches established by McCarty (2011) with respect to language policy and ethnographic research certainly weigh heavily in our positions. Hornberger and Johnson (2011) ask "What kinds of data are necessary to show that there is a connection" between macro-level policy and local language practice (275). To this end, we ventured to maintain an "ethnographic eye on how linguistic resources are actually employed" (275) via a plethora of observation, interviews, documents, and mini-surveys; field notes and videotaped lessons; life histories, retrospectives, diaries, and blogs—practices that are likely unsheddable—where our choice and use of methods is wide-ranging and eclectic (Shi-xu, 2014: 362).

Still, we acknowledge that rigid adherence to so-called traditional ethnography may not be perfectly suited to studying the multi-sited and multilayered nature of policy. Indeed, Canagarajah (2006) elevates our need to challenge elitist clinging to paradigms and ideologies regarding language policy; therefore, we posit that such includes self-reflection regarding our own Northern-trained practices. Indeed, in the spirit of the Global South, we question Eurocentric approaches as being limiting, suggesting we may need to push the envelope beyond the norm of establishing research praxis as invented, imposed, and controlled by unintended colonialists, endeavoring not to recommit the sin of what Bourdieu (1991) called "the illusion of linguistic communism" where we might "[ignore] the social-historical conditions that established a particular set of linguistic practices as dominant and legitimate" (Ndhlovu & Makalela, 2021: 79).

Regarding hegemony in educational research, Dwyer and Baez (2015) write that authors often

> distinguish (a) the producer of knowledge from (b) its objects and users: students and teachers. The latter, while participating regularly in the studied phenomena, may be considered unqualified in the debate about this knowledge. (12–13)

We therefore suggest, in a number of cases, those reporting without research methodology may indeed be qualified, or at least worthy of attention. In other words, the arbiters of the epistemology, particularly originating from the Global South, must engage with interlocutors with boots on the ground since they themselves are closer to the phenomena than the usual judges.

With these tenets in mind, in this volume we turn, for example, to Bratić and Vuković-Stamatović who turned away from Europe and to Asia as a lens for evaluating their Montegrin context. We put ourselves at risk with Northern colleagues when we display a small in-program survey from a middle-tier institution in Japan or informal blogs from Western Africa. However, perhaps even worse, if we omitted them, we would risk ignoring, erasing, or invisibilizing (Ndhlovu & Makalela, 2021) these key stories and their important orientations. Thus, we find we need to lift voices not yet invited into a fraternity of peers, not yet exhibiting credentials or wielding the syntax under which research techniques purportedly necessitate, especially those invented and controlled by colonialists or imposed by elite researcher gatekeepers.

From a Northern perspective, we may appear to color outside the lines. Doing so of course does not mean that we accept data haphazardly. It is still appropriate for us to self-reflect, as Shi-xu (2014) does, attending to information "grounded in local cultural contexts yet still open to disciplinary dialogue as a way "to achieve or maintain harmonious relationship" with others through attending to others' interests, incorporating differences, avoiding conflicts, balancing powers, etc." (364).

Two Key Overarching Themes

With these perspectives in mind, I offer in this chapter the following concepts for examination:

1. That administrators aim high for content and English, and
2. a typical scenario where English as a Medium of Instruction (EMI) has become a worldwide problematic phenomenon.

The authors report that not all is right with implementation of EMI. Indeed, their narratives suggest that EMI without language support does not make education easier for really anyone.

Administrators Aim High for Content and English

A key finding in this volume is that the observed authorities promote English as good for everyone—not only because one then communicates with more people, but because, as Coyle (2015) points out,

> When we stand back and look at results obtained in countries which have put a lot of emphasis only on developing literacy in the first language, results show that it simply hasn't impacted across the curriculum and achieved its full potential. (89)

This message is not lost on policymakers. There appears to be a planet-wide call for citizens to conduct business in English and with dexterity. In their chapter, Birdal and Vural declare the "influence of the global status of English … is evident in the incorporation of English in the school curriculum as a compulsory subject." For Farag and Yacoub, this goal suggests that graduates speak English beautifully, as virtuosos are desired in government, commerce, and media.

While English has been linked to students' position in society, several authors indicated that leadership has alluded to altruistic narratives. Ramírez Lamus observes academics in Colombia promoting multilingualism, linguistic diversity, and cultural pluralism. Owusu and Sterzuk describe how English helps Ghanaian citizens gain access to globalized concepts while transcending in-country linguistic barriers. Ruas and Djau note English advancement promotes peace building in three African countries. Finally, Seilstad shows how Ohio offers schools and districts flexibility in how they address "languaculturally sustaining programming for adolescent newcomers" within English-centric contexts.

Promoting access to curriculum has also been reported. In countries like Turkey and Colombia, Birdal and Vural, as well as Ramírez Lamus, report that officials have pushed the age of initial English learning to primary school grades. In Florida, Dwyer and O'Gorman-Fazzolari refer to a consent decree determining that multilingual students are to have access to all scholastic material. Meanwhile, Bratić and Vuković-Stamatović found that their students lauded the goals of high English achievement.

In sum, ministries are posturing their educational systems, from primary school matriculation through university graduation, where students master their major in English. EMI is the ideal, and many ministries are confident enough in this objective that they mandate it.

But do policymakers follow through?

Typical EMI Scenario

Fabricant and Brier (2016) noted that institutions

> will be increasingly assessed on the basis of their ability to contain tuition increases while graduating a great percentage of their undergraduates more rapidly. That is a recipe for both fiscal and curricular degradation.

Throughout this book, we see a similar story, one that occurs almost anywhere: We have goal content, the stuff we all want to learn. Ultimately, we want to be at ease with professional content in both our home language and English. Naturally, the easiest way to learn that content is through our mother tongue. Therefore, an administration—perhaps university leadership, a school district, or an education ministry—decides it wants to educate its citizenry such that it resonates as the brightest in the world.

But there's a problem: Funds toward publishing materials in the home language overwhelm budgets. No matter! Since we all need English anyway, administrators decide, "Hey, let's just learn the content along with English" and operate with materials that already exist. It's a win-win: Students graduate with expertise related to their major *and* strong English (Fig. 13.1).

To accomplish this, though, we can no longer focus exclusively on the desired content, which is expressed in *content objectives*. We must also attend to relaying content in an L2 (second language), which requires concentration on *language objectives* (Fig. 13.2).

To assert that the combo of content and language is realized, administrations hire content area specialists (CASs) who can explain their fields in academic English. However, administrators soon understand that

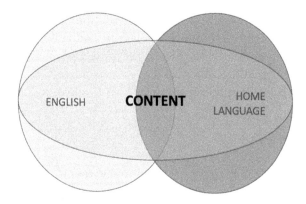

Fig. 13.1 The goal: mastering content in both one's home language and English

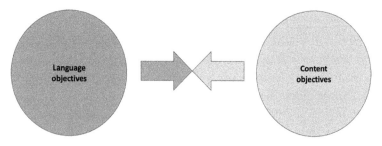

Fig. 13.2 EMI syllabus planning: attention to both language and content objectives

CASs are rarely trained to build both subject-area content and the English needed to navigate that content. No problem! ELTs are usually nearby. They get summoned: "Hey! Would you like to help?"

"Sure!" the ELTs shout. "We would be delighted."

The administrator introduces CASs to ELTs. Everyone is excited. After all, the interaction highlights interdisciplinary collaboration among seemingly disparate parties on campus. EMI is born! (Fig. 13.3)

Meetings are scheduled. The CAS lays out their syllabus—one tightened over years so its layout is efficient and robust. Week by week, unit by unit, and assignment by assignment, outcomes match objectives, and articulation between this class and other program classes makes sense.

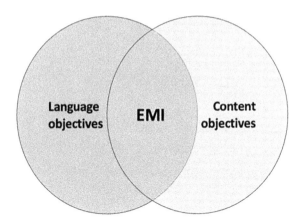

Fig. 13.3 EMI: convergence of both language and content objectives

We then often see the following: Classes belong to the content-area prof; after all, the class code is linked to their credential. The ELT is not credentialed in this area and knows only a smattering of the material. Meanwhile, few find it problematic that the CAS lacks credentialing in English language teaching. The CAS is in the front of the room. The ELT is in the back of the room.

Discussion of the syllabus begins. The ELT observes that the syllabus includes content objectives; it does not however address students' varying English proficiencies or *language development*. The ELT asserts the incorporation of language objectives and multicultural considerations into the course, an action that augments the syllabus. However, the administration has provided no extra time, additional credits, or supplemental funding. The CAS winces: "Nope! There isn't enough time. All those content elements are vital." Furthermore, fusing in language objectives will affect not only one single class but all subsequent classes.

Occasionally professional development in ELT is made available for CASs. Meanwhile, the ELT may be asked to take a workshop or even a class in the content area. Still, the disparity is clear: CASs will not have sufficient facility to assist students with language objectives, and ELTs will be asked to address content with which their students have more experience.

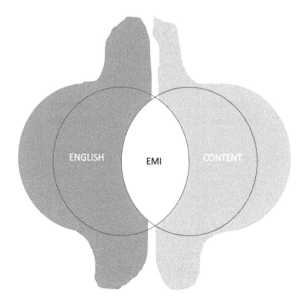

Fig. 13.4 Collaborative EMI: equitable smushing and negotiation of language and content objectives

Conceptually, we ponder EMI where ESL lithely seeps into symbiotic teamwork with content (Fig. 13.4).

However, instead of a melded version of EMI, the ESL smushes into the content. Where ESL is supposed to happen, content maintains its position, necessitating that ESL pedagogy and cultural considerations ooze to the side, unlikely that it will be sopped back into the class (Fig. 13.5).

ELTs are now left out of conversations with CASs, who may argue that decisions regarding language objectives in *their* course is a matter of academic freedom.

Smush and Poof!

Bratić and Vuković-Stamatović (this volume) relay that European Union policymakers have linked the emphasis on content to their perception that English has become the academic lingua franca of the E.U., thereby

13 So … What's the Interface? The Specter of Smush and Poof

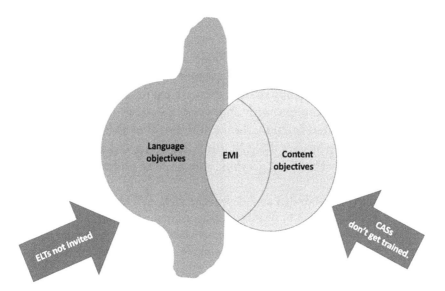

Fig. 13.5 Content area specialist dominant EMI: content objectives maintained with language objectives tangentially addressed

mandating its use. This decision comes despite obvious complications, including the presupposition that students have a command of general English. Seemingly ministries worldwide are cool with (a) neoliberal motivations of increased employability considering the prevalence of English in the global market, and (b) welcoming students whether they have appropriate English proficiency or not.

To this end, our authors report that administrators are saying:

We need the same number of classes.
We need the same number of lessons.
The composite time spent in class and in the program will be the same.
We require that CASs and ELTs collaborate.
We will not provide extra resources.

Pecorari and Malmström (2018) write that "EMI has become a setting in which English skills are not specified as a curricular outcome, are rarely planned, and are not systematically taught, but nonetheless are expected to be acquired" (502). Our book's contributors underscore this reality.

Education ministers promote additional fantasy objectives without resources to achieve them. *Smush!* It is as if they just want all these objectives to materialize by magic: *Poof!* Kelderman (2012) wrote that administrators posture these constraints as merely requesting efficiency and productivity, asking faculty to offer greater bang for their buck.

Advancing L2 content with shortened ESL contribution has been brewing for decades. In 2003, the TESOL Board of Directors published a position statement (see TESOL 2021) regarding independent certificate programs by establishing a minimum sense of professionalism:

> TESOL recommends that an independent TESL or TEFL certificate program should be taught by qualified teacher educators and offer a balance of theory and practice regarding pedagogy and methodology, including a minimum of 100 instructional hours plus a supervised practice teaching component.

This statement unconsciously undercut TESOL's (2019) five standards of teacher education, inadvertently legitimizing certificate programs' focus on language, instruction, and perhaps some assessment, but ignoring sociocultural contexts and professionalism altogether. In other words, TESOL has demurred, as Burns (2018) warns, to mandates of legislatures, ministries, and accreditors to broadcast success in designated outcomes—acts that perpetuate anti-intellectual vocationalism and promote social efficiency-style instrumentalism (71), while marginalizing the intricacies of its own profession by ticking off lists of predetermined learning objectives, which of course are content-based but not language-based.

Bullying

As Ekembe elegantly articulates in his chapter, some teachers have foundational knowledge but no power; thus, leadership wishing to maintain colonial practice can smother teachers with work and limit resources. If teachers are cast into overwhelming contexts, set up to fail, and then blamed for the outcomes, we see them vulnerable to bullying by administrations in the following fashions:

1. Administrative expectations of Poof!
2. Large classes
3. English proficiency as gatekeeper

Administrative Expectations of Poof!

Perhaps the most egregious outcome reported by our colleagues is one of administrative abuse. Farag and Yacoub report that Egyptian teachers are inundated with professional development obligations regarding Communicative Language Teaching (CLT); however, they are simultaneously pressured to achieve high marks on non-CLT-related assessments and then criticized for students' lower marks. Their observations evoke those of Samuel (2014), who writes that teachers are then seen as villains, as the ones who cause poor performance, particularly after government purportedly supports professional development.

Birdal and Vural reported that the decision in Turkey to lower the age for learning English was made without attention to class hours, texts, teacher training, or characteristics of younger learners. In addition, ELTs find professional development short on intriguing activities that motivate younger learners. Similarly, Ramírez Lamus observes that many Colombian teachers lack English proficiency in the first place, suggesting that decision makers enacted bilingually laced goals without establishing a competent workforce. In both cases, authors say that teachers endure negative consequences when students fail to perform to unrealistic expectations.

While Seilstad demonstrated how teachers may reveal an array of attitudes regarding multilingualism, Farag and Yacoub detailed how those teachers experienced with navigating policy (Frost, 2008) can be the most informed advocates for students but have little recourse. We can recall Dina's confession:

> The ministry says do this and do not do this and we have to listen … We simply cannot follow what is mandated upon us. We need to make a living; we don't possess the privilege or the luxury to object or ask for change.

Indeed, we see little comment in our chapters regarding how to improve EMI. Even on occasions, as Ekembe observes, when leadership is cool with new progressive ideas, some teachers may *not* possess foundational knowledge and find themselves resistant to new knowledge. Still, what we do see is that teachers worldwide feel as Yaseen does (as reported by Farag and Yacoub) where

> teachers do not even come to a realization they should have a voice … And if they know, they don't have time to express their voices.

Large Classes

The larger the class, the more complicated it becomes.

In South Sudan, Morjakole describes literal smushing of students. Classroom space may so constrained that teachers direct cooperative learning activities outdoors, providing it's not raining. Indeed, the usefulness of a seasoned teacher's toolbox of activities and strategies is seemingly inversely proportional to class size. Morjakole witnessed schools where five students share desks built for three. Some students share chairs. Others sit on the floor. Chairs actually disenfranchise some students whereas benches allow for flexibility. Morjakole calls such smushing a form of "triple discomfort," where students

1. are squeezed into the walls of the room,
2. are surprised when they are called on, and
3. feel less safe when speaking in front of peers.

In Egypt, Farag and Yacoub report teachers serving as the tug-of-war rope between MoE demands of student portfolio construction and its ultimate demand of successful test scores. The larger the class, the harder it is to be on top of portfolios and the easier it is to prioritize test prep over portfolio development.

As we consider large attendance in insufficient spaces, we must ask ourselves, What is the threshold number of students where teachers exclaim, "This is just too much!" Years ago, West (1960) suggested the number was around 30. Colleagues in the Global South clearly would find 30 a luxury. Morjakole indicates that South Sudan's teachers argue that 50 is the number where they feel overwhelmed but between 70 and 85 is the asymptote where a class is absolutely unmanageable.

English Proficiency as Gatekeeper

Several authors indicate that administratively set English proficiency levels can become gatekeepers to student progress. Bratić and Vuković-Stamatović showed how students are on their own in achieving the required English proficiency milestone for graduation. Since ESL coursework may not be included in their program, students may pass all content-related coursework but still not graduate if they cannot afford extracurricular English classes. Owusu and Sterzuk explained that in Ghana concepts of literacy apply exclusively to English but no other language, an act that stratifies children depending on whether they live in urban and rural areas. Similarly, Ramírez Lamus laments that in Colombia the term *bilingual* refers only to Spanish plus English rather than Spanish plus any other language.[1] Finally, Dwyer and O'Gorman-Fazzolari shared an instance where a multilingual student can only make Valentine's cards for their family after first completing majority language tasks based on vocabulary they haven't learned yet.

So … What's the Interface?

Our colleagues and their interlocutors emphasize concern that the resonance of their jobs needs serious boost. While initial orientations of "Hey, let's really add English on" are enthusiastically initiated, ongoing CAS/ELT partnerships rarely work out. Ministries eschew accommodations. CASs often end up uninterested in participating. Meanwhile, ELTs work so hard they have no fuel remaining to offer resistance. EMI success is thus dependent upon students engaging in extracurricular exercise to

---

[1] Kuchah Kuchah (2016) also details a national sense of bilingualism in Cameroon that is based on French/English rather than multilingual stances, including local languages.

achieve graduation requirements, a condition leaving financially strapped students behind.

To achieve students' mastery of English-delivered content, rarely does a single expert stand out as able to mesh content and language fully. We see that successful EMI necessitates overt logically scheduled attention on not only content but also language. Success in modern day EFL is dependent upon well-trained ELTs but is inadequate regarding approaches to content. EMI is dependent upon CASs who seldom attend to language. The symbiotic nature of this interface is obvious: both need one another; one is incomplete without the other.

Language Practices Generally Ignored

In the spirit of Global South proclivity, Ndhlovu (2015) suggested looking out for language practices that are generally ignored. To that end, Ruas and Djau observe in Western Africa that colleagues find coursebooks exported as part of colonialism to be irrelevant to their students' lives. Furthermore, they suggest that purposeful steering away from Eurocentrically imposed attitudes to PARSNIPS[2]-type topics may not be in their communities' best interest. Instead, they suggest there may be space for new "African pedagogy," more specifically operationalizing conversations regarding serious local social issues—including FGM, HIV, and Koranic school street-begging—which may actually be in line with the spirit of revolutionary leader Amilcar Cabral.

Similarly, Owusu and Sterzuk front Osei's experience with a lesson on a Western stove. In their story, Osei, in quiet noncompliance of the Ghanaian ministry's English-only wishes, operates both multilingually and multiculturally, offering students a chance to attend to their own background knowledge regarding stoves in their own homes. When Osei asked higher order questions, namely students' orientations toward advantages and disadvantages of each stove, Osei allowed students to use Twi in navigating the information while adding English on.

---

[2] Politics, alcohol, religion, sex, narcotics, -isms, and pork.

Osei's translanguaging in Ghana was not so different from Ms Popov's cushioned talk in Ohio, as reported by Seilstad as stemming from Pérez and Enciso's (2017) proposed cushioned, contextualized, extensive, and radical approach. Ms Popov was the only teacher Seilstad found, who was willing to ask students to engage in home language reference, defending the action by saying

> It enriches them. They learn from each other and like this interaction.

Still, Seilstad concedes, noting that

> despite the possibility of creating radical languaculturally-sustaining programming for adolescent newcomers, the focal program is "English-centric".

Colonial Schooling and "Epistemic Violence"

McCarty et al. (2011) referred to "coercive English" (35)—moments English is forced on communities such that locals begin forgetting their home language—as "epistemic violence." As Ndhlovu and Makalela (2021) called out versions of additive bilingual education as "subtle manifestation of coloniality" (77), we wondered if we might see similar versions of sociolinguistic injustice within EMI structures.

In countries like Japan, Egypt, Turkey, and Colombia, there is little chance that Japanese, Arabic, Turkish, or Spanish face diminished implementation. However, in Colombia and other parts of Africa, there is clear danger that local languages are invisibilized through national policy. In Ghana, Owusu and Sterzuk showed the ministry's reverence of English as students are only recorded as "literate" if literacy is demonstrated in English. Similarly, Ramírez Lamus showed how bilingualism in Colombia refers only to Spanish and English, but never to any indigenous language found within the country. In Florida, officials make curriculum harder and the teachers do their best, but not in their home language and without reference to content localized to their neighborhood.

In the cases of Ohio and Ghana, colleagues did observe occasional subversive uses of home language. But only a few! Egyptian and Floridian teachers were nearly unanimous in showing that they know what to do—at least they have the training and credential suggesting that they do—but they feel they can't do it. At the end of the day, their job description shifts to a reality: their students must pass the tests.

There's little question, though, that colonial schooling entails large classes. Morjakole illustrates push and pull environments in South Sudan. If a teacher in an overcrowded school somehow achieves unexpectedly higher marks from their students, the school can expect to lose that teacher to an NGO unless it keeps class size to a minimum. In Egypt, school quality seems related to school enrollments and tuition cost. Thus, the more a school is enrolled, the more teachers must rely on rote memorization. And the more in-class quality drops, the more likely a teacher, already with a higher pupil load, must take on extracurricular tutoring to make ends meet.

A common theme revealed in several chapters is that teachers not only feel segregated from decision-making procedures, but also feel compelled to contort their habits in responding to new demands. In Japan, Unser-Schutz et al. complain that while MEXT has raised the number of subject classes taught in English to improve internationalization and foreign student enrollment, Rissho University's international faculty feel that they have been isolated from one another, with little recourse in offering feedback to ministry officials. Meanwhile, Birdal and Vural demonstrate how Turkey's lowering the age of English instruction without attention to teacher professional development suddenly had seasoned teachers feeling like novices. Teachers then felt they must figure out, on the fly, new in-class activities, games, cultural constructs, and motivational techniques.

Under EMI, the colonial matrix of administrative power is seemingly maintained, if not emboldened, meaning that "the ways that colonially invented versions of languages [including English as a medium of instruction] continue to be used as a technology of political control, manipulation, and subtle cultural normalization" (Ndhlovu & Makalela, 2021: 75). This conclusion would likely disappoint Hornberger and Johnson (2011) who argued that "educators … are not simply cogs in the machine of dominant discourses, the wheels of which are turned by hegemonic language policies – they can agentively interpret, appropriate, and/or ignore such policies in creative ways" (285). A finding in our volume is that teachers often feel they have little agency in the decision making or even the energy to grasp or demand any.

For Ndhlovu and Makalela (2021), our contributors' experiences might evoke South African environments where English is purportedly promoted as neutral. Instead, these EMI practices "effectively [amount] to the production and reproduction of the very same colonial matrices of power, and epistemological hegemonies that are disconnected from the 'qualitative' multilingual practices of real people in real life' (14). Painter (2011), meanwhile, would likely argue that administrative emphasis on English is anything but neutral, representing instead neoliberal arguments supporting internationalism and marketability but still reflecting interests of the elite. In other words, observations from our authors support a notion that EMI ends up being more of a divider than a uniter.

Critiques of EMI

Authors of this volume indicate that language development is not a curricular focus of EMI; however, it is an expected outcome, thereby confirming Byun et al.'s (2011) observations that administrators generally do not prioritize language development even if students show insufficient English proficiency. This call for additional efficiency without allocating resources leaves administrators open to critique, and there has been plenty. Cammarata and Tedick (2012) proclaim that "second languages are not learned by osmosis, as decades of research studies in one-way immersion contexts have consistently shown" (262). Indeed, observers have complained that placing L2 students into environments without trained teachers yields dissatisfying results (Ellis, 2015).

It is crucial, then, that we also acknowledge that potentially *decolonizing* actions may exist, even in EMI settings. We have seen, for example, that EMI professors' lack of pedagogical training becomes critical. Evans and Morrison (2011) affirmed that students look to professionally trained guidance regarding in-class actions like notetaking, following discussions, understanding specialist vocabulary, faster reading comprehension, clear pronunciation, writing academically, and meeting institutional and disciplinary requirements. For students to garner that support, Gierlinger (2016) details class elements that can assist L2 learners, attending to *SALT*: Strategic learning, All language practices, Literacy (multi-modal), and

Topic relevant language. When these elements are not present, many (including Björkman, 2011; Dimova & Kling, 2018) argue that in-class effectiveness is sacrificed in EMI settings when multilingual and multicultural contexts are ignored, even when students show strong English proficiency. In fact, Duff (1997) and Met and Lorenz (1997) observed that lack of support, especially in non-language-based courses, can inhibit L2 students' ability or willingness to explore abstract concepts. In other words, Margić and Vodopija-Krstanović (2017) found that EMI courses were far more effective when linguistic and cultural support were provided.

A stark outcome of this book is the observation that—regardless of venue, north or south, rich or poor—the administrative world is mostly OK with bad EMI. The result is the invisibilizing of those who must suppress linguistic and cultural contributions of their own communities. The trend against responsible ELT, via smush and poof practices, is likely in the hands of leadership who impede it—a result that not only preserves the power of the powerful but purposefully implants margins against the poor, rendering the ELT world more colonialized and colonizing than it was even a decade ago.

Solutions/Future Inquiry

Walkinshaw, Fenton-Smith, and Humphreys (2017) argue that "EMI is a more nuanced concept operating on continua of usage at varying levels including institutional, course, and classroom" (6). Thus, it may be difficult to achieve what Pecorari and Malmström (2018) called the Goldilocks zone where there the balance of content and ESL is just right. The clearest solution for successful EMI is to augment time and reallocate appropriate pedagogical roles. Doing so would allow time for students to process both the new content *and* the linguistic and multicultural underpinnings that ground their new content learning and allow them to express it in both their home language and in English.

This of course is a chimera.

In the meantime, we endeavor to approach Goldilocks. Macaro (2018) notes that, in many EMI settings, some form of language support may be available to students, including English for Academic Purposes courses

(Dearden, 2018; Lee & Lee, 2018). Dafouz and Smit (2020) proposed *Road Mapping*, where the following checklist applies to conceptualizing integrated content learning:

Ro   Roles of English
AD   Academic Disciplines
M   (Language) Management
A   Agents
P   Practices
P   Processes
In   Internationalization
G   Glocalization

Kim, Kweon, and Kim (2016) showed Korean administrators who worried about students in EMI classes, suggesting that even if students had English experiences, they were likely not academic. To address such shortcomings, one institution established a three-week intensive English camp for incoming freshman with the lowest standardized test scores. The researchers reported that students found navigating lecture vocabulary most difficult but still preferred content-integrated classes to language-focused classes.

Administrators also worry about CASs' English proficiency. Thus, some institutions have developed professional development and internal assessment procedures (Dimova & Kling, 2018) based on simulated or actual teaching within specific academic contexts (Farnsworth, 2013). Dwyer and O'Gorman Fazzolari welcome the professional development but warn that while such training may positively change attitudes, it does not necessarily lead to in-class language-based adjustments later. As it turns out, Seilstad's experience shows that when a rainbow of policy choices is offered, some credentialed teachers will still opt for less linguaculturally sustaining pedagogy.

If administrative simplicity points to English, then we can only expect colonialistic systems to dominate and support only those who can afford to navigate them. Therefore, we look at this volume as a call for teachers to congregate and establish advocacy in the name of their students. Similarly, we call on administrators to rethink the constraints they regularly demand. After all, ELTs should have a rightful place in EMI. Birdal and Vural state, "it is vital to establish constant cooperation [among] teachers, policymakers, researchers, and academics who specialize in teacher education." We will need to ask leadership, "Are you really cool with failing students?" Politically, administrators will say "Of course not." Reality is likely otherwise. Thus, we must ask, and ask, and then ask again. Otherwise, ELTs will make the same mistake they are complaining about, hoping that ministries, departments of education, and content area specialists will suddenly spark *noblesse-oblige* and allow time, budget for additional resources, and reciprocate professional respect—and that all will happen as if by magic: Poof!

References

Björkman, B. (2011). Pragmatic strategies in English as an academic lingua franca: Ways of achieving communicative effectiveness? *Journal of Pragmatics, 43*(4), 950–964.
Bourdieu, P. (1991). *Language and symbolic power* (G. Raymond & M. Adamson, Trans.; edited and introduced by J. B. Thompson). Polity Press.
Brown, M. E., & Ganguly, S. (2003). *Fighting words: Language policy and ethnic relations in Asia*. MIT Press.
Burns, J. (2018). *Power, curriculum, and embodiment: Re-thinking curriculum as counter-conduct and counter-politics*. Palgrave Macmillan.
Byun, K., Chu, H., Kim, M., Park, I., Kim, S., & Jung, J. (2011). English-medium teaching in Korean higher education: Policy debates and reality. *Higher Education, 62*(4), 431–449.
Cammarata, L., & Tedick, D. J. (2012). Balancing content and language in instruction: The experience of immersion teachers. *The Modern Language Journal, 96*(2), 251–269.
Canagarajah, S. (2006). Ethnographic methods in language policy. In T. Ricento (Ed.), *An Introduction to language policy: Theory and method*. Blackwell.
Connell, R. (2007). *Southern theory: The global dynamics of knowledge in social science*. Allen & Unwin.
Coyle, D. (2015). Strengthening integrated learning: Towards a new era for pluriliteracies and intercultural learning. *Latin American Journal of Content and Language Integrated Learning, 8*(2), 84–103.

Dafouz, E., & Smit, U. (2020). *ROAD-MAPPING: English medium education in the internationalised university*. Palgrave Macmillan.

Dearden, J. (2018). The changing roles of EMI academics and English language specialists. In Y. Kırkgöz & K. Dikilitaş (Eds.), *Key issues in English for specific purposes in higher education*. Springer.

Dimova, S., & Kling, J. (2018). Assessing English-medium instruction lecturer language proficiency across disciplines. *TESOL Quarterly, 52*(3), 634–656.

Duff, P. A. (1997). Immersion in Hungary: An ELF experiment. In R. K. Johnson & M. Swain (Eds.), *Immersion education: International Perspectives* (pp. 19–43). Cambridge University Press.

Dwyer, E., & Baez, B. (2015). Critiquing the research of others. In J. D. Brown & C. A. Coombe (Eds.), *The Cambridge guide to research in language teaching and learning*. Cambridge University Press.

Ellis, N. (2015). Implicit and explicit language learning: Their dynamic interface and complexity. In P. Rebuschat (Ed.), *Implicit and explicit learning of languages* (pp. 3–23). John Benjamins.

Erling, E. J., Adinolfi, L., & Hultgren, A. K. (2017). *Multilingual Classrooms: Opportunities and challenges for English medium instruction in low and middle income contexts*. The British Council.

Evans, S., & Morrison, B. (2011). The first term at university: Implications for EAP. *ELT Journal, 65*(4), 387–397.

Fabricant, M., & Brier, S. (2016). How cost-cutting and austerity affect public higher education. *Clarion*. At www.psc-cuny.org/clarion/october/2016

Farnsworth, T. L. (2013). An investigation into the validity of the TOEFL iBT speaking test for international teaching assistant certification. *Language Assessment Quarterly, 10*, 274–291.

Fillerup, M. (2008). Building bridges of beauty between the rich languages and cultures of the American Southwest: Puente de Hózhó Trilingual Magnet School. In M. Romero-Little, S. J. Ortiz, & T. L. McCarty (Eds.), *Indigenous languages across the generations – Strengthening families and communities*. Arizona State University Center for Indian Education.

Frost, D. (2008). "Teacher leadership": Values and voice. *School Leadership and Management, 28*(4), 337–352.

Gierlinger, E. M. (2016). *Whatever the CLIL cuisine, a pinch of SALT will help! On teaching content and language through a language-aware CLIL model*. Found at https://clilingmesoftly.files.wordpress.com/2016/11/portland_salt_presentation_2017_03-18_blog.pdf

Hornberger, N., & Johnson, D. C. (2011). Ethnography of language policy. In T. L. McCarty (Ed.), *Ethnography and language policy*. Routledge.

Hu, G. (2005). English language education in China: Policies, progress, and problems. *Language Policy, 5*, 5–24.

Hymes, D. (1980). Qualitative/quantitative research methodologies in education: A linguistic perspective. In D. Hymes (Ed.), *Language in education: Ethnolinguistic essays*. Center for Applied Linguistics.

Kelderman, E. (2012, January 22). States push even further to cut spending on colleges. *Chronicle of Higher Education*

Kim, E. G., Kweon, S.-O., & Jeongyeon, K. (2016). Korean engineering students' perceptions of English-medium instruction (EMI) and L1 use in EMI classes. *Journal of Multilingual and Multicultural Development, 38*(20), 1–16.

Kuchah, K. (2016). English-medium instruction in an English-French bilingual setting: Issues of quality and equity in Cameroon. *Comparative Education, 52*(3), 311–327.

Lee, K., & Lee, H. (2018). An EAP professional development program for graduate students in an English-medium instruction context. *TESOL Quarterly, 52*(4), 1097–1107.

Macaro, E. (2018). *English medium instruction*. Oxford University Press.

Macedo, D. (2006). *Literacies of power: What Americans are not allowed to know*. Westview.

Margić, B. D., & Vodopija-Krstanović, I. (2017). *Uncovering English-medium instruction: Glocal issues in higher Education*. Peter Lang.

McCarty, T. L. (2011). *Ethnography and language policy*. Routledge.

McCarty, T. L., Romero-Little, E., Warhol, L., & Zepeda, O. (2011). Critical ethnography and indigenous language survival. In T. L. McCarty (Ed.), *Ethnography and language policy*. Routledge.

Met, M., & Lorenz, E. B. (1997). Lessons from U.S. immersion programs: Two decades of experience. In R. K. Johnson & M. Swain (Eds.), *Immersion education: International Perspectives* (pp. 243–264). Cambridge University Press.

Mignolo, W. D., & Walsh, C. E. (2018). *On decoloniality: concepts, analytics, praxis*. Duke University Press.

Miligan, L. O., & Tikly, L. (2016). English as a medium of instruction in postcolonial contexts: Moving the debate forward. *Comparative Education, 52*(3), 277–280.

Ndhlovu, F. (2015). *Hegemony and language policies in Southern Africa: Identity, integration, development*. Cambridge Scholars.

Ndhlovu, F., & Makalela, L. (2021). *Decolonising multilingualism in Africa: Recentering voices from the global south*. Multilingual Matters.

Nomlomo, V., & Vuzo, M. (2014). Language transition and access to education: Experiences from Tanzania and South Africa. *International Journal of Educational Studies, 1*(2), 73–82.

Painter, D. (2011). *The Monolingual Drone: Language and critical psychology, Part 1.* Found at https://southernpsychologies.wordpress.com/2011/12/03/the-monolingual-drone-language-and-critical-psychology-part-1/

Pecorari, D., & Malmström, H. (2018). TESOL and English medium instruction. *TESOL Quarterly, 52*(3), 497–515.

Pérez, A. H., & Enciso, P. (2017). Decentering whiteness and monolingualism in the reception of Latinx YA literature. *Bilingual Review/Revista Bilingüe, 33*(5). Found at http://bilingualreview.utsa.edu/index.php/br/article/view/182

Ramírez Lamus, Daniel (2015). *Foreign language education in Colombia: A qualitative study of Escuela Nueva.* Florida International University dissertation.

Samuel, M. (2014). South African teacher voices: Recurring resistances and reconstructions for teacher education and development. *Journal of Education for Teaching: International Research and Pedagogy, 40*(5), 610–621.

Shi-xu. (2014). Cultural dialogue with CDA: Cultural discourse studies. *Critical Discourse Studies, 11*(3), 360–369.

Teachers of English to Speakers of Other Languages International Association. (2019). *Standards for initial TESOL Pre-K-12 teacher education programs.* TESOL.

Teachers of English to Speakers of Other Languages International Association. (2021). *Tips for evaluating independent certificate programs.* Found at https://www.tesol.org/enhance-your-career/career-development/beginning-your-career/tips-for-evaluating-independent-certificate-programs

Tuhiwai Smith, L. (2012). *Decolonizing methodologies: Research and indigenous peoples* (2nd ed.). Zed Books.

Walkinshaw, I., Fenton-Smith, B., & Humphreys, P. (2017). EMI issues and challenges in Asia-Pacific higher education: An introduction. In B. Fenton-Smith, P. Humphreys, & I. Walkinshaw (Eds.), *English medium instruction in higher education in Asia-Pacific: From policy to pedagogy.* Springer.

West, M. (1960). *Teaching English in difficult circumstances.* Longmas, Green.

Index[1]

A

Abdel-Nasser, Gamal, 60, 61
Acculturation, 171, 175
Adolescent newcomer program, 128–129, 132, 133, 143
Affective discomfort, 116
Age of instruction, 43, 54
Apprenticeship of observation, 52
Appropriate formula, 108
Assessing Montenegrin tertiary ELT policies, 229
Assimilation, 175, 194
assimilationist, 169–195
Attention span, 43, 44, 46, 47, 49
Attitudes, 246, 250, 252, 253, 259, 261
Australia, 2

B

Beliefs, 245–246, 250, 251
Bilingual, 283, 285
Bilingualism, 194
Bottom-up, 9, 14
British Council, 153, 154
Building background, 175, 190–191

C

Cameroon, 12, 243–262
Challenges in classroom practice, 41, 52, 55
Classroom density, 107–108
Classroom noise, 110
Classroom practice, 41, 43, 44, 48–55

---

[1] Note: Page numbers followed by 'n' refer to notes.

Classroom procedures, 255, 259
Class size, 107–110, 112–118
Code breaking, 174–175, 188–190
Code-mixing, 92, 98, 99
Code-switching, 92, 98, 99
Cognitive Academic Language Learning Approach (CALLA), 174
Colombia, 9
Colombian Framework for English (COFE), 153
Colonialist, 271–273
Common European Framework of Reference (CEFR), 153, 157, 159
Communicative approach, 62, 71, 72
Communicative exchanges, 110
Communicative jigsaw, 122
Communicative Language Teaching (CLT), 5, 8, 107–123, 281
Communicative tasks, 109
Community needs, 2, 5
Comparative case study methodology, 86
Competence, 249
Congested classrooms, 117
Consent decree, 274
Constraints, 122
Content and language integrated learning, 289
Content area specialists (CASs), 275–279, 283, 284, 289, 290
Content-based learning, 32
Content objectives, 275–279
Context, 243–246, 248–251, 253, 255, 256, 258, 259, 261, 262
Continuing Professional Development (CPD), 246–247, 257–258, 261
Create change, 215
Credential, 273, 277, 285
Credit weight, 252, 253, 259
Critical language-policy research, 155, 156
Cultural pluralism, 154–156, 274
Curriculum, 5, 6, 9, 11, 12, 40–43, 47, 50–55, 89, 90, 96
Curriculum reforms, 252, 256–257, 259, 261

Decentralization, 6
Democratic Republic of Congo (DRC), 11, 203–218
Deviation score, 22
Differentiated attention, 109
Difficult circumstances, 107, 109
Diffusion of English, 154, 155, 160, 164, 166
Diffusion of English paradigm, 154, 155, 160, 164, 166
Discourse analysis, 133, 134

Ecology of languages paradigm, 154, 155
Education quality, 60, 78
Egypt, 6
Elementary school, 9
ELT mandatory exit level in tertiary education, 236
ELT policies, 39–42, 85–100, 243–262
ELT policies and higher education legislation, 226
ELT policies and practices, 59–80

English as a foreign language (EFL), 1, 5, 12, 108–111, 243, 249, 261
English as a medium of instruction, 269, 273, 286
English as a Second Language (ESL), 110
English-centric, 127–144
English for Academic Purposes (EAP), 288
English instruction in Turkey, 42–44
English Language Teaching (ELT), 116, 122, 123
English medium instruction (EMI), 1–5, 7, 12, 13
English-only instruction, 88, 90, 94–96, 99
Environment, 208, 210, 213, 215, 216
Escuela Activa Urbana, 152, 153, 164
Escuela Nueva, 151–153, 157–159, 162–165
ESOL Endorsement, 174
ESOL strategies, 172–177, 180–194
Estándares básicos de competencias en lenguas extranjeras inglés, 154, 159, 164, 166n2
Ethnography, 133, 134
Evidence, 2, 3, 5–7, 9, 11, 12
Experimental schools, 63, 65
Exploratory, 111

Flexible language policy, 143
Florida Consent Decree, 169–195
　Consent Decree, 169–172, 194, 195
Florida Department of Education (FDOE), 170, 174

Foreign language education reform, 42
Francophone, 249
Fundación Escuela Nueva Volvamos a la Gente, 152, 158
Funds of knowledge, 175, 194

García Márquez, Gabriel, 151
Gatekeeper, 273, 283
Gender equity, 210, 216
General education (GE), 32, 33
Ghana Education Service (GES), 87
Ghanaian language (s), 87–89, 98
Globalization, 3
Global Journal, 152
Grammar-based teaching, 5, 6
Guinea Bissau, 11, 203–218
Gurōbaru-jinzai (global talent), 22, 23

Hegemony, 154
Hegemony of English, 154–156, 160
Higher education, 1, 5, 12
Higher-order thinking skills, 176
High school, 9, 12
Home languages, 3, 9, 175, 191
Humanizing teaching, 79
HundrED, 152

IATEFL Global Issues SIG (GISIG), 205, 210, 216
Immigration/immigrants, 8
Impact assessment, 4

Imperialism
  cultural, 154, 155
  linguistic, 154–157
Implementing tertiary ELT policies, 222, 228–233, 235–237
Imported policies, 73
Incompatibility, 110
Indigenous languages, 85, 87, 90, 98, 100
Innovation, 2, 4–7, 9–14
In-service training, 43, 45, 51, 53–55
Instrumental, 271
Intentions, 246–248
Interactive learning, 117
Inter-American Bank Development Bank, 152
Internationalization, 21–24
International schools, 65, 77

Japan, 5, 6, 21–34
Japanese Ministry of Education (MEXT), 21–26, 28–34

Languaculturally, 274, 289
Language-Based Approach to Content Instruction (LACI), 173
Language brokering, 175
Language-in-education policy, 86–89, 92, 100
Language learning, 249, 257
Language objectives, 275–279
Language policy, 1–14, 39–42

Large classes, 282–283
Latinidad, 175
Learner-centerd approaches, 109
Learning achievement, 109
Learning goals, 67
Learning theory
  behaviorism, 130
  cultural-historical, 130, 131, 143
  dialogic, 129, 131, 143
  sociocultural, 129–131, 143
Lesson preparation, 174, 180, 188, 193
Lingua franca, 39, 40
Linguicism, 154
Linguistic diversity, 274
Linguistic imperialism, 154–157
Linguistic resources, 98, 99
Listening comprehension, 188
Local materials, 215
Lower-middle-income countries, 68

Mainstream classes, 169–195
Materials, 41, 43, 46, 49, 50, 52, 53
Medium of Instruction (EMI), 85–88, 95, 243, 269, 273, 275–279, 282–290
Mid-tier universities, 22, 25, 26, 33, 34
The Minister of Education, 62, 67, 74
Ministry of Education (MoE), 22
Mode of enforcing English speaking, 94–95
Monocultural, 194
Montenegro, 12
Mother tongue, 3, 5, 87–92, 94, 95, 97

Multicultural Education Training and Advocacy (META), 170
Multilingual and multicultural contexts, 85–100, 288
Multilingualism, 2, 3, 7, 8, 274, 281
Multimodal techniques, 176, 187

National Development Plan, 152
The National English Language Curriculum Framework Grades, 59
NESs, 187, 190, 192, 193
1994 General Law of Education, 160
Non English speaker status, 154, 165, 271

Official language, 85, 87, 89, 92, 97, 99
Ottoman Empire, 60
Over-centralization, 76, 78
Owu-Ewie, C., 85, 88

PARSNIP topics, 205
Perceived behavioural control (PBC), 246–248, 250, 251, 257
Perceptions, 243–262
Performance, 68, 71, 72
Periphery, 157, 166n3
Policy, 250
Policy implementation, 244, 247, 250, 251, 257, 259, 261
Policy innovation, 244, 245, 247, 248, 250, 251, 257, 259–262

Policymakers, 40, 54, 87, 89, 100, 271, 274, 275, 278
Policy making, 41
Poof, 269–290
Poorly resourced, 108
Portfolios, 66, 67, 71, 73–75, 78
Practice, 245, 247, 250, 252–254, 257, 258, 261, 262
Praxis, 122
Product model of English, 59
Professional development (PD), 66, 67, 71, 75, 78
Proficiency, 160, 161, 164, 170, 174, 176, 177, 187, 188, 190, 192, 194, 243, 247, 256, 258, 259, 277, 279, 281, 283, 287–289
Programa de Fortalecimiento al Desarrollo de Competencias en Lenguas Extranjeras (PFDCLE), 153
Programa Nacional de Bilingüismo (PNB), 153, 157, 159–161, 164

Radical languaculturally sustaining programming, 143
Realities of implementation, *see* Striking a balance
Relevant, 243
Remedial education, 21, 24–25
Representative students, *see* Student sampling
Resistance, 155–157, 245, 248, 250
Responsible ELT, 153–157, 271, 288
Road Mapping, 289

Index

S

SALT, 287
Sampling of students, 119, 122
School policy, 113
Senegal, 11, 203–218
Sheltered Instruction Observation Protocol (SIOP), 173
Smush, 269–290
South Africa, 2, 8
Specially Designed Academic Instruction in English (SDAIE), 174
Structured English Immersion (SEI), 174
Student perception of tertiary ELT policies, 231
Student sampling, 119, 122
Supreme Court Decisions
  Castañeda v. Pickard, 128
  Lau v. Nichols, 127

T

Target language, 109
Teacher agency, 244
Teacher and student respondents, 212
Teacher education programs, 43, 53, 54
Teacher pay, 63, 68–69
Teacher perception of tertiary ELT policies, 228, 235–237
Teacher-pupil ratios (TPR), 107, 108, 113
Teacher responsibility, 252, 254–255, 259, 262
Teacher training, 45, 51, 53, 55
Teacher voice, 67–68, 71, 75–76
Teaching context, 111, 122
Teaching English as a Foreign Language (TEFL), 280
Teaching English to Speakers of Other Languages (TESOL), 280
Teaching to the test, 71–73
Tertiary ELT, 221–237
Tertiary ELT in Europe, 225–227
Tertiary ELT in Montenegro, 221–237
Teritiary ELT policies, 221–237
TESL, 280
Top-down, 5, 9, 161–162, 164, 271
Top down policies, 23, 25, 34
Transitional process, 112
Translanguaging, 92, 175, 187
Translation, 94
Transportation, 245, 261
Triple discomfort, 282
Turkey, 6
Tutoring, 75–77, 79
Twi and English, 91–94

U

UK, 13
UNICEF, 152
United States (USA), 2
Universal language, 160
Unser-Schutz, Giancarla, 21
USA, *see* United States
USAID, 152

W

Well-resourced, 108
World Bank, 152
World-class Instructional Design and Assessment (WIDA), 174, 175

Y

Young learners, 40, 41, 43, 44, 46, 51, 53

Lightning Source UK Ltd.
Milton Keynes UK
UKHW021008050323
418016UK00004B/33